A DESCRIPTIVE CATALOGUE OF ORIENTAL MANUSCRIPTS AT ST JOHN'S COLLEGE, OXFORD

A DESCRIPTIVE CATALOGUE OF ORIENTAL MANUSCRIPTS AT ST JOHN'S COLLEGE OXFORD

EMILIE SAVAGE-SMITH

WITH CONTRIBUTIONS BY

GEERT JAN VAN GELDER
PETER E. PORMANN
SAMIRA SHEIKH
TIM STANLEY
EDWARD ULLENDORFF

OXFORD
UNIVERSITY PRESS

OXFORD
UNIVERSITY PRESS

Great Clarendon Street, Oxford OX2 6DP

Oxford University Press is a department of the University of Oxford.
It furthers the University's objective of excellence in research, scholarship,
and education by publishing worldwide in

Oxford New York

Auckland Cape Town Dar es Salaam Hong Kong Karachi
Kuala Lumpur Madrid Melbourne Mexico City Nairobi
New Delhi Shanghai Taipei Toronto

With offices in

Argentina Austria Brazil Chile Czech Republic France Greece
Guatemala Hungary Italy Japan South Korea Poland Portugal
Singapore Switzerland Thailand Turkey Ukraine Vietnam

Published in the United States
by Oxford University Press Inc., New York

First published 2005

British Library Cataloguing in Publication Data
Data available

Library of Congress Cataloging in Publication Data
Data available

ISBN 0–19–920195–1

1 3 5 7 9 10 8 6 4 2

Printed in Great Britain
on acid-free paper by
Antony Rowe Ltd.,
Chippenham, Wiltshire

ACKNOWLEDGEMENTS

One of the pleasures in completing a project is the opportunity it provides to thank formally all the people who have been a part of the effort and assisted in various ways.

First and foremost I wish to thank my collaborators who contributed to the volume. Professor Geert Jan van Gelder, present Laudian Professor of Arabic and Fellow of St John's College, has transformed a mere catalogue into a volume of far wider interest by providing a fascinating essay on the incidental Arabic poetry found in these manuscript – which is to say, the poetry that various owners over the years jotted down on the margins or endpapers. A unique study, so far as I am aware.

Professor Edward Ullendorff, Emeritus Professor of Ethiopian Studies, provided the entry for the two Ethiopic items, with the assistance of Dr Girma Getahun who utilized the wonders of computer programs to transform the entry into a form that could be used in the final formatting of the catalogue. Dr Peter E. Pormann, Junior Research Fellow in Oriental Studies at Merton College, prepared the Hebrew and Syriac entries and in the process discovered that one of the Hebrew items was a copy of material in the archives at Merton, which he proceeded to publish in detail. Tim Stanley, Curator of the Middle East Collections at the V&A Museum in London, wrote the analysis of the Turkish letter and carefully laid out the historical arguments for its date and significance. Samira Sheikh, a doctoral candidate in Gujarati history at Wolfson College, kindly studied the Gurajati navigational guide and map, which in the event proved so interesting that she also has produced a full study of the document that will be published elsewhere. To the entries supplied by my collaborators, I added paper and binding descriptions, information on provenance, and similar data, and edited the entries to conform, more or less, with the format used in the first half of the catalogue (covering Arabic and Persian manuscripts). I sincerely apologize to them for any errors I may thereby have introduced.

Others were also instrumental in seeing this volume through to completion. It was felt that a second set of eyes to look over the transcriptions of passages from manuscripts would aid in eliminating the inevitable human errors. Accordingly, Colin Wakefield, Deputy Keeper of the Oriental Collections at the Bodleian Library, agree to check all the Arabic and Persian transcriptions, while Peter Glare, of the Dictionary of Medieval Latin from British Sources, proofed the Latin, consisting mostly of seventeenth- and eighteenth-century notes added to manuscripts. Similarly, Dr Sebastian Brock, recently retired Reader in Syriac Studies and Professorial Fellow of Wolfson College, checked the Syriac entry, and Dr Alison Salvesen, University Research Lecturer in Biblical Studies, the bilingual Hebrew–Latin manuscript. Since two people had already looked at the Ethiopic volume, another person seemed unnecessary, while it was impossible to find a second for the Gujarati item, it being quite difficult to find one in the first place. The careful and patient reading of all of these people is gratefully acknowledged here.

Two people gave generous assistance with some of the Arabic and Persian material, though so much time has now passed that they may well have forgotten: Professor Wilferd Madelung, former Laudian Professor of Arabic and Fellow of St John's, helped me in identifying some material, and Dr Nadia Jamal, Instructor in Arabic at the Oriental Institute, aided the interpretation of a troublesome bit of Arabic.

Throughout the project, the staff of the library at St John's College have been most kind and helpful to all of us. The late Angela Williams, Assistant Librarian at the time the project began, was always eager to discuss the manuscripts and keen to see work on them proceed. The present Assistant Librarian, Mrs Catherine Hilliard, has been a model of efficiency and helpfulness in settling the numerous questions that arose toward the end of the project, while Mrs Ruth Ogden, Library Administrator, has throughout cheerfully greeted us upon entrance to the library and always without complaint provided any manuscript that was needed. It has indeed been a pleasure to be able to work in the library of St John's College.

Last, but by no means least, I wish thank the fellow librarian of St John's College, Dr Peter Hacker, for asking me to undertake and organize the catalogue, and the bursar, Dr Anthony Boyce, for making the work just that much more enjoyable for us all.

E. Savage-Smith

The Oriental Institute, Oxford
June 2004

CONTENTS

LIST OF COLOUR PLATES

(*between pages* 76 *and* 77)

Photographs (*Plates* I, IV–XXI) © Christopher Phillips
Photographs (*Plates* II, III) © Ashmolean Photographic Studio

LIST OF BLACK AND WHITE PLATES

(*between pages* 108 *and* 109)

Photographs © Christopher Phillips

ABBREVIATIONS

Ahlwardt, *Berlin*

W. Ahlwardt, *Die Handschriften-Verzeichnisse der königliche Bibliotheken zu Berlin: Verzeichniss der arabischen Handschriften*, 10 vols. (Berlin: A. Ashner, 1887–99)

Alumni Oxoniensis–i

Joseph Foster, *Alumni Oxoniensis: The Members of the University of Oxford, 1500–1714* (Oxford: Parker & Co., 1892)

Alumni Oxoniensis–ii

Joseph Foster, *Alumni Oxoniensis: The Members of the University of Oxford, 1715–1866* (Oxford: Parker & Co., 1888)

Bernard, *Catalogi*

Edward Bernard, *Catalogi librorum manuscriptorum Angliae et Hiberniae* (Oxford, 1697), ii: 59–63

Brockelmann, *GAL*

C. Brockelmann, *Geschichte der arabischen Litteratur*, 1st edn., 2 vols. (Leiden: Brill, 1889–1936). Page references will be to the first edition, with the page numbers of the second edition (Leiden: Brill, 1943-9) given in parentheses

Brockelmann, *GAL* S

C. Brockelmann, *Geschichte der arabischen Litteratur, Supplement*, 3 vols. (Leiden: Brill, 1937–42)

Costin, *History of St. John's College*

W. C. Costin, *The History of St. John's College, Oxford, 1598–1860* (Oxford: Oxford University Press, 1958)

Coxe

H. O. Coxe, *Catalogus Codicum MSS. Collegii S. Johannis Baptisæ*, part II, section 6, in H. O. Coxe, *Catalogus codicum MSS. qui in collegiis aulisque Oxoniensibus hodie adservantur* (Oxford: e typographeo Academico, 1852)

Coxe-supplement-1

St. John's College, Oxford: Summary Catalogue of Manuscripts 213–310, Being a Supplement of Coxe's Catalogue of 1852 [up to 1956] [unpublished typescript of supplement prepared by H. M. Colvin, kept in College library]

Coxe-supplement-2

St. John's College, Oxford: Summary Catalogue of Manuscripts Acquired or Listed since 1956, Forming the Second Supplement to Coxe's Catalogue of 1852 [unpublished typescript of supplement prepared by H. M. Colvin in 1979, kept in College library]

DNB

Dictionary of National Biography

DSB

C. C. Gillispie and Frederic L. Holmes (eds.), *Dictionary of Scientific Biography*, 18 vols. (New York: American Council of Learned Societies and Charles Scribner's Sons, 1970-90)

EI^2
H. A. R. Gibbs, B. Lewis, Ch. Pellat, C. Bosworth, et al. (eds.), *The Encyclopaedia of Islam*, 2nd edn., 11 vols. (Leiden: E. J. Brill, 1960–2002)

EncIr
Ehsan Yarshater (ed.), *Encyclopedia Iranica*, 10 vols. (London: Routledge & Kegan Paul and Costa Mesa: Mazda, 1983 to present)

Gunther, *Early Science in Oxford*
R. T. Gunther, *Early Science in Oxford* (Oxford: Oxford University Press, 1959)

Hanna, *St John's Catalogue*
Ralph Hanna, *A Description Catalogue of the Western Medieval Manuscripts of St. John's College, Oxford* (Oxford: Oxford University Press, 2002)

ḤKh
Ḥājjī Khalīfah (Kātib Çelebī), *Kashf al-ẓunūn: Lexicon bibliographicum et encyclopœdicum*, ed. G. Flügel, 7 vols. (Leipzig: Typis Frider. Chr. Guil. Vogeli/London: Richard Bentley for the Oriental Translation Fund of Great Britain and Ireland, 1835–58)

James, *After Timur*
David James, *After Timur: Qur'ans of the 15th and 16th centuries*, Khalili Collection of Islamic Art iii (London: Azimuth Editions/Oxford: Oxford University Press, 1992)

King, *Catalogue*
David A. King, *A Catalogue of the Scientific Manuscripts in the Egyptian National Library, Part II: A Descriptive Catalogue of the Scientific Collections Arranged Chronologically According to Subject Matter (Arabic-Persian-Turkish): Indexes of Titles and Authors*, American Research Center in Egypt, Catalog 4 (Cairo: General Egyptian Book Organization in collaboration with the American Research Center in Egypt, 1986)

King, *Survey*
David A. King, *A Survey of the Scientific Manuscripts in the Egyptian National Library*, American Research Center in Egypt, Catalog 5 (Winona Lake, Ind.: Eisenbrauns for the American Research Center in Egypt, 1986)

Maddison and Savage-Smith, *Science, Tools & Magic*
F. Maddison and E. Savage-Smith, *Science, Tools & Magic*, Khalili Collection of Islamic Art xi (London: Azimuth Editions/Oxford: Oxford University Press, 1997)

NPAM
'Codices Arabici Mohammedani', pp. 60–407 and 433–9, in *Catalogi codicum manuscriptorum Orientalium Bibliothecae Bodleianae. Pars seconda Arabicos complectens. Confecit Alexander Nicoll. Editionem absolvit et catalogum Urianum aliquatenus emendavit E. B. Pusey* (Oxford: e typographeo Academico, 1835)

Pearson, *Oriental Collections Great Britain*
J. D. Pearson, *Oriental Manuscript Collections in the Libraries of Great Britain and Ireland* (London: The Royal Asiatic Society, 1954)

Pearson, *Oriental Manuscripts Europe*
J. D. Pearson, *Oriental Manuscripts in Europe and North America* (Zug: Inter Documentation Company AG, 1971)

Pointer, *Oxoniensis Academia*
John Pointer, *Oxoniensis Academia: or, the Antiquities and Curiosities of the University of Oxford* (London: Printed for S. Birt and J. Ward. Sold also by J. Fletcher, and J. Barrett at Oxford, and T. Merrill at Cambridge, 1749)

Quiring-Zoche, *VOHD*
Rosemarie Quiring-Zoche, *Arabische Handschriften, Teil III*, Verzeichnis der orientalischen Handschriften in Deutschland, XVII, B, 3 (Stuttgart: Franz Steiner, 1994)

Schoeler, *VOHD*
Gregor Schoeler, *Arabische Handschriften, Teil II*, Verzeichnis der orientalischen Handschriften in Deutschland, XVII, B, 2 (Stuttgart: Franz Steiner, 1990)

SEB I
E. Sachau, completed by Hermann Ethé, *Catalogue of the Persian, Turkish, Hindûstânî and Pushtû Manuscripts in the Bodleian Library. Part I: The Persian Manuscripts* (Oxford: Clarendon Press, 1899)

SEB II
Hermann Ethé, *Catalogue of the Persian,Turkish, Hindûstânî and Pushtû Manuscripts in the Bodleian Library. Part II: Turkish, Hindûstânî, Pushtû and Additional Manuscripts* (Oxford: Clarendon Press, 1930)

SEB III
A. F. L. Beeston, *Catalogue of the Persian, Turkish, Hindûstânî and Pushtû Manuscripts in the Bodleian Library. Part III: Additional Manuscripts* (Oxford: Clarendon Press, 1954)

Sellheim, *VOHD*
Rudolf Sellheim, *Materialien zur arabischen Literaturgeschichte, Teil I*, Verzeichnis der orientalischen Handschriften in Deutschland, XVII, A, 1 (Wiesbaden: Franz Steiner, 1976)

Sezgin, *GAS* I
Fuat Sezgin, *Qur'ānwissenschaften, Ḥadīṯ, Geschichte, Fiqh, Dogmatik, Mystik bis ca 430 H.*, Geschichte des arabischen Schrifttums 1 (Leiden: E. J. Brill, 1967)

Sezgin, *GAS* V
Fuat Sezgin, *Mathematik bis ca 430 H.*, Geschichte des arabischen Schrifttums 5 (Leiden: E. J. Brill, 1974)

Sezgin, *GAS* VI
Fuat Sezgin, *Astronomie bis ca 430 H.*, Geschichte des arabischen Schrifttums 6 (Leiden: E. J. Brill, 1978)

Sezgin, *GAS* VII
Fuat Sezgin, *Astrologie – Meteorologie und Verwandtes bis ca 430 H.*, Geschichte des arabischen Schrifttums 7 (Leiden: E. J. Brill, 1979)

Sezgin, *GAS* X
Fuat Sezgin, *Mathematische Geographie und Kartographie im Islam und ihr Fortleben im Abendland. Historische Darstellung, Teil I*, Geschichte der arabischen Schrifttums 10 (Frankfurt am Main: Institut für Geschichte der Arabisch-Islamischen Wissenschaften an der Johann Wolfgang Goethe-Universität, 2000)

Sobieroj, *VOHD*
Florian Sobieroj, *Islamische Handschriften. Teil 5. Thüringen*, Verzeichnis der orientalischen Handschriften in Deutschland XXXVII, 5 (Stuttgart: Franz Steiner, 2001)

Storey, *PL* II_1
C. A. Storey, *Persian Literature: A Bio-bibliographical Survey, Volume 2, Part1: A. Mathematics, B. Weights and Measures, C. Astronomy and Astrology, D. Geography* (London: Luzac, 1958)

Storey, *PL* II_3

C. A. Storey, *Persian Literature: A Bio-Bibliographical Survey, Volume 2, Part 3: F. Encyclopaedias and Miscellanies, G. Arts and Crafts, H. Science, J. Occult Arts* (London: Royal Asiatic Society, 1977)

Suter, Die Mathematiker

Heinrich Suter, *Die Mathematiker und Astronomen der Araber und ihre Werke*, Abhandlungen zur Geschichte der Mathematischen Wissenschaften mit Einschluss ihrer Anwendungen, X (Leizig: B.G. Teubner, 1900)

Wagner, *VOHD*

Ewald Wagner, *Arabische Handschriften, Teil I*, Verzeichnis der orientalischen Handschriften in Deutschland, XVII, B, 1 (Wiesbaden: Franz Steiner, 1976)

INTRODUCTION

The twenty-six 'Oriental' manuscripts in the library of St John's College—that is, those which are not Latin or Greek or European vernaculars—are a very mixed group. Most are Arabic or Persian treatises, but there also Syriac, Hebrew, Turkish, Ethiopic, and Gujarati items. Therefore, the first level of organization within this catalogue is by language. The twenty-one Arabic and Persian manuscripts, containing thirty-four separate items, are sub-grouped by subject, the majority falling within the categories of astronomy and mathematics. For the other languages, the number of manuscripts were so small that they did not merit subdivision by subject. The intention of this catalogue is to provide a full description of each item within each manuscript. It is in essence a *catalogue raisonné*, in which as much information as currently available is given regarding the identification and significance of the material.

Only one of the items here catalogued has been described previously in any published modern-language catalogue. In 1697 Edward Bernard included sixteen of the Oriental manuscripts in his union catalogue of British libraries, *Catalogi librorum manuscriptorum Angliae et Hibernia*. These volumes were simply given numerical shelfmarks within two chests, called 'Abacus ij' and 'Abacus iij', in which they were stored. In 1852 H. O. Coxe assigned the modern shelfmark numbers up to 212 to all the manuscripts at St John's College at that time, also providing short Latin descriptions for the manuscripts. Two supplements to the Coxe catalogue of St John's manuscripts were prepared by H. M. Colvin, one completed in 1956 and the other in 1979, but both remain unpublished in typescript and available only in the library of the College. The entries provided by Colvin tend to be very short indeed, though the copy kept in the library has been annotated over the years as various scholars have examined some of the items.

Some individual manuscripts have attracted more attention in print, in particular the bilingual Latin–Hebrew manuscript containing four books of the Old Testament, which the cataloguer of the Latin manuscripts at St John's College, Ralph Hanna, amongst others, has described from various standpoints (see MS 143, Entry 35). Several readers in past years left notes on particular manuscripts with the library, and these have proved useful and are for the most part noted in the catalogue entries in this volume. The notes made by Adrian Brockett on the *Qur'ān*s in the collection were particularly useful. By and large, however, the items here catalogued have not been described previously in any detail.

These Oriental manuscripts came to be at St John's College through a number of avenues. Fifteen came to the College through the donation of Archbishop William Laud (d. 1645). Of these fifteen, eight had been in the collection of Sir Kenelm Digby (d. 1665), whose *ex libris* is often crossed out. (See the Index of Previous Owners and Donors for details.) Edward Bernard (d. 1697), Savilian Professor of Astronomy from 1673 to 1691, was seriously interested in Middle Eastern manuscripts (*Alumni Oxoniensis*-i, 115; *DNB*).

In 1667 Bernard gave to the College the bilingual Hebrew–Latin volume of four books of the Old Testament (MS 143). He also acquired an Arabic translation of Ulugh Beg's fifteenth-century astronomical tables (MS 91) specifically for the College (according to an inscription in the volume dated 1682), though the volume entered the College technically through the donation of Archbishop William Laud, whose *ex libris* dated 1640 is in the volume. John Pointer (d. 1754) of Merton College bequeathed to St John's College miscellaneous collections of autographs and palaeographic curiosities, among which are to be found a Hebrew conveyance of land (MS 253, item 51), the Turkish letter (MS 253, item 7), and the Gujarati navigational guide (MS 254, item 54).

The Syriac manuscript (MS 70) was given to the College in 1639 by Matthias Turner. This may be the same Matthias Turner who was at Balliol College from 1618 to 1632 and rector of Dynedor, Herefordshire, from 1631 until an specified time (*Alumni Oxoniensis*-i, 1521). A *Qur'ān* (MS 215) was given to the College by William Stoddard (or Stoddart) who was a Fellow of St John's from 1828 until 1853, during which time he also served as bursar (1841) and vice-president (1844). From 1853 until his death in 1856 he was chaplain of St John's College and vicar of Charlbury, Oxfordshire (*Alumni Oxoniensis*-ii, 1357). Another *Qur'ān* (MS 304) was given in 1769 to the College by Charles Stafford Playdell (or Pleydell), who unfortunately has not otherwise been identified.

The unillustrated but illuminated copy of the *Maqāmāt* by al-Ḥarīrī (MS 370), made for the Maronite Christian Arab community in Syria, was in the collection of John Trott before entering that of the College, and it is presumed that John Trott was the donor, though there may have been an unknown intermediary. According to the bookplate in the volume, dated 1806, Trott held a BA from St John's College, Cambridge, though his name does not occur in the *Alumni Cantabrigiensis* by J. A. Venn. It is unknown when or by what route the Ethiopic manuscript came to be at St John's College.

Each manuscript, or each item contained in a manuscript, has been assigned an Entry Number. The Concordance of Manuscripts (Appendix I) provides the title(s) and author(s) for each manuscript according to shelfmark, with corresponding entry numbers. This concordance serves as the guide to all items in a given manuscript. The Concordance by Author (Appendix II) provides the names of the authors with the corresponding titles of treatises, the shelfmark (manuscript number), and the entry number. The Concordance of Dated Manuscripts (Appendix III) presents the date given in a colophon, the name of the copyist, the place of copying when known, and the corresponding shelfmark and entry number.

THE FORMAT OF THE ENTRIES

Following each entry number, the shelfmark (manuscript number with item number if appropriate) is given, followed by the title and the author, if known. Under the rubric CONTENTS there is a general discussion of the nature of the treatise being catalogued, evidence for identifying the author, and any distinctive features of this particular copy. This section also includes references to other known copies and any editions or translations that have appeared.

The PHYSICAL DESCRIPTION portion of the entry begins with the number of leaves (folios) comprising the item being catalogued. In manuscripts written in languages reading from left to right, the two sides of a folio are designated r (*recto*) and v (*verso*), while in manuscripts reading from right to left, such as Arabic, Persian, and Hebrew, the sides of a folio are referred to in the order read as 'a' and 'b'. In the case of the bilingual Latin–Hebrew manuscript (MS 143), while the Hebrew is written right to left, the manuscript has been bound as if reading from left to right.

There follows a transcription of the beginning and ending of the copy. Line numbers are given as subscripts. In the case of the Turkish letter (Entry No. 37) and the Gujarati navigational guide (Entry No. 41) the transcribed openings and closing are not given, but a detailed analysis of each is provided. If the copy is signed or dated, the colophon is transcribed, and if the copy is undated or unsigned then a suggestion is made as to the possible date of copying.

A statement of the language of the text is followed by the dimensions of the copy, with height given first (the size of the text area is in parentheses), and the number of lines per page. That is followed immediately by the evidence given in the manuscript itself for the title and the author. There then may occur detailed listing of the sections, or tables, comprising the copy.

The general type of script is then specified (for example, Naskh or Maghribī, in the case of Arabic and Persian manuscripts) and an indication of size given. The latter (in the case of Arabic and Persian items) has been done by using terms that correspond to the following measurements of the letter ط occurring in the text:

very large	> 10 mm
large	8–10 mm
medium large	6–7 mm
medium small	4–5 mm
small	2–3 mm
very small	< 2 mm

It is also noted if undotted letters (*muhmal*) have small carons over them or minuscule letters underneath, and other distinctive features of the hand are recorded. An indication of ink colour and the coloration of headings is also provided.

A separate paragraph is devoted to paper description. The colour of the paper has been determined by comparing pages toward the inner part of the manuscript (not water damaged or soiled, if possible) with fan decks of colour samples using the 'Munsell system' (formerly known as the Centroid Colour Charts devised by the US National Bureau of Standards). Fan decks in the 5Y and 10YR range were used. These were grouped into six sets, and when a paper in a manuscript fell within the following range of colour samples in a set, the general colour name assigned to that set was given the paper in the catalogue entry. This was done in an attempt to introduce some quantification, even if rather primitive, to what is a highly subjective evaluation. The six colours have been defined as follows:

Ivory	5Y/9/0.5–1.0; 5Y/8.5/0.5–1.0; 10YR/9/0.5–1.0; and 10YR/8.5/0.5–1.0
Cream	5Y/8.5/1.5–3.0 and 5Y/9/1.5–3.0
Beige	10YR/9/1.5–2.0 and 10YR/8.5/2.0–4.0
Biscuit	10YR/7.5/1.5–2.0 and 10YR/8/1.5–3.0
Brown	10YR/7.5/2.5–4.0 and 10YR/7/2.5–4.0
Grey	5Y/6.5–8/0.5 and 10YR/6.5–8/0.5

The thickness of the paper was measured with a micrometer and a range of values given. Because of the variation in all papers, the range of values for a paper is significant, and not a single value. The opaqueness, or translucency, of the paper is assigned a value on the Sharp Scale of Opaqueness. The latter is a recently devised method (named after its originator, Henrietta Sharp) by which the translucency of paper can be categorized in terms of the number of folios required before the outline of a dowel held behind the folio(s) is no longer visible when illuminated from behind with a constant light of 60 watts at an approximate distance of 15 cm. The laid lines are described as well as the chain lines (if there are any) and the occurrence of watermarks noted (sometimes with a description of the watermark when it was sufficiently visible).

Under *Marginalia and owners' notes*, the occurrence of any marginalia is noted, as well as any evidence for authorship of the annotations and sometimes transcriptions of important or interesting parts. This section does not include former owners' *ex libris*, for those are discussed in the section titled *Provenance*.

Volume contents enumerates every item in the volume and its extent, as well as any miscellaneous leaves. This enumeration occurs only once for those manuscripts with multiple items, in the entry marked MAIN ENTRY in the Concordance of Manuscripts (Appendix I).

Under *Binding* a general description of the binding, pastedowns, and endpapers is given. When a binding is described as having 'modern' pastedowns or endpapers, it is meant that these items were probably placed in the volume when it was last bound or rebound. No attempt has been made to give a specialist description of Near Eastern bindings. Many of these manuscripts, in fact, have been rebound in European bindings of no particular historical importance. The binding of the Ethiopic manuscript (MS 228), in wooden boards, is of particular interest, as is the dark-brown leather pouch in which it was kept. The items from the Pointer collection (MSS 253 and 254) essentially have no bindings.

Under *Provenance* all the available information about previous owners is given. These include owners' stamps and handwritten *ex libris* wherever these occur in the volume.

Under *References*, the entry numbers in the 1697 catalogue of Edward Bernard and that of H. O. Coxe in 1852 are provided first. For those manuscripts not in these two early catalogues, most are in the unpublished typescript supplements to Coxe prepared by H. M. Colvin, and these are duly noted. Other published citations or descriptions of a manuscript are also given at this point, including the entries in John Pointer's *Oxoniensis Academia* and, for MS143 (the bilingual Latin–Hebrew volume), the Hebrew catalogue descriptions of D. Neugebauer, Malachi Beit-Arié, and Ralph Hanna as well as the recent description by J. Olszowy-Schlanger.

In the transcription of Arabic and Persian texts, the following conventions have been used:

bold	rubricated words
[n.d.]	undotted; unless otherwise specified, pertains only to preceding word.
< >	damage; hole, gap, lacuna
≪... ≫	erasure or deletion in text
[...]	illegible
[sic]	as written in text
[؟]	reading and/or meaning of preceding word uncertain
[=]	correction or expansion of a term by the editor
{ }	superfluous writing in the text; word(s) written twice
(( ))	gloss or correction written in text, above the word, or outside the line
{{ }}	catchword

Any vocalization is that given in the manuscript itself, but not all vocalization given in a manuscript is reproduced. In general, the orthography of a manuscript has been retained, even when it deviates from standard modern practices.

I

CATALOGUE

1

ARABIC AND PERSIAN MANUSCRIPTS

Emilie Savage-Smith

ASTRONOMY

Entry No. 1

MS 175 (item 3)

TITLE: [*al-Shakkāzīyah*]

الشكازية

AUTHOR: Abū Isḥāq Ibrāhīm ibn Yaḥyá al-Zarqāllu al-Ṭulayṭulī (d. 493/1100)

CONTENTS: This is a treatise on the use of a particular universal instrument usually called (in other copies) *al-ṣafīḥah al-shakkāzīyah*. The author, the Andalusian astronomer al-Zarqāllu, was famous for devising the universal astrolabic plate and the universal astrolabe. Al-Zarqāllu, or Zarqēllo, wrote at least two versions of a treatise concerned with this instrument, one version in 100 chapters and the other in 61 chapters. It is the latter version that appears to be represented here.

Four other copies of this treatise are recorded; the copy at St John's College has not been noted in the literature. The other copies are: Cairo, Dār al-Kutub, MS *hay'ah* 40 (54 fos., undated *c.*950/1543) attributed to al-Zarqāllu; Istanbul University Library, MS A4800, where it is also attributed to al-Zarqāllu; Cairo, Dār al-Kutub, Taymūr MS *riyāḍah* 131, item 4 (pp. 14–40) copied in 1186/1722 in Maghribī script with no author given; and Rabat, Royal Library, MS 6667, pp. 20–48 also attributed to al-Zarqāllu. See King, *Catalogue*, 528 entry 4.6.1 item 2; King, *Survey*, 50 entry B87; and Roser Puig,

'Concerning the *Ṣafīḥa Shakkāziyya*', *Zeitschrift für Geschichte der Arabisch-Islamischen Wissenschaften*, 2 (1985), 123–39.

The treatise consists of 61 unnumbered chapters (*bābs*). In the Cairo copy, the first chapter is called a *faṣl* with 60 subsequent numbered chapters. The beginning and ending of the St John's copy differ from the Cairo copy, Taymūr MS *riyāḍah* 131, but the section headings appear to be identical. The Istanbul copy was not available for comparison.

This treatise was translated into Hebrew and Latin; see J. Millás Vallicrosa, *Don Profeit Tibbon: Tractat de l'Assafea d'Azarquiel*, Biblioteca Hebraico-Catalana iv (Barcelona: Editorial Alpha, 1933). See also David A. King, 'On the Early History of the Universal Astrolabe in Islamic Astronomy, and the Origin of the Term "Shakkāzīya" in Medieval Scientific Arabic', *Journal for the History of Arabic Science*, 3 (1979), 244–57, esp. 253 n. 21. For Zarqāllu, see Brockelmann *GAL* i. 472–3 (623) and S i. 862 [treatise not cited]; Suter, *Die Mathematiker*, no. 255; and J. Vernet, 'al-Zarqālī', in *DSB*, xiv. 592–5.

PHYSICAL DESCRIPTION:

28 leaves (fos. 12b–39b)

Beginning (fo. $12b_{1-8}$):

وسلم تسليما

بسم الله ...

قال ابو اسحاق ابراهيم بن يحيى النقاش
المعروف بابن الزرقال رحمه الله وعفا عنه

اما بعد حمد الله الذي لا يحاط بمعلوماته ولا يدرك كنــز ذاته [؟] ... فاني رايت الناس فى القديم والحديث قد اعدوا الات علمية لمعرفة الاوقات واختلاف الليل والنهار فى الطول القصر على كل افق ...

Ending (fo. $39b_{15-19}$):

... وتعرف بما اجتمع الارتفاع كما كان فهو الارتفاع لوقت العصر وهو اخر وقت الظهر وان اردت على ظل الزوال اربعا وعشرين اصبعا التى هى قامتان وعملته بالمجتمع لارتفاع كان ذالك .

تمت بحمد الله وتوفيقه

This item was apparently copied by the same copyist as transcribed the first item in the volume, which was completed by Abū al-Qāsim ibn Muḥammad ibn ʿAlī al-Khaddām al-Andalusī on 23 Rabīʿ II 915 [= 8 Aug. 1509]. See Entry No. 9.

Arabic. Dimensions: 19.9 × 14.8 (text area 14.6 × 9.5) cm; 20 lines per page. The author is named at the beginning of the text Abū Isḥāq Ibrāhīm ibn Yaḥyá al-Naqqāsh, known as Ibn al-Zarqāl. The title is not given in this copy.

The first *bāb* (fo. 13b) is titled: باب في تسمية الرسوم الموضوعة فى وجه الصفيحة المشتركة بجميع لعروض و من ظهرها

The second *bāb* (fo. 14b): باب فى معرفة درجة الشمس من برجها

The third *bāb* (fo. 14b): باب فى معرفة اخذ ارتفاع الشمس بالنهار والكواكب بالليل

The fourth *bāb* (fo. 15a): باب فى معرفة وضع الشمس فى جزيها من برجها فى وجه الصفيحة

The next to the last *bāb* (fo. 39a): باب فى معرفة الارتفاع من قبل الظل المبسوط والمنكوس

The final *bāb* (fo. 39b): باب فى معرفة ظل الزوال فى كل يوم وهو ظل نصف النهار ومعرفة وقت الظهر والعصر .

The medium-small script is superficially Maghribī, but the dotting of the letter *fā'* is almost always above the letter rather than beneath. The text is written in dark-brown ink with headings written in a larger and extended script. Folio 13b is written by a different hand. The last word or two on the verso is often repeated at the beginning of the next folio and there are occasional catchwords; some of the folios may be out of sequence or missing.

The beige, stiff paper has a thickness of 0.12–0.14 mm and an opaqueness factor of 5. There are fine vertical laid lines, single chain lines, and watermarks (a thin hand with a flower at the end of the index finger). The paper is water damaged around the edges, particularly at the bottom. The outer margins of fos. 7–16 have one or two columns of small indentations or prickings; their purpose is unknown, but they were not apparently for ruling the text.

Marginalia and owners' notes: There are a few marginalia in different hands and some interlinear correction of the text. Folios 36a and 37a have marginalia whose ink has corroded so as to appear to be goldsprinkled.

Volume contents: The volume consists of 74 leaves. Folio 1a, in addition to two lines giving the Basmala, has five owners' notes. Folios 1b–10a (item 1, Entry No. 9) is an anonymous treatise titled *Risālat al-jāmi'ah lil-'uruḍ kullihā*; fo. 10b has the continuation of the note on zodiacal houses, written in the same hand as item 1, which began on fo. $10a_{16}$ immediately after the colophon. Folios 11a–12a (item 2, Entry No. 11) are anonymous astronomical tables and diagrams; fos. 12b–39b (item 3) is the treatise by al-Zarqāllu here catalogued; fos. 40a–43b (item 4, Entry No. 12) is a collection of trigonometric and calendric tables. Folio 44a contains miscellaneous notes, including a recipe and some poetry; for the latter, see Part II below ('Incidental Arabic Poetry', item VI). Folios 44b–56a (item 5, Entry No. 7) is a treatise on sundials by Ibn Abī al-Fatḥ al-Ṣūfī; and fos. 56b–74 (item 6, Entry No. 13) contain various calendric and astronomical tables and diagrams. There is one preliminary leaf of later paper which has been attached to a recent leaf forming one of the three (otherwise blank) front endpapers; This preliminary leaf has a Latin annotation reading *Abu Isaac Ibrahim ben Bechi, 1. De Motu solari et calculo diurno et horario. 2. Mahumed ben Mahumed de Longitudine et Latitudine locorum aliquot*; a second Latin hand, initialled L.R., has written *1. Ibrahim Ben Jahia Alnacash, Abu Isaac, vulgo B. Zarcalli, Cordubensis*; there are also earlier catalogue nos.: *Abaciij No. 20, C.38*, and [pencilled] *175*. Folio 74b has five poems and a line of prose; see Part II below ('Incidental Arabic Poetry', items VII–XI).

Binding: The volume is bound in a European library binding of dark-brown leather over pasteboards; the covers have frames of two single fillets. The pastedowns and final endpapers are European marbled paper, in maroon, dark blue, and yellow.

Provenance: The volume came to the College through the donation of Archbishop William Laud (d. 1645). Prior to that it was in the collection of Sir Kenelm Digby (d. 1665).

On fo. 1a, in addition to two lines written by different hands giving the Basmala, there are five owners' notes. One undated entry for Muḥammad ibn Qāsim known as (*yukanná bi-*) Abū ʿAmr al-Andalusī al-Wadiyāshī [or al-Wādiyāshī] al-Dārī, who also drew the circular diagrams on fos. 40b and 41a which he dated Rabīʿ II 917 [= June–July 1511] 'during the reign of Sulṭān Yazīd'). A second undated entry notes its transfer from Muḥammad ibn Qāsim to Muḥammad Abū Ḥafṣ ʿUmar ibn . . . [?]; and a third, defaced, is for . . . ibn ʿAbd Allāh. At the bottom is the *ex libris* of Digby, now inked over; and above the latter is the *ex libris* of Laud, dated 1639.

References

Coxe, 57 entry CLXXV, item 1. It was also enclosed on a typescript list (of items moved from one of the cabinets) appended at the back of the copy of the Coxe catalogue kept in the College library.

Bernard, *Catalogi*, B.20 (*in abaco secundo*).

Pearson, *Oriental Collections Great Britain*, 49 (no description given).

Pearson, *Oriental Manuscripts Europe*, 308 (no description given).

Entry No. 2

MS 103

TITLE: *Tawḍīḥ al-Tadhkirah* | *Sharḥ al-Tadhkirah*

The Explication of the 'Memoir' | *Commentary on the 'Memoir'*

توضيح التذكرة | شرح التذكرة

AUTHOR: Niẓām al-Dīn al-Ḥasan ibn Muḥammad ibn al-Ḥusayn, usually known as al-Aʿraj al-Nīsābūrī (*fl.* 711/1311)

CONTENTS: This manuscript is the earliest recorded copy of al-Aʿraj al-Nīsābūrī's commentary on Naṣīr al-Dīn Ṭūsī's *al-Tadhkirah fī 'ilm al-hay'ah* ('Memoir on the Science of Astronomy').

Naṣīr al-Dīn al-Ṭūsī (d. 672/1274) composed a general introduction to astronomy titled *Kitāb al-Tadhkirah fī 'ilm al-hay'ah*, intended as a summary for the non-specialist and consequently devoid of mathematical proofs. It comprised four parts (*bābs*): (1) an introduction to the mathematical and physical principles involved, (2) a discussion of the configuration of the skies, (3) a discourse on the configuration of the earth and its astronomically determined features, and (4) a chapter on the size of the earth and celestial bodies, and the distances between them. These chapters have 2, 14, 12, and 17 subsections (*faṣl*s) respectively. A number of commentaries were subsequently prepared on this treatise.

On 1 Rabīʿ I 711 [= 18 July 1311] Niẓām al-Dīn al-Ḥasan ibn Muḥammad ibn al-Ḥusayn, usually known as al-Aʿraj al-Nīsābūrī, completed the commentary on the *Tadhkirah* that is preserved in this manuscript. This copy now at St John's was made forty years after its composition and appears to be the earliest recorded copy.

For other copies: See Oxford, Bodleian Library, Oriental Collections, MS Arab. e. 122, copied in 1064/1654; London, BL, APAC, MS Add. 7472. *Rich.*, copied in 1062/1651; Paris, BNF, MS arabe suppl. 963; Leiden, Universiteitsbibliothek MS 1010 Warn.; Najaf, Āyat Allāh al-Ḥakīm Library, MS 649; Brockelmann, *GAL*, i. 511 (675); Suter, *Die Mathematiker*, 161 no. 395; King, *Survey*, no. G38; and F. J. Ragep, *Naṣīr al-Dīn al-Ṭūsī's Memoir on Astronomy (al-Tadhkira fī 'ilm al-hay'a)*, 2 vols., Sources for the History of Mathematics and Physical Sciences 12 (Berlin: Springer-Verlag, 1993), i. 60 no. 3. King (*Survey*, no. G38) gives three Cairo manuscripts which are really photocopies of other manuscripts: Dār al-Kutub, MS *hay'ah* 54 is a photocopy of Paris, BnF, arabe 2510, and Dār al-Kutub, MSS *hay'ah* 66 and 88 are two sets of photos of a manuscript in the Damietta Institute.

The commentary by al-Aʿraj al-Nīsābūrī was apparently very popular (see ḤKh, ii. 268 no. 2856). He also wrote a commentary on another work of Naṣīr al-Dīn al-Ṭūsī's. For al-Aʿraj al-Nīsābūrī's compositions, see Brockelmann, *GAL* ii. 200 (256) and S ii. 273; and King, *Survey*, nos. G32 and G38.

For al-Ṭūsī's treatise, see F. J. Ragep, *Naṣīr al-Dīn al-Ṭūsī's Memoir on Astronomy,* cited above.

PHYSICAL DESCRIPTION:

174 leaves (3b–48b, 51a–52b, 55a–66b, 69a–76a, 77a–180a)

Beginning (fo. $3b_{1-12}$):

بسم الله ... الحمد لله الذى جعلنا من المتفكرين فى خلق الارض والسموات ... **وبعد** فان احوج خلق الله
تعالى الى غفرانه الحسن بن محمد النيسابورى يعرف بنظام نظم الله احواله يقول من المعلوم ان العلوم ...

Ending (fo. $180a_{13-18}$):

... والقول الصحيح وجعل ما لقيت فى توضيح هذا الكتاب من عرق الجبين وكد اليمين تبصرة للمتفكرين
فى ملكوت السموات والارضين وتذكرة للهاملين [؟] فى عجيب صنع رب العالمين ووسيلة لى يوم الدين
وسببا لرضى ارحم الراحمين فان الاعمال بالنيات وبها تجلب البركات وتنال الدرجات والحمد لمبدع الكل
والصلوه على الهادى تلى اقوم السبل والسلام على من اتبع الهدى .

Colophon (fo. $180a_{19–23}$, with most diacritical dots missing), illustrated in Plate 1:

تم الكتاب بعون الملك الوهاب يوم الاربعا من شهر رمضان
المبارك عمت ميامنه لسنه اثنتين وخمسين وسبعماية على يد العبد
الضعيف النحيف الفقير الى الله الغني وهو اعظم الناس جرما
واضعفهم جرما عبد الله القيصري رزقه الله علما نافعا وغفر له
ولجميع المسلمين بفضله وكرمه .

The copy was completed on 4 Ramaḍān 752 [= 25 Oct. 1351] by ʿAbd Allāh al-Qayṣarī.

Arabic. Dimensions: 25 × 17 (text area 17.8 × 11.5) cm; 23 lines per page. At the beginning of the text, fo. $3b_{11–12}$, the name of the commentator is given as al-Ḥasan ibn Muḥammad al-Nīsābūrī, known as (يعرف بـ) Niẓām. On folio 3a a later hand has written *sharḥ-i Tadhkirah-i Niẓāmī | 200*. The name of the treatise being commented upon, *Kitāb al-Tadhkirah*, is given at $3b_{15}$, with its author given in the following two lines as Naṣīr al-Dīn Muḥammad ibn Muḥammad al-Ṭūsī. On fo. $4a_{14}$ the commentator states that he has titled the treatise *Tawḍīḥ al-Tadhkirah.*

A note written vertically alongside the colophon on fo. 180a (illustrated in Plate 1) transcribes three lines that the copyist states were written at the end of the exemplar. These lines supply the information that the author completed the composition on the first of the month of Rabīʿ I in the year 711 [= 18 July 1311]:

هذا صوره ما كان مكتوبا فى اخر الاصل
و قد اتفق فراغى من تاليف هذا الكتاب غرة ربيع الاول من شهور سنة احدى عشرة
وسبعماية هلالية رحم الله من اذا نظر [فيه] دعالى بالخير وانا افقر خلق الله تعالى
الى غفرانه الحسن بن محمد يعرف بنظام النيسابورى نظم الله احواله فى
الدارين

The treatise is transcribed in a medium-small Naskh script using a dark-brown ink, with headings in a tomato red. The passages being commented upon are introduced by *qāla* ('he said') or *qawluhu* ('he says'), written in red, with *aqūlu* ('I say') introducing the commentary. There are numerous diagrams drawn with a very fine pen using black ink and labelled in the same tomato red. The text area is frame ruled. There are catchwords. The original volume consisted of 22 numbered quires of eight folios each, except the last which has only six. Quire annotations can be seen on fos. 120, 136, 144, 152, 160, and 168, the latter labelled the 21st; only traces of quire numberings can be seen earlier in the volume.

The stiff, beige, almost matt-finished paper has a thickness of 0.17–0.21 mm and an opaqueness factor of 4 or occasionally 5. It is quite fibrous and there is considerable creasing. On most of the leaves no laid or chain lines can be distinguished, but on a few there are traces of horizontal laid lines and some chain lines (possibly in groups of threes). The paper is water stained at the bottom corners, with slight damp staining and foxing throughout. The edges have been trimmed from their original size.

Marginalia and owners' notes: Collation notes are found throughout the volume (e.g. fo. 4a) and marginal corrections marked صح. There are also annotations in other hands, some designated ظ ; some of the annotations have been partially cut off as the paper edges were trimmed.

Volume contents: The volume consists of 182 leaves, with two front and two back endpapers placed at the time of the last binding (i–ii + 1–182 + iii–iv). Folio 2 is blank except for an annotation on the recto written in a Persian hand: *sharḥ-i Tadhkirah-i al-Ḥasan al-A'raj*; on the verso there is a Latin note (*Commentarius De Elementis Astronomiœ*) and one Arabic *dūbayt* ('quatrain') and two distichs; for the poetry see Part II below, 'Incidental Arabic Poetry', items II–IV). Folio 1 (of different paper, clearly having chain lines in groups of threes) is blank except for a Turkish *ex libris* on the recto and, on the verso, a tiny illegible note in the upper left corner. Folio 3a has six owners' notes and a stamp.

Folios 49 and 50 are small slips of modern paper (18.7 × 5.6 and 16.5 × 5.5 cm) that have been bound, upside down, into the volume; they contain some casually written Persian notes with a mathematical diagram reproducing that on fo. 52a in the text). Folios 53 and 54 are loose sheets of modern paper (17.5 × 11.5 and 18.5 × 13.8 cm), one of which has a diagram reproducing that on fo. 52a of the text while the other has a number of miscellaneous Persian notes and poetry written in several different directions on the paper. Folios 67 and 68 are in fact one loose sheet of modern paper (14.5 × 21 cm), folded in half; Persian notes are written on one side of the folded paper. Folio 76b is blank.

Folios 180b and 181 are blank except for a St John's College bookplate on the verso of fo. 181. Folio 182 is later paper (with chain lines in groups of twos alternating with threes) and is blank except for three separate Persian verses; it also has the pencilled numeration *169*, apparently having been taken from another volume.

Binding: On fo. 2a staining from an envelope flap belonging to an earlier binding can been detected. The volume is at present bound in a European binding identical to that of MS 122 (Entry No. 23), made of pasteboards covered with a light-brown suede leather; the spine has five cords. The covers have blind-stamped rectangular designs of acanthus leaves on one side of two fillets, with repetitive flower-head and leaves on the other side and a large tulip at each corner. The same design, but impressed on a shiny, mottled brown leather, can be seen in the binding of MS 107 (Entry No. 32). The front and back endpapers, of identical paper, are blank except for a slip of paper attached to fo. i which has a Latin note regarding the contents and the date of copying. The back paper pastedown has the bookplate of St John's College. The front pastedown has pencilled at the bottom *ol. 1867. III.35*, as well as having pasted onto it another piece of paper with the following Latin annotation:

Commentarius
in
Elementa Astronomica
insignis Philosophi & Mathematici
Nassir Eddini Tusæi, qui floruit
tempore Chalîfæ Mostásemi, circa
an. Hej. 660, X^ti^. 1261.
incerto Auctore.

Vid. Hydij Præfat. ad Tab. Ulugh Beig.
Epistolam Ioan Gravij. binis Tabulis
Geograph. præfixam, & D'Herbelot.
Bibliothec. Orient. p. 665.col.2.

Quidam verò Arabs (in chartis vacuis libro præfixis, & alibi) tribuit Opus Astronomicum, quod hîc explicatur, Alhasani, fil. Mohammedis, Nisaburensi, sed minùs, ut videtur, rectè. Qui Arabicè scit, paginam J^mam.^ consulat.

Hoc Exemplar scriptum videtur (nam verba ærae obscura sunt) an Hej. 752. X^ti^. 1352.

Provenance: The manuscript came to the College through the donation of Archbishop William Laud (d. 1645) and before that was in the collection of Sir Kenelm Digby (d. 1665).

On fo. 3a, there is a six-line owner's note written at the centre of the page, signed ʿAbd al-Raḥīm ibn ʿAlī ibn Mu'ayyad al-Rūmī al-Amāsī in the city of Constantinople on the first of the month of Dhū al-Ḥijjah 890 [= 9 Dec. 1485], as well as an undated circular stamp with the same name (ʿAbd al-Raḥīm ibn ʿAlī ibn Mu'ayyad). At the top of the same page there is a note stating that the volume was amongst the gifts of Sultan Mehmet Murād Khān to one Ibn Ilyās. On this same folio there is also an obliterated Arabic owner's note, the *ex libris* of Digby (crossed out), and an undated *ex libris* of Archbishop Laud with a later annotation of its donation to St John's College.

On fo. 1a there is an undated *ex libris* reading, in Arabic: '*ṣāḥibuhu* Muʿallim Zādah Efendī, teacher in the Khanjarīyah [?] Madrasah and then *qāḍī* in the Victorious Army in the Province of Rumeli'. On folio 2a there is the numeral ١۴٠ [140].

References

Coxe, 31 entry CIII; it is also included on a typescript list (of items moved from one of the cabinets), appended at the back of the Coxe catalogue kept in the College library.
Bernard, *Catalogi*, C.35 (*in abaco tertio*).
Pearson, *Oriental Collections Great Britain*, 49 (no description given).
Pearson, *Oriental Manuscripts Europe*, 308 (no description given).

Entry No. 3

MS 156B (item 1)

TITLE: *Kitab al-Sirr al-maktūm fī al-'amal bi-l-zīj al-manẓūm*

The Hidden Secret concerning the use of 'the versified zīj'

AUTHOR: [attributed to] Abū al-Fidā', Ismā'īl ibn 'Alī ibn Maḥmūd ibn Muḥammad ibn Taqī al-Dīn 'Umar ibn Ayyūb, al-Malik al-Mu'ayyad 'Imād al-Dīn (d. 732/1331)

CONTENTS: This is a treatise on astronomy in two chapters (*maqālahs*). The first, titled *fī ḥisāb al-jadāwil*, 'on the computation of the tables', consists of short didactic poems summarizing procedures, each followed immediately by a prose explanation (*al-tafsīr*). The second *maqālah* apparently consists only of tables.

The author is given as 'Imād al-Dīn Ismā'īl ibn Zayn al-Dīn 'Umar Sulṭān Ḥamāh, which has been interpreted as referring to the Syrian prince, ruler of Ḥamāh, historian, and geographer Abū al-Fidā', though it is a somewhat unusual designation if it does refer to Abū al-Fidā'. There has been no study of this treatise and its possible relationship to his historical and geographical writings. Arabic bio-bibliographic sources do provide some examples of his efforts at poetry, however, and it is known that he produced a versification of a juristic work. For Abū al-Fidā', see H. A. R. Gibb, 'Abu 'l-Fidā' in *EI*[2], i. 118–19.

In one table (on fo. 88a) the authority of one *al-shaykh al-imām* 'Alā' al-Dīn ibn al-Shāṭir *al-muwaqqit* is cited (الشيخ الامام علاي الدين بن الشاطر الموقت). This is not, presumably, a reference to the famous Damascene astronomer 'Alā' al-Dīn 'Alī ibn Ibrāhīm Ibn al-Shāṭir al-Dimashqī (*fl. c.*1350). In several tables, the latitude of 34° is specified.

Only one other copy of this treatise is recorded, and that is an incomplete transcription made by Edward Bernard from this manuscript in St John's College. It is now in the Bodleian Library, Oriental Collections MS Bodl. Or. 218, item 1 (fos. ia and 1a–13a); see NPAM, 301 entry CCCII and corrections in NPAE 547. The Bodleian manuscript (but not the St John's original) was cited by Suter, *Die Mathematiker*, 160 no. 392.

The copyist of the manuscript, 'Alī ibn Yūsuf al-Qudsī, states that he was a muezzin at the Umayyad mosque in Damascus and a pupil of Shams al-Dīn Abū 'Abd Allāh Muḥammad ibn Muḥammad al-Tīzīnī, the timekeeper of the Umayyad mosque. The latter was an important Syrian astronomer, several of whose treatises are preserved today. For Muḥammad ibn Muḥammad al-Tīzīnī (*fl. c.*899/1494), see King, *Survey*, no. C95, and Suter, *Die Mathematiker*, 186 no. 450.

PHYSICAL DESCRIPTION:

82 leaves (fos. 1a–17b, 19a–23b, 29a–83b, 87a–90a_5)

Title page (fo. 1a):

كتاب السر المكتوم فى العمل بالزيج المنظوم
، تاليف الشيخ الامام العالم العلامة ، وحيد دهره ،
وفريد عصره ، عماد الدين اسمعيل بن زين الدين
عمر سلطان حماه ، رضي الله عنه وارضاه ،
وجعل الجنة مثواه ، بمنه
وطوله ، وقوته ،
وحوله
امين
م
وحسبنا الله ونعم الوكيل

A later (17th-century?) hand has added in the middle of the title page the following Latin note: Tabulæ Astronimicæ Omadaddin Ismaelis Regis Hamah. Liber elegantissimè scriptus, et quovis auro preciosior.

Beginning (fos. $1b_1$–$2a_5$):

بسم الله . . . رب يسر يا كريم. الحمد لله المتفرد بالقدرة في الانشا والايجاد ، . . . **اما بعد** فان هذا قانون لـتقويم الكواكـب وغيرها من الاعمال النجوميه وعظم فخره وعظم قدره ، منعش الاذهان العبقه بالذكآ والالباب ، وناطق بحكم بدايع الاقوال وفصل الخطاب ، . . . وقصمت مشكلات معانيه من الحفاظ بطلا ، مع ان الرسايل المنظومه فيه علي ما هي مبرهنه لم يكن بينها وبين ما دون في غيره من الزيجات نسبة بالسهولة وقـرب العمل والاختصار ولا يكاد يتحقق ذلك الا من كثر نظره في الكتب المولفه في ذلك وجعلته مقالتين **الاولي** في حساب والجداول **والثانيه** في علل ذلك وبراهينه وبالله استعين .

في نقل سني الروم الي الايام
، اذا ما سنيّ الروم حصلت تامة ، فتضربها في هآطاب تقسم ،
، لذاك علي ستين من بعد ضربه ، فتحميل ايام السنين فاحكم ، . . .
التفسير
تضرب السنين الفارسيه في **٢١٩١٥** وتقسم المبلغ علي **٦٥** فتحصل ايام تلك السنين . . .

Colophon (fo. $90a_{1-5}$), illustrated in Plate 2:

ووافق الفراغ من نسخ الزيج المنظوم وما يليه من الجدوال نهار الاربعا سابع المحرم الحرام سنه **٨٩٧** علي يد العبد الفقير الراجي عفو ربه القدير علي بن يوسف القدسي الموذن بالجامع الاموي تلميذ الشيخ شمس الدين ابي عبد الله محمد بن محمد التيزيني الموقت بالجامع الاموي غفر الله له ولوالديه ولمالكه ولمن نظر فيه ودعا له بالمغفره ولجميع المسلمين امين والحمد لله وحده وصلى الله على سيدنا محمد وآله وسلم .

The copying of the *Zīj manẓūm* and associated charts was completed on 7 Muḥarram 897 [= 10 Nov. 1491] in Damascus by ʿAlī ibn Yūsuf al-Qudsī, *al-mu'adhdhin bi-l-Jāmiʿ al-Umawī* [muezzin at the Umayyad mosque] and pupil of *al-shaykh* Shams al-Dīn Abū

ʿAbd Allāh Muḥammad ibn Muḥammad al-Tīzīnī, *al-muwaqqit bi-l-Jāmiʿ al-Umawī* [the timekeeper at the Umayyad mosque].

Arabic. Dimensions: 20.8 × 15.2 (text area 14.6 × 10.5) cm; 21 lines per page. Author's name is given on the title page: ʿImād al-Dīn Ismāʿīl ibn Zayn al-Dīn ʿUmar Sulṭān Ḥamāh. The title is also provided on the title page.

The text is written in a medium-small Naskh script using black ink, with headings in red and red teardrop text-stops. The *tā' marbuṭah* is nearly always ligatured to the preceding letter. The text throughout is written with frames of two thin red lines; occasionally the last letter or two of a word occurring at the end of a line is written outside the text frame. There are catchwords.

The two gilt circular decorative medallions at the top of fo. 1a have been cut from another manuscript and placed at the top of the page.

The treatise as now bound is out of sequence and possibly defective. Moreover, fos. 24–8 and 84–7 have been inserted from other compilations, further confusing the sequence of the folios. The correct sequence in which the folios comprising the first item should be read are the following: 1–17b, 81a–83b, 29a–80, 19–23, 87–90a$_5$. A later hand has added the text on the lower half of fo. 90a and the table on fo. 90b, along with notes on other folios; these have been dealt with as a group under item 2 (Entry No. 16).

A number of the ten-folio quires are labelled with numbers spelt out in words. These quire annotations, along with the catchwords (which are missing from most of the folios having tables), allow an approximate reconstruction of item 1 as follows:

Quire 1: fos. 1–9.

Quire 2: fos. 10–17 and 81–2 (fo. 10 labelled ثانى). The first *maqālah* of the present item ends at the bottom of fo. 17a (وهذا اخر المقالة الاول). It is unclear where the subsequent *maqālah* starts and ends, for most of the remainder appears to consist of tables.

Folio 17b consists of an untitled table giving values for six planets plus one of the lunar nodes. It is possible that it was added by a later hand.

Folios 81–82 consist of four tables:

81a: جدول الايام المعظمة فى الاسلام على الاشهر العربية

81b: جدول التوقيعات وطلوع المنازل بالفجر فى الاشهر الرومية

82a: بقيه التوقيعات وطلوع المنازل فى الاشهر الرومية

82b: جدول اهات الكواكب المعدله للاتصالات والانتقالات تدخل بالبعد الى تحت البهت

Quire 3: fos. 83 and 19–35 (fo. 83 labelled ثالث). This quire is defective, having eight leaves only.

83a: بقيه الاهات للكواكب والاتصالات والانتقالات وجزويهما وساعات البعد

[untitled table] :83b

29a: جدول حركة وسط الشمس والاوج في السنين الفارسيه | جدول حركة الجوزهر في السنين الفارسيه

29b: جدول حركة القمر فى التاريخ الفارسي الناقص

30a: جدول حركة الشمس والقمر والجوزهر فى الايام والشهور الفارسيه

30b: جدول حركة الشمس والقمر والجوزهر فى الشهور والايام الفارسيه

31a: جدول حركة الشمس والقمر والجوزهر فى الشهور والايام الفارسيه

31b: جدول حركة الشمس والقمر والجوزهر فى الشهور والايام الفارسيه

32a: جدول حركة الشمس والقمر والجوزهر فى الشهور والايام الفارسيه

32b: جدول حركة الشمس والقمر والجوزهر فى الشهور الفارسيه

33a: جدول حركة الشمس والقمر والجوزهر فى الشهور والايام الفارسيه

33b: جدول حركة الشمس والقمر والجوزهر فى الشهور والايام الفارسيه

34a: جدول حركة الشمس والقمر والجوزهر فى الشهور الفارسيه والايام

34b: جدول حركة الشمس والقمر والجوزهر فى الشهور والايام الفارسيه

35a: جدول حركة الشمس والقمر والجوزهر فى الشهور والايام الفارسيه

35b: جدول حركة الشمس والقمر والجوزهر فى الشهور والايام الفارسيه

Quire 4: fos. 36–45 (fo. 36 labelled رابع)

36a: تتمه جداول حركة الشمس والقمر والجوزهر في الشهور الفارسية

36b: جدول تعديل الشمس يوخذ بمركزها ويزاد عليه ابداً والاوج ايضاً

37a: جدول تعديل الشمس يوخذ بمركزها ويزاد عليه ابدا والاوج ايضاً

37b: جدول تعديل الشمس يوخذ بالمركز ويزاد عليه وعلي الاوج ابداً

38a: جدول تعديل الشمس يوخذ بالمركز ويزاد عليه وعلي الاوج ابداً

38b: جدول تعديل الشمس يوخذ بالمركز ويزاد عليه ابداً وعلي الاوج

39a: تتمة جدول تعديل الشمس يوخذ بالمركز ويزاد عليه ابدا وعلي الاوج

39b: جداول التعديل الاول ودقايق النسب للقمر يوخذ بالمركز ويزاد على الخاصه ابدا

40a: جدول التعديل الاول للقمر ودقايق النسب يوخذ بالمركز ويزاد على الخاصه ابدا

40b: جدول التعديل الاول للقمر ودقايق النسب يوخذ بالمركز ويزاد على الخاصه ابدا

41a: تتمه جداول التعديل الاول للقمر ودقايق النسب يوخذ بالمركز ويزاد على الخاصه ابدا

41b: جدول التعديل الثاني للقمر وتعديل الاختلاف يوخذ بالخاصه المعدّله

42a: جداول التعديل الثاني للقسر وتعديل الاختلاف يوخذ بالخاصه المعدّله

42b: جداول التعديل الثاني للقمر وتعديل الاختلاف يوخذ بالخاصه المعدّله

43a: جداول التعديل الثاني الاختلاف للقمر يوخذ بالخاصه المعدّله

43b: جداول التعديل الثاني للقمر وتعديل الاختلاف يوخذ بالخاصه المعدّله

44a: بقية جداول التعديل الثاني للقمر وتعديل الاختلاف يوخذ بالخاصه المعدّله ابدا
44b: جدول مركز زحل يجمع بالسنين الفارسيه لطول **فد**
45a: جدول خاصة زحل يجمع بالسنين الفارسيه وهو لطول **فد**
45b: جدول اوج زحل يجمع بالسنين الفارسيه لطول **فد**

Quire 5: fos. 46–55 (fo. 46 labelled خامس)

46a: جدول التعديل الاول لزحل يزاد على المركز وينقص من الخاصه من هذا الجانب
46b: جدول التعديل الاول لزحل يزاد على المركز وينقص من الخاصه من هذا الجانب
47a: جدول التعديل الثاني لزحل يوخد بالخاصه ويزاد على الاوج من هذا الجانب
47b: جدول التعديل الثاني لزحل يوخد بالخاصه ويزاد على الاوج من هذا الجانب
48a: جدول دقايق النسب لزحل | جدول اختلاف زحل يزاد من هذا الجانب
48b: اختلاف زحل يزاد من هذا الجانب | دقايق النسب لزحل
49a: جدول مركز المشتري يجمع بالسنين الفارسيه وهو لطول **فد**
49b: جدول خاصة المشتري يجمع بالسنين الفارسيه وهو لطول **فد**
50a: جدول اوج المشتري يجمع بسنين الفرس المجموعه والمبسوطه لطول **فد**
50b: جدول التعديل الاول للمشتري يزاد على المركز وينقص من الخاصه من هذا الجانب
51a: جدول التعديل الاول للمشتري يزاد على المركز وينقص من الخاصه من هذا الجانب
51b: جدول التعديل الثانى للمشتري يوخد بالخاصه المعدله ويزاد على الاوج من هذا الجانب
52a: جدول التعديل الثانى للمشتري يوخد بالخاصه ويزاد على الاوج من هذا الجانب
52b: جدول دقايق النسب للمشتري | جدول اختلاف المشتري يزاد من هذا الجانب
53a: جدول دقايق النسب للمشتري | اختلاف المشتري يزاد من هذا الجانب
53b: جدول مركز المريخ تجمع بالسنين الفارسيه المجموعه والمبسوطه والشهر واليوم لطول **فد**
54a: جدول خاصة المريخ تجمع بالسنين المجموعه والمبسوطه والشهر واليوم لطول **فد**
54b: جدول اوج المريخ تجمع بالسنين الفارسيه المجموعه والمبسوطه والشهر واليوم لطول **فد**
55a: جدول التعديل الاول للمريخ يزاد علي المركز وينقص من الخاصه من هذا الجانب
55b: جدول التعديل الاول للمريخ يزاد علي المركز وينقص من الخاصه من هذا الجانب

Quire 6: fos. 56–65 (fo. 56 labelled سادس)

56a: جدول التعديل الثاني للمريخ يزاد علي الاوج من هذا الجانب
56b: جدول التعديل الثاني للمريخ يزاد علي الاوج من هذا الجانب
57a: دقايق النسب للمريخ | اختلاف المريخ يزاد من هذا الجانب
57b: دقايق النسب للمريخ | اختلاف المريخ يزاد من هذا الجانب
58a: جدول المركز للزهره يجمع بالسنين الفارسيه المجموعه والمبسوطه والشهر واليوم لطول [**فد**]
58b: جدول خاصه الزهره يجمع بالسنين المجموعه الفارسيه والمبسوطه والشهر واليوم لطول **فد**

59a: جدول اوج الزهره تجمع بالسنين الفارسيه المجموعه والمبسوطه والشهر واليوم لطول **فد**

59b: جدول التعديل الاول للزهره يزاد علي المركز وينقص من الخاصه من هذا الجانب

60a: جدول التعديل الاول للزهره يزاد علي المركز وينقص من الخاصه من هذا الجانب

60b: جدول التعديل الثاني للزهره يزاد علي الاوج من هذا الجانب

61a: جدول التعديل الثاني للزهره يزاد علي الاوج من هذا الجانب

61b: دقايق النسب للزهره | اختلاف الزهره يزاد من هذا الجانب

62a: دقايق النسب للزهره | اختلاف الزهره يزاد من هذا الجانب

62b: جدول مركز عطارد يجمع بسنين الفرس المجموعه والمبسوطه والشهر واليوم

63a: جدول خاصه عطارد يجمع بالسنين الفارسيه المجموعه والمبسوطه والشهر واليوم

63b: جدول اوج عطارد يجمع بالسنين الفارسيه المجموعه والمبسوطه والشهر واليوم

64a: جدول التعديل الاول لعطارد يزاد علي المركز وينقص من الخاصه من هذا الجانب

64b: جدول التعديل الاول لعطارد يزاد علي المركز وينقص من الخاصه من هذا الجانب

65a: جدول التعديل الثاني لعطارد يزاد علي الاوج من هذا الجانب

65b: جدول التعديل الثاني لعطارد يزاد علي الاوج من هذا الجانب

Quire 7: fos. 66–78. Both fo. 66 and fo. 75 are labelled سابع 'seventh'. Since there are 13 leaves in this section, it is evident that this quire has been corrupted. It is possible that some of the tables in this section belong to some of the defective quires (quires 3 and 8) but since there are no catchwords associated with the tables, it is not possible to determine the quire structure without disbinding the manuscript.

66a: دقايق النسب لعطارد | اختلاف عطارد يزاد من هذا الجانب

66b: دقايق النسب لعطارد | اختلاف عطارد يضرب ويزاد من هذا الجانب

67a: جدول حركة الراس يجمع بالسنين الفارسيه المجموعه والمبسوطه والشهر واليوم

67b: جدول حركة الكيد يجمع بالسنين الاسكندريه المجموعه والمبسوطه والشهر واليوم

68a: جدول ما يزاد على كردجات الكواكب والنيرين والراس والكيد والاوج

68b: جدول تعديل الايام بلياليها يوخد بتقويمها وينقص الخارج منه | تعديل الثالث وهو الخامس عند مامون

69a: العرض الاول للزهره شمال ابدا | دقايق الحصص لعرض الزهره | العرض الثانى للزهره

69b: دقايق حصص العرض | الثالث للزهره | العرض الثالث للزهره

70a: العرض الاول لعطارد جنوبى ابدا | دقايق حصص العرض الثانى لعطارد | العرض الثانى لعطارد

70b: دقايق حصص العرض الثالث لعطارد | العرض الثالث لعطارد

71a: دقايق حصص المشترى | عرض المشتري في الشمال

71b: دقايق حصص المشتري | عرض المشتري فى الجنوب

72a: دقايق حصص زحل | عرض زحل في الشمال

72b: دقايق حصص زحل | عرض زحل في الجنوب

73a: دقايق حصص المريخ | عرض المريخ في الشمال

73b: دقايق حصص المريخ | عرض المريخ في الجنوب

74a: جدول معرفه عرض القمر فى البروج الاثنى عشر

74b: جدول عرض ما بين النيرين | جدول رويه الهلال

75a: جدول كسوف الشمس معبترا

75b: جدول يعرف منه خسوف القمر والله اعلم بالغيب

76a: جدول حركه القمر فى البروج ليوم تدخل بالدرجه الى تحت البرج تجد السير

76b: جدول حركة القمر فى البروج لساعة تدخل بالدرجه الى تحت البرج تجد السير

77a: جدول حركة الشمس فى البروج ليوم تدخل بالدرجه وبالبرج تجد السير

77b: جدول حركة الشمس المختلفه لساعه تدخل بالدرجه لتحت البرج تجد السير

78a: جدول مطالع البروج لعروض البلدان وساعات البلدان

78b: جدول الميل | جدول الجيب

Quire 8: fos. 79–80 and 19–23 (7 leaves)

79a: جدول منازل القمر في البروج الاثني عشر

79b: **تنبيه** اذا اردت معرفة كسوف الشمس فانظر يوم الاجتماع ان كان الشمس والقمر مع الراس او مع الذنب ...

80a: **جدول لمعرفة خسوف القمر** وطريق العمل به ان تدخل بالبعد بين القمر والعقدتين ...

80b: جدول في معرفة ممازجات الكواكب بعضها ببعض

19a: جدول مركز الشمس واوجها على السنين الفارسيه المجموعه والشهر اليوم والساعه

19b: جدول مركز القمر وخاصته ووسطه على السنين الفارسيه والشهور والايام

20a: تتمه مركز القمر وخاصته ووسطه على الايام والساعات

20b: جدول مركز زحل وخاصته فى السنين الفارسيه والشهور الايام والساعات

21a: جدول مركز المشتري وخاصته فى السنين الفارسيه والشهور الايام والساعات

21b: جدول مركز المريخ وخاصته فى السنين الفارسيه والشهور الايام والساعات

22a: جدول مركز الزهره وخاصتها فى السنين الفارسيه والشهور الايام والساعات

22b: جدول مركز عطارد وخاصته فى السنين الفارسيه والشهور الايام والساعات

23a: جدول مركز الجوزهر فى السنين الفارسيه فى الشهور الايام والساعات

23b: **باب** فى معرفة اصول يعرف بها سنى اليهود وشهورهم واعيادهم من هذين الجدولين وهو ان تاخذ الماضي من سنى الاسكندر ذي القرنين الي الوقت الذى تريد معرفة راس سنة اليهود فيه ...

There is a catchword at the bottom of fo. 23b, and the Latin annotation at the bottom: *Quis* [= *Quae*] *hic deesse videntur postponuntur tabulis* [=*tabulae*] *2*[dae] *de cognitione anni Judaici.*

Quire 9: fos. 87–90, and possibly more. Quire numbering stops with تاسع on fo. 87. The quire structure of the rest of the volume in undetermined.

$87a_{1-15}$: غرب ولو كان علي صفر يكون ثاني غد اول شهر اليهود ... ويتلوه الجداول لمعرفة سنى اليهود .

$87a_{16-24}$: فايده ... [added in later hand]

87b: جدول محازير اليهود يعرف منه راس سنة اليهود وموقعها فى اول يوم من ايلول

88a: او ااب من شهور الاسكندر حساب الشيخ الامام علاي الدين بن الشاطر الموقت

88b: هذا الجدول الثانى يعرف منه اوايل شهور اليهود واعيادهم

89a: تتمة الجدول الثاني لمعرفه اعيادهم من ايام الاسبوع وصفات سنيهم وشهورهم ابدا

89b: جدول يستخرج منه صوم النصاري وفطرهم فاحتفظ به ترشد

The treatise ends on fo. 90a, at line 5. Immediately thereafter there are tables that are part of another collection, catalogued here as item 2 in the volume (see Entry No. 16).

The stiff, beige-biscuit, semi-glossy paper has a thickness of 0.23–0.28 mm and an opaquness factor of 3 or 4. It is quite fibrous and has indistinct vertical laid lines with traces of chain lines (possibly in alternating groups of twos and threes). The paper is slightly worm-eaten and the edges have been trimmed from their original size. Folios 84–103 are water stained in the gutter and the upper half.

Volume contents: The volume consists of 103 leaves, with three preliminary leaves and two endpapers (i–iii + 103 + iv–v). Folios 18a, 24a, 92a, and 93b are blank except for frames for text and a mutilated small Arabic note in the upper corner of 18a; fo. 28a is completely blank. Folios 1–17, 19–23, 29–83, 87–$90a_5$ (item 1) form the treatise on astronomy attributed to Abū al-Fidā' here catalogued. Folios 18b, 28b, 84–6, $90a_6$–91b, 92b–93a, 94a–103a (item 2, Entry No. 16) contain a miscellaneous collection of astronomical tables and notes scattered throughout the volume apparently written by one later owner. Folios 24b–26b (item 3, Entry No. 17) are miscellaneous astronomical tables and discourses; and fo. 27 (item 4, Entry No. 18) is a short anonymous treatise on knowledge of solar eclipses. Folio 103b has three short anonymous *bābs* on astronomical topics, written in brown ink (different hand from rest of volume) in a cramped and irregular script with no regard to straight lines.

The first two preliminary leaves (i–ii) are relatively modern blank front endpapers. The third preliminary folio (iii) is of paper somewhat similar to that of the main treatise, but not identical. It has the numeral *awwal* in the upper left corner, indicating that the leaf was intended to be the first folio of the first quire when the quires were numbered (though it is not usual for the first quire to be numbered). On it are a series of short chapters (labelled *bāb* or *faṣl*) concerned with astronomy, occupying 22 lines on the recto and 14 lines on the verso, all written in the same rather cramped and awkward Naskh script (different from main text and using a different ink). The folio is guarded, and in the gutter it is pasted to a strip of paper having two vertical lines giving a recipe.

Folios iv–v are endpapers, blank except for a handwritten *ex libris* of St John's College and the shelfmark *156B*. The back pastedown has the College bookplate.

The front pastedown has the annotation *olim Ab.III.67.*[*1899.*] as well as a shelfmark *156*; there are also two small slips of scrap paper (with notes from a sermon on the back) pasted onto the front pastedown; on these scraps are notes apparently used in the preparation of the entry published by Coxe: [1st paper, 9.4 × 6 cm] *Liber Secreti absconditi de Astronomia carmine conficienda: auctore Omadeddin Ismael B. Zaineddin Omar, Sultano Hamae. Tabulae astronomicae.* [2nd paper, 9.0 × 6 cm] *Tabulae mensium Arab. Copt. Graec. & Jud. Arabice.*

Binding: The volume is bound in a European version of an Islamic binding made of dark-green leather. The covers and envelope flap have frames formed of a broad band of blind-stamped undulating grape vines, within an outer frame formed of two blind-stamped fillets. The numeral *156* is stamped in gold at the top of the spine. The doublure of the envelope flap and the front edge lining is brown cloth. There are relatively modern paper pastedowns and endpapers.

Provenance: The volume came to the College through the donation of Archbishop William Laud (d. 1645); his *ex libris*, dated 1637, occurs on fo. 1a. On the same folio there are three obliterated owners' notes.

The volume is now designated as MS 156B to distinguish it from another manuscript which had inadvertently been given the same number in the catalogue by Coxe.

References

Coxe, 48 entry CLVI.B.

Bernard, *Catalogi*, assigned the number 103 to the volume.

Entry No. 4

MS 155 (item 1)

TITLE: [not given]

AUTHOR: [not given]

CONTENTS: This is an anonymous and incomplete set of Arabic astronomical tables.

Ibn al-Shāṭir al-Dimashqī is cited in some of the tables, though no precise alignment with other available tables known to have been compiled by Ibn al-Shāṭir has been found. On Ibn al-Shāṭir, a Damascene astronomer (*fl. c.*1350), see Suter, *Die Mathematiker*, 168 no. 41; David King, 'Ibn al-Shāṭir', in *DSB*, xii. 357–64. For his importance in the development of planetary theories, see the references given in D. King, *World-Maps for*

Finding the Direction and Distance to Mecca: Innovation and Tradition in Islamic Science (London: al-Furqān Islamic Heritage Foundation/Leiden: Brill, 1999), 43–4 n. 90.

In one table, the latitude of Egypt (Miṣr, latitude 54° 30') is given.

It is evident from numbers placed on each table that there were originally 23, though tables 5–6, 14–15, and 20–1 are now missing and two tables carry the number '9'. The titles of the tables are as follows:

1: الجدول المجرد لاستخراج سني التواريخ الاربعة وشهورها من ايام الاسبوع

2: جدول العلامات للتاريخ العبري للسنين العبريه [*sic*]

3: جدول مواليد السنين العبريه وشهورها والصوم والاعياد والمواسم من ايام الاسبوع

4: جدول استخراج التواريخ الاربعه بعضها من بعض تدخل بالتامه والشهر اليام [؟ = الايام] والله اعلم

7: جدول اعياد المسلمين ومواسمهم المشهورة في السنين العربيه الهلاليه والله تعالي اعلم [not completed]

8: جدول التوقيعات ومواسم النصاري اليعاقبة [table not filled in]

9: وطلوع المنازل والانوا ومداخلة الشهور السريانيه [table not filled in]

9: على راي المغاربة في السنة القبطيه والله تعالى اعلم

10: جدول اوج [*sic*] الشمس والكواكب الخمسة رصد بن الشاطر الدمشقي

11: جدول وسط الشمس لطول ند ل مصر رصد بن الشاطر والله تعالي اعلم

12: جدول تعديل الشمس رصد بن الشاطر والله تعالي اعلم من هنا يزال علي الوسط

13: جدول وسط القمر لطول ند ل مصر رصد بن الشاطر الدمشقي والله تعالي اعلم

16: جدول تعديل القمر الاول ودقايق النسب رصد بن الشاطر والله تعالي اعلم

17: جدول تعديل القمر الثاني واختلاف البعد الاقرب للقمر ايضا رصد بن الشاطر الدمشقي والله تعالي اعلم

18: جدول مقوم الراس لطول ند ل مصر رصد بن الشاطر الدمشقي والله تعالي اعلم

[19]: جدول عرض القمر ودقايق النقل من المايل لفلك البروج رصد بن الشاطر الدمشقي والله تعالي اعلم

22: جدول تعديل زحل الاول ودقايق النسب لابن الشاطر الدمشقي عفد الله تعالى عنه

23: جدول تعديل زحل الثاني واختلاف البعد الاقرب لابن الشاطر الدمشقي عفي الله تعالى عنه

PHYSICAL DESCRIPTION:

9 leaves (fos. 1a–9b; old pages 1–18):

Beginning (fo. 1a):

الجدول المجرد لاستخراج سني التواريخ الاربعة وشهورها من ايام الاسبوع

[Titles of left-hand column:]

الفاضل العربي من | الشهور العربيه | الفاضل القبطي من| الشهور القبطيه | الفاضل السرياني من| شهور روميه بسيطه | شهور سنة كبيسه روميه | الشهور الفارسيه

[Instructions for using the table are written on four sides around the edges.]

Ending (fo. 9b (old p. 18), righthand margin):

... ان دخلت بالخاصه من اسفل الجدول والله تعالي اعلم تمت .

The copy is undated and unsigned. The nature of the paper, ink, and script suggest a date of the 17th century. The same hand copied the second item in the volume (Entry No. 10), which has a table for the position of the sun at the latitude of Aleppo for the year 1028/1618, said to be recently observed.

Arabic. Dimensions: 21.3 × 13.9 (text area 17 × 10.2) cm; lines per page vary. No compiler or author is given. Ibn al-Shāṭir al-Dimashqī is cited in tables 10–13, 16–19, and 22–3. In table 18 (fo. 8a, old p. 15) the latitude of Egypt/Miṣr is specified (54° 30').

The text is written in a variable (small to medium), somewhat awkward, but consistent Naskh using black and red inks. The text area has not been ruled, but the tables are divided into rows and columns. The texts are written in tables whose cells are delineated by red- and black-inked lines; occasionally there is writing around the perimeter of the table. There are no catchwords. The volume has been recently foliated; there are pencilled pagination numerals enclosed by parentheses.

The pale, cream, glossy paper has a thickness of 0.11–0.13 mm and an opaqueness factor of 3. There are vertical laid lines with nearly indistinct fine single chain lines. There are traces of small watermarks (a letter B; a trefoil). There is slight soiling from thumbing and dampness.

Marginalia and owners' notes: There are no annotations in this item. The second item in the volume (Entry No. 10) has Latin marginal annotations, apparently (according to a note on the third preliminary leaf) by John Greaves, Savilian Professor of Astronomy (d. 1652).

Volume contents: The volume consists of 17 folios plus 3 preliminary leaves and 2 endpapers (i–iii + 17 + iv–v). Folios 1a–9b is the item here catalogued, while fos. 11b–17a (item 2, Entry No. 10) contain an anonymous set of Arabic calendric conversion tables. Folios 10ab, 11a, and 17b (old pp. 19–21 and 34) are blank except for frames formed of two black-inked lines (old pp. 19–21 and 34). Folio iii consists of a piece of paper roughly contemporary with that used for the treatise (blank except for two black-inked frames); on iiia there is the note *For Dr. Banbrige*. A piece of paper similar to that used for the more recent endpapers has been pasted to the verso of fo. iii, on which there is the following Latin notation:

MSS. 155. Collatio Mensium Arabicorum, Cophticorum, Græcorum, & Judaicorum. Vide pag. 1. ubi habes hunc titulum doctissimi ipsius Pocockij [a later hand has crossed out the last two words, and written in pencil: Gul. Laudi manuscriptum]. Nec non Tabulæ quædam Astronomicæ. Omnia imperfecta. In margine passim occurrunt Notæ Viri eruditissimi Joan. Grauij, Prof. Astronom. Sauil.

At the top of fo. 1a there is a Latin note, presumably in the hand of Greaves: *Collatio mensium Arabicorum, Cophtiticorum* [*sic*], *Græcorum et Judaicorum.*

The two endpapers (fos. iv–v) and the first two preliminary leaves (fos. i–ii) are blank modern endpapers, of the same paper as the pastedowns.

Binding: The volume is bound in a European binding of pasteboards covered with brown leather. The covers have frames formed of two gold fillets. There are five cords on the spine, with two gold fillets either side of each cord. The pastedowns are modern and are blank except for annotations of the manuscript number and a bookplate for St John's College and *E Libris Coll. Di. Jo. Bapt. Oxon.* on the back pastedown.

Provenance: No information is available on the provenance of the volume. It was possibly from the collection of John Greaves, Savilian Professor of Astronomy (d. 1652), and after that possibly in the collection of 'Dr. Banbrige [= Bainbridge?]'. The note on the verso of fo. iii, however, suggests it might have been in one of the donations of Archbishop Laud (d. 1645); see Hanna, *St John's Catalogue*, p. xxiii n. 16, where he groups the manuscript amongst those in the Laud donation.

References

Coxe, 48 entry CLV.

Bernard, *Catalogi*, M.67 (*in abaco tertio*).

Entry No. 5

MS 151 (item 1)

TITLE: [*Zīj-i jadīd-i sulṭānī*]

[*The New Tables of the Sultan*]

[زيج جديد سلطانى]

AUTHOR: Ulugh Beg ibn Shāhrukh ibn Tīmūr Gurgān (d. 853/1449)

CONTENTS: This is a copy, completed in 1532, of Ulugh Beg's astronomical and chronological tables (*zīj*) in the second, or revised, version. The treatise consists of a preface and four chapters (*maqālahs*) with numerous charts.

Ulugh Beg ibn Shāhrukh was governor of Transoxania from 1409 to about 1448 (812–52 H) when he succeeded to the throne of Herat but was soon thereafter, in 1449 (853 H), slain by his own son. Ulugh Beg compiled the tables in Samarqand with the assistance of Qāḍī Zāde al-Rūmī and Ghiyāth al-Dīn Jamshīd. The latter died during the early stages of the work and was replaced by ʿAlī ibn Muḥammad al-Qūshjī. The astronomical tables (*zīj*) were compiled in Persian and were later translated into Arabic. For an Arabic version, see St John's College MS 91 (Entry No. 6). The first, or original, version of the *zīj* was compiled by Ghiyāth al-Dīn Jamshīd and was called *Zīj-i Ulugh Beg* or *Zīj-i khāqānī*. This second edition was revised on the basis of observations made by Ulugh Beg himself in the observatory of Samarqand between 1420 and 1438 (823–41 H) and is usually titled *Zīj-i jadīd-i sulṭānī* or 'The New Tables of the Sultan'.

This copy now at St John's was one of three manuscripts employed by Thomas Hyde in an edition made in 1665 of the tables of longitudes and latitudes of the fixed stars from the third *maqālah* (*Tabulae longitudinis et latitudinis stellarum fixarum ex observatione Ulugh Beighi ... jam primum luce ac Latio donavit, & commentariis illustravit, Thomas Hyde ... In calce libri accesserunt Mohammedis Tizini tablulae declinationum & rectarum ascensionum. Additur demum elenchus nominum stellarum* (Oxford: typis Henrici Hall academiae typographi, 1665); reprinted in *Syntagma dissertationum quas olim auctor doctissimus Thomas Hyde separatim edidit. Accesserunt nunnula ejusdem opuscula hactenus inedita ... Omnia diligente recognita a G. Sharpe* (Oxford: e typographeo Clarendoniano, 1767). The other two manuscripts used by Hyde are both in the Bodleian Library: Oriental Collections, MS Pococke 226 and MS Saville 46.

An earlier edition of these same detached portions (tables of fixed stars from the third *maqālah*, the text of the first *maqālah*, and tables giving latitudes and longitudes of towns from the second *maqālah*) was published, together with a Latin translation, by John Greaves. For this edition Greaves employed a manuscript in his possession and now also in the Bodleian Library (Oriental Collections, MS Greaves 5) and probably also St John's College MS 91 (Entry No. 6, an Arabic translation) which has Greaves's annotations. Greaves published these portions in *Insigniorum aliquot stellaru longitudines, et latitudines ex astronomicis observationibus Ulug Beigi, nunc primum a J. Gravio publicatae* (Oxford, 1648, appended to John Bainbridge's *Canicularia*); in *Epocae celebriores, astronomis, historicis, chronologis Chataiorum, ... ex traditione Ulugh Beigi ... Eas primus publicavit, recensuit, et commentariis illustravit J. Gravius* (London: typis Jacobi Flesher, et prostant apud Cornelium Bee, 1650); and in *Binae tablulae geographicae una Nassir Eddini Persae altera Ulug Beigi Tatari opera et studio J. Gravii ... publicatae* (London: typis Jacobi Flesher, et prostant apud Cornelium Bee, 1652).

The Persian introductory material was published by Louis-Amélie Sédillot in Paris in 1847 as *Prolégomènes des tables astronomiques d'Oloug-Beg publiés avec notes et variantes, et précédés d'une introduction* (Paris: Firmin Didot Frères, 1847) and again in 1853 as *Prolégomènes des tables astronomiques d'Oloug-Beg, Traduction et commentaire* (Paris: Firmin Didot Frères). The tables of fixed stars from the third maqālah were edited and translated into English in 1917 by E. B. Knobel as *Ulugh Beg's Catalogue of Stars. Revised from all Persian manuscripts existing in Great Britain, with a vocabulary of Persian and Arabic words* (Washington, DC: The Carnegie Institution of Washington, 1917).

Despite the evident importance of this treatise, there has been no complete edition or translation published. The treatise opens with quotations from the *Qur'ān* 25: 61–2, followed by Persian summaries. It is for this reason, perhaps, that there has been some confusion as to whether this present manuscript was an Arabic or Persian one. Coxe stated in his 1852 catalogue listing of the St John's manuscripts that it was a Persian manuscript with three distinct, anonymous, parts (Coxe, 46 entry CLI). Annotations added to the copy of Coxe's catalogue kept in the library of St John's College state (incorrectly) that the text is Arabic rather than Persian. Although there has been no modern and full analysis of Ulugh Beg's *Zīj-i jadīd-i sulṭānī* and all its constituent parts and tables, it appears that fos. 1b–131b of the present manuscript constitute one treatise, with two anonymous Persian astronomical compilations making up the rest of the volume.

For other copies: see Storey, *PL* II_1, 67–72 no. 104; King, *Survey*, 157 no. G49; Brockelmann, *GAL* ii. 212–13 (275–6) and *GAL* S ii. 298; SEB I, nos. 1515–18; SEB II, no. 2368; and SEB III, no. 2731.

PHYSICAL DESCRIPTION:

131 leaves (fos. 1b–131b)

Beginning (fo. 1b):

بسم الله ... **تبارك الذي جعل في السمآء بروجا وجعل فيها سراجا وقمرا منيرا وهو الذي جعل الليل والنهار خلفة لمن اراد ان يذكر او اراد شكورا** مالك الملكي كه مصباح صباح **وجعلنا سراجا وهاجا** افروختهٔ جكمت اوست ورايت آية ...

Ending (fo. 131b, chart):

جدول سهام مستعمله در تحاويل ومواليد وغير اينها بر اشهر وجوه ... سهم الموحت ل | ح | **فق** | من الطالع

Colophon (fo. 131b bottom of table), illustrated in Plate 3:

تمت الكتابت في اواخر جمادى الآخرة من سنة ٩٣٨

The copy was completed toward the end of Jumādá II 938 [about 25 Jan. 1532].

Persian. Dimensions: 21.5 × 14.8 (text area 15.0 × 9.1) cm; 21 lines per page. Ulugh Beg ibn Shāhrukh ibn Tīmūr Gurgān is named on fo. $2a_2$. Qāḍī Zāde Rūmī and Ghiyāth al-millah wa-al-dīn Jamshīd are named on fo. $2a_{18-21}$, and ʿAlī ibn Muḥammad al-Qūshjī on fo. $2b_6$. The title is not given. The text was identified by comparison with manuscripts in the Bodleian Library, esp. MS Greaves 5, where the text is the same, though some of the charts and tables differ.

The copy is written in a careful, probably professional, medium-large Naskh script. The text is written in dense black ink with headings in red and portions of the charts in red. There is little trace of the frame ruling; fo. 43b has been ruled with hardpoint. Folios 1b–

2a are fully vocalized, and there is considerable vocalization elsewhere. The final leaf of each ten-leaf quire has a catchword (e.g. fo. 10b, 40b, with some missing). The folios are numbered in Arabic numerals with a later foliation in pencilled Western numerals.

The copy is incomplete. Folios 5a–16b contain the preface and the first *maqālah*, consisting in this instance of five *bāb*s with the fifth *bāb* having 12 *faṣl*s. The second *maqālah*, in 22 *bāb*s, is on fos. 16b–28b, with three tables and an unfinished one occupying fos. 29a–30b. The third *maqālah*, in 13 *bāb*s, occupies fos. 31a–43b, followed by charts on fos. 44a–116b. The first *bāb* of the fourth *maqālah*, in 7 *faṣl*s, is on fos. 117a to 120a. Tables occupy fos. 120b–123b; the second *bāb* of the fourth *maqālah* is on fos. 124a–b. Tables occupy fos. 125a–131b.

The glossy, beige paper has a thickness of 0.12–0.17 mm and an opaqueness factor of 5. It has occasional thin patches and creasing. There are indistinct vertical laid lines, with single chain lines (slightly varying spacing), and watermarks (several designs, including a circle with double perimeter and two small circles inside, a vase (?), and a hand). The edges have been trimmed from their original size. There is some foxing and a few wormholes.

Marginalia and owners' notes: There are considerable marginalia in several hands. Some of them, as on fos. 6b–8a, 120a, 125b–127a, and 128a, are concerned with medical procedures and unrelated to the text. On fo. 120a a later hand has entered a recipe in Arabic useful for sufferers of melancholia. Recipes are also written in the margins of 125b–127a and 128a. Other recipes are written in a different hand on fo. 1a, where one Shaykh Wafā' al-Qūnawī is quoted. On fo. 92b a 6 × 6 magic square has been added by a later hand, while on fo. 124b two magic squares have been drawn, one 8 × 8 and the other 6 × 6; on fo. 180a there is a 10 × 10 magic square added by the same hand as placed the other magic squares.

Volume contents: The volume consists of 180 leaves with one preliminary leaf and one back leaf (i + 180 + ii). Folios 1b–131b (item 1) contain the *zīj* of Ulugh Beg, here catalogued; fos. 132a–148a (item 2, Entry No. 14) are a Persian/Arabic astronomical miscellany; and fos. 149a–180b (item 3, Entry No. 15) are a collection of astronomical and calendric tables. Folio 148b is blank, except for a quotation from the *Qur'ān* 41: 29–30 added later in a casually written hand. Folio 1a has 23 lines of text, surrounded by extensive marginalia, all added later and concerned with medical and magical recipes. The bottom seven lines of fo. 1a are more carefully written than the rest, and in these lines one Shaykh Wafā' al-Qūnawī is quoted.

Both the front and back endleaves are of vellum; the back one (fo. ii) is blank except for annotation *M.S.S. 151* and pencilled foliations note. The front vellum leaf (fo. i) is blank on one side; on the verso, there are the annotations *N°. 151* and [*ol. 1898.66.Abac.iij. M.*] added by later hands, as well as the following note:

Hali ben Mahumed
1. Compendium Chronolog: de calculo et annis Arabicis, Persic: Romanis

2. Et Astronom: de Motuum coelestiū calculo. Et longitud: et Latitudine Syderum.
3. Item Tabulæ cuilibet Planetæ singularis.

Both vellum endleaves were taken from another manuscript, for this Latin description does not apply to this manuscript, and the use of vellum in Islamic secular manuscripts is very uncommon.

Binding: The volume is bound in pasteboard covers and envelope flap covered with brown leather. The covers are taken from an older Middle Eastern binding; the spine, edges, fore-edge flap, and envelope flap are products of a European restoration. The covers each have a scalloped ogival blind-stamped medallion, filled with a design of intertwined flowers and vines; The frame is blind stamped and consists of two fillets filled with *S*-stamps. The lining of the fore-edge flap and envelope flap is light-red-brown buckram. The front pastedown is multicoloured marbled paper; on top of the front pastedown there has been pasted a small piece of paper (9.4 × 6 cm) with a Latin note repeating all the information given in Latin on the front vellum leaf (fo. i). The back pastedown is a dark-yellow-green paper on which there is written a small horoscope, some mathematical calculations, and a number of Turkish quatrains (some of which have been crossed out); over some of these notes the bookplate for St John's College has been placed. There are no endpapers.

Provenance: It came into the College through the donation of Archbishop William Laud (d. 1645), whose *ex libris* and the date of 1639 are entered at the bottom of fo. 1a. On fo. 70b there is an undated owner's stamp (negative), circular with an internal square. Two lenticular negative owners' stamps are on fo. 133a, both undated, one reading *ṣāḥib al-faqīh* Anvarī *al-ḥaqīr*.

References

Coxe, 46 entry CLI, item 1, where author given as ʿAli b. Mohammad'. Appended to the Coxe catalogue kept in the College library, there are two pages of handwritten notes signed by E. B. Knobel and dated May 1916, in which Knobel corrects the earlier identification by Coxe and records all the variants that Thomas Hyde noticed in his edition of 1665, placing ticks alongside those variants that he (Knobel) had verified and correcting Hyde's errors.

Bernard, *Catalogi*, M.66 (*in abaco tertio*); elsewhere Bernard assigns a number 104 to *Ejusdem [Ologbegi] tabulae astronomicae*, which might refer also to this manuscript; see Hanna, *St John's Catalogue*, 338.

Entry No. 6

MS 91

TITLE: [*Zīj-i jadīd-i sulṭānī*]

[The New Tables of the Sultan]

[زيج جديد سلطانى]

AUTHOR: [Ulugh Beg ibn Shāhrukh ibn Tīmūr Gurgān (d. 853/1449)]

CONTENTS: An Arabic translation of Ulugh Beg's astronomical and chronological tables (*zīj*) in the second, or revised, version. The treatise consists of a preface and four chapters (*maqālah*s) with numerous tables. The translation was made in 1536 (943 H) by Yaḥyá ibn ʻAlī al-Rifāʻī al-Shāfiʻī for Shams al-Dīn Muḥammad ibn Abī al-Fatḥ al-Ṣūfī al-Miṣrī, a well-known astronomer in Cairo who may still have been living at that time.

Using the Arabic translation prepared for him by al-Rifāʻī, Ibn Abī al-Fatḥ al-Ṣūfī undertook a recension of the *Zīj-i jadīd-i sulṭānī* of Ulugh Beg titled *Zīj al-Ṣūfī*. Al-Ṣūfī died, however, before he could complete the recension of the fourth *maqālah*; a complete copy of the *Zīj al-Ṣūfī* in Ibn Abī al-Fatḥ al-Ṣūfī's own hand is now in Tehran (see King, *Survey*, 82 no. C98).

For a copy of the original Persian version of Ulugh Beg's *zīj*, see St John's MS 151, item 1 (Entry No. 5).

This copy at one time belonged to John Greaves, who has annotated it and filled several of the otherwise blank folios with notes (see Plate 4). It is likely that he used it (along with a Persian manuscript then in his possession, now Bodleian Library, Oriental Collections, MS Greaves 5) in the editions and Latin translations of portions of Ulugh Beg's *zīj* which he prepared. For Greaves's editions of the tables of fixed stars from the third *maqālah*, the text of the first *maqālah*, and tables giving latitudes and longitudes of towns from the second *maqālah*, see *Insigniorum aliquot stellaru longitudines,et latitudines ex astronomicis observationibus Ulug Beigi, nunc primum a J. Gravio pubicatae* (Oxford, 1648, appended to John Bainbridge's *Canicularia*); *Epocae celebriores, astronomis, historicis, chronologis Chataiorum, ... ex traditione Ulugh Beigi ... Eas primus publicavit, recensuit, et commentariis illustravit J. Gravius* (London: typis Jacobi Flesher, et prostant apud Cornelium Bee, 1650); and *Binae tablulae geographicae una Nassir Eddini Persae altera Ulug Beigi Tatari opera et studio J. Gravii ... publicatae* (London: typis Jacobi Flesher, et prostant apud Cornelium Bee, 1652).

For other copies: See Storey, *PL* II_1, 71 no. 194 ('Arabic translation (i)'); King, *Survey*, 84 no. C99; Brockelmann, *GAL* ii. 213 (276) and *GAL* S ii. 298; and NPAM, 239 no. 273 and 289 no. 289(2).

PHYSICAL DESCRIPTION:

93 leaves (fos. 2b–12a, 13a–47a, 48a–49a, 50a–93b)

Beginning (fo. $2b_{1-20}$):

بسم الله ... الحمد لله الذي جعل العلم شمسا حرس من الكسوف شعاعه ...، **وبعد** فيقول الفقير الى الله تعالى يحى ابن علي الرفاعى ، الشافعى اشار الي شيخنا الاستاذ العالم ، العلامه ، البحر الفهامه ، سيدنا الشيخ

شمس الدنيا والدين شمس ، الدين ابن ابى الفتح الصوفى ، اطال الله بقاه ونفع به وبعلومه ، سيبويه اهل زمانه وبطليموس اوانه من هو الان امام اهل زمانه كاشف الغطا عن العلوم الهندسية والحسابية وغيرها من جميع الفنون ، لازال منهلا عذبا ، ... بعد ان اظهر من دخآير الشريفة واكنافه اللطيفه ، زيج السلطان ابن السلطان ابن السلطان السعيد الشهيد الغ بيك ... ∴ **قال** المولف وابتد[ئ] بقوله تعالى تبارك الذي جعل فى السما بروجا وجعل فيها سراجا وقمرا منيرا ، ...

Ending (fo. 93b, table):

ذابح	بلع	سعود	اخبيه	مقدم	موخر	رشا
ط كر نــى	**نــى نــى ا**	**نــى كب ن**	**يا يه مد**	**يا مخ لو**	**ﻫ ا كر**	**ﻫ يد يح**

The copy was completed on 20 Ṣafar 939 [= 21 Sept. 1532].

Colophon (fo. 47a$_{12–18}$), illustrated in Plate 5:

وكان الفراغ من تعليق هذا
الكتاب في نهار الجمعه سابع
عشرين صفر الخير من شهور
سنه تسع وثلاثين وتسعمايه
وصلى الله على سيدنا محمد
واله وصحبه اجمعين
تم

Arabic. Dimensions: 26.4 × 18.0 (17.2 × 11.0) cm; 21 lines per page. At the beginning of the treatise it is stated that it was translated from the Persian into Arabic by Yaḥyá ibn ʿAlī al-Rifāʿī al-Shāfiʿī for Shams al-Dīn ibn Abī al-Fatḥ al-Ṣūfī. Ulugh Beg is named on fo. 2b$_{12}$ as the author of the treatise.

The copy is imperfect. The preface and the first four *bāb*s of the first *maqālah* occupy fos. 2b–9b. The fifth *bāb*, fos. 10a–12a, is incomplete and missing the 12 *faṣl*s. A lacuna occurs after 12a, and fo. 12b is blank except for numerous pencilled notes apparently by John Greaves. The second *maqālah*, in 22 *bāb*s, occupies fos. 13a–26b; the third *maqālah*, in 13 *bāb*s, fos. 26b$_{15}$–41a; and the fourth *maqālah*, in two *bābs* the first of which has seven *faṣl*s, fos. 41a$_{20}$–47a. The tables (incomplete) occupy fos. 48a–49a (some not completed) and fos. 50b–93b. The text on fo. 50a has been added by a later hand (15 lines plus margin) as an explanation for some of the following tables.

The text is written in a careful and fluid medium-large Naskh script, with ascending and descending strokes sometimes reaching into nearby rows and with an exaggerated top to the letter *kāf*. The text on fos. 2b–47a is more carefully written than the tables. The text area has been frame ruled. It is written in black ink with headings in red and some red over-lining and a few red text-stops. The tables and text on fos. 50a–93b are written within frames of doubled red lines, and the same frames continue on fo. 94 which is otherwise blank. There is an Arabic-numeral foliation beginning with the numeral for 2 on fo. 3a; two leaves were labelled with the numeral for 27. Consequently the recent pencilled foliation (in Western numerals) is off by a factor of 1 until fo. 29 when it is thereafter off by a factor of 2.

The glossy beige paper has a thickness of 0.15–0.18 mm and an opaqueness factor of 3 or 4. It is quite fibrous with occasional inclusions and thin patches. There are horizontal laid lines and chains lines in groups of threes (e.g. fo. 41). The paper is worm-eaten near the bottom, and the edges have been trimmed from their original size.

Marginalia and owners' notes: There are marginalia in several hands, sometimes extensive, including corrections apparently by the copyist. On fo. 13a there is a small mathematical diagram in the margin, with a larger one on fo. 13b. On fos. 4b–5a the margins of the first *maqālah* are filled with pencilled notes made by John Greaves; fo. 4b is illustrated in Plate 4. A virtually identical hand can be seen in Bodleian Library, Oriental Collections, MS Greaves 5, where John Greaves filled the volume with extensive annotations. Folio 12b (otherwise blank) is filled with closely written pencilled Latin notes (54 lines), apparently also by Greaves, as is also the top of fo. 94a.

Volume contents: The manuscript consists of 94 leaves, two endleaves and two front flyleaves, blank except for the St John's College bookplate (i–ii + 1–94 + iii–iv). Folios 47b, 49b, and 94b are blank. Folio 2a is blank except for one casually written distich and the following statement (in a different European-Arabic hand, fully vocalized, possibly written by Greaves):

بعد فهذا زيج وضعته علي مقتضي اوساط صحتها الشيخ ابو الوفا محمد بن احمد البوزجاني واصحابه بارصاد متواليه وامتحانات صدرت منهم بعد رصد المامون وقد اوردها صاحب الزيج العلاني مدعيا لثلثة انصافه انها مرصودة بالات اتخذ هو بنفسه من غير اشتهادة بالرصد واني وجدت في تصنيف البوزجاني جدولا مشتملا علي هذه الاوساط تنقلتها

For the panegyric distich, see Part II below ('Incidental Arabic Poetry', item I). Folio 12 is covered with 54 lines of pencilled notes in Latin concerned with the contents of the book; 94a is blank except for red-inked text frames and nine lines of pencilled Latin notes; the notes were apparently written by John Greaves.

Folio 1, of slightly different paper, has on one side an unfinished table concerning the moon and planets (written in two different hands, both different from that of the main text and tables), over which someone has written that the volume is the *zīj* of Ulugh Beg (زيج سلطاني الوغ بك). On the verso of fo. 1, inside the framed area, there is written: *Astronomica Ulug Beigi in Linguam Arabicam conversa. Novem folia iam prope ab initio desiderabis.*

Binding: The volume is bound in a European binding (repaired) of pasteboards covered with mottled brown leather. The covers have a central frame of four fillets with scallops interspersed with palmettes; at each corner of the central frame are large blind-stamped flower-heads. The covers also have narrow outer frames of two fillets. The spine (five cords) is undecorated. The pastedowns and endpapers (fos. ii–ii, iii–iv) are modern. The numeral *91* has been inked on the fore-edge of the manuscript.

On the back pastedown there is the bookplate of St John's College and the shelfmark. Attached to the front pastedown there is a paper having the following annotations in an 18th-century hand (writer unidentified):

> The Tables of Ologbeg, or Ulug-Beig, were originally written in the Persic language, [deletion]. We have here two Sets of them. The first Set consists of 4 Books, the first whereof was printed, in Persic and Latin, by M^r^. John Greaves, Professor of Astronomy, in the year 1650, under the title of Epochæ Celebriores. This Book in this Arabic Translation of it is very imperfect, almost half of it being wanting. The other 3 Books of this Set were never printed; nor any part of the Second Set, concerning the Motions of the Planets. This Arabic Translation, so far as it goes, seems to have been of great use to M^r^. Greaves in translating the Epochæ Celebriores, as appears by his learned & curious manuscript Notes in several places of it. And if, as D^r^. Bernard intimates in his Memorandum, page 2^d^. the rest of the Arabic Mst. of Ologbeg remains in St. John's College Library, it is a great curiosity, and would be very useful towards understanding the Persic Original. But perhaps the Dr. by the Word Ms^t^. means only the 2^d^. Set of these Tables, which may have been bound up with the first, as we here have them, since his Time; and not the whole Collection of Ulug-Beig's Astronomical Tables. But of this *Q[uaere]*.
>
> The Copy of the first Set of these Tables was taken an. Hej. 939. i.e. about A.D. 1532. as appears by the date at the end of it; but when the Second was transcribed, is uncertain, there being no date to it; and it seems to be wrote in a different hand.
>
> Ulug-Beig, King of Parthia and India, & Grandson of Tamerlan the Great, whose name these Tables bear, died an. Hej. 853, i.e. 1449 of the X^ti^. Æra. The Tables were drawn up by him and the other great Mathematicians of his Court 12 years before, viz. an. Hej. 841.
>
> For a further Account of this Author, see Mr. John Greaves's Epistle prefix'd to his Binæ Tabulæ Geographicæ,—Dr. Hyde's Preface to Ulug-Beig's Long. & Lat. of the Fix'd Stars,—and D' Herbelot's Bibliothec. Orient. p. 914, 935.

Provenance: The manuscript came to the College through the donation of Archbishop William Laud (d. 1645). Prior to that it was in the collection of Edward Bernard (d. 1696), the Savilian Professor of Astronomy, who had acquired it from the collection of John Greaves (d. 1652) via the intermediary of one Mr Stubs.

At the top of fo. 3a there is the following note written in light brown ink:

> Procurd this, by good chance, of Mr Stubs, frō ye relict of Dr Greaves, to compleate ye Ms^t^. of Ologbeg in Arabic in St Johns College Library in Oxford. (Nov. 2. 1682. E Bernard [)].

At the time that Edward Bernard acquired this manuscript there was in fact no Arabic copy of Ulugh Beg's *zīj* in the library of St John's College, but only the Persian version (MS 151, see Entry No. 5). It would appear that Edward Bernard was confused as to whether MS 151 was an Arabic or a Persian version.

At the bottom of fo. 2a there is written: *Liber Guil: Laud Archiepi Cant: & Cancellar. Vniuersit: Oxon. 1640.*

References

Coxe, 25 entry XCI. Appended to the copy of the Coxe catalogue in the College library is a page of notes signed by E. B. Knobel, dated May 1916, concerned with MS 151 and MS 91. In these notes he identified the pencilled marginalia in MS 91 as being those of John Greaves.

Bernard, *Catalogi*, B.22 (*in abaco tertio*).

Entry No. 7

MS 175 (item 5)

TITLE: *Nuzhat al-nāẓir fī waḍ' khuṭūṭ faḍl al-dā'ir*

نزهة الناظر في وضع خطوط فضل الداير

AUTHOR: Ibn Abī al-Fatḥ al-Ṣūfī al-Miṣrī, Shams al-Dīn Muḥammad (*fl.* 878/1473)

CONTENTS: This treatise on sundial theory was written in 878/1473 by a well-known Egyptian scholar and astronomer who may have still been living in 943/1536. It consists of a brief introduction (*muqaddimah*), two chapters (*bāb*s), and an appendix (*khātimah*) that has an extensive table called *al-jadwal al-mushtarak.*

For the author, see Brockelmann, *GAL* S ii. 159 (this treatise is not cited); and Suter, *Die Mathematiker*, nos. 447 and 460 (confused).

For other copies: see King, *Catalogue*, 588–9 entry 4.7.14 item 1; and King, *Survey*, 83 no. C98, 4.7.14.

PHYSICAL DESCRIPTION:

13 leaves (fos. 44b–56a)

Beginning (fo. $44b_1$–$45a_5$):

بسم الله ... يقل [*sic*] العبد الفقير الى الله تعالى محمد بن محمد الصوفى لطف الله به الحمد لله الذي امد (؟) البسيطه بطل انعامه الوريف [line 9] ... وبعد فلما كان علم الوقت من علوم الدين الواجبة على المكلفين ... وكان الجدول المشترك الذى ابتكرناه كفيلا بوضعها فى البسايط والمنحرفات والمرتفعات والمايلات ... فخاطبنى من لا يسعنى مخالفته [fo. 45a] ان اضع عليه مختصرة شاملة لكفية [= لكيفية] انشا الجدول واستخراج اعماله ... **وسميتها** نزهة الناظر فى وضع خطوط فضل الداير ... **ورتبتها** على مقدمة وبابين وخاتمة ...

Ending of 2nd chapter (fo. $48b_{16\,-\,\text{margin}}$):

وكان **الغرض** ان نورد هنا ما يتعلق بالمايلات والاسطوانات وغير ذلك عملا وحسابا ... لكن اوضحنا ذلك فى رسلتنا [= رسالتنا] الكبرى المسمات [*sic*] بالدر المتناثر فى رسم خطوط فضل الداير والله اعلم .

The treatise ends on fo. 56a with a chart filled with numerals.

Arabic. Dimensions: 19.9 × 14.8 (text area *c.*14.5 × 9 variable); 18–19 lines per page. The author is given at the beginning as Muḥammad ibn Muḥammad al-Ṣūfī, and the title is given on fo. $45a_3$.

The copy is unsigned and undated. The general appearance of the paper, ink, and script, as well as other items in the volume, suggest the first half of the 16th century.

In this copy the divisions of the treatise are as follows:

[المقدمة] فى انشا الجدول وما بتعلق بذلك [fo. $45a_5$]
الباب الاول فى البسايط وما يتعلق بها [fo. $45a_9$]
الباب الثانى فى المنحرفات [fo. $46b_6$]
الخاتمة [fo. 49a, tables]

The text is written in Maghribī script, but not the same hand as copied items 1 and 3 in the volume. It is written in black ink with headings in red. The text area has been ruled with hardpoint.

The beige paper is different from that of rest of volume (watermarked) though similar; it has a thickness of 0.14–0.16 mm. The paper is quite soiled through thumbing and is water damaged around the edges, particularly at the bottom.

Marginalia and owners' notes: There are carefully written marginalia in several hands (marked ظ صح). On fo. 45a there is a lengthy gloss (ط) filling the margins, written upside down and in an awkward Naskh with traces of Maghribī characteristics. It begins:

مثال ذلك الداير من الفلك ه درج فرضناه [؟] ارتفاع واستخرجنا ظله المنكوس فكان ...

The gloss continues in the same hand on fos. 45b–46a, with that on fo. 45b beginning:

ط | فصل فى معرفت الارتفاع والظل والسمت من فضل الداير مثال ذلك ....

In the margin of 46a the gloss ends:

... وهو من كتب عمدت الذاكر لوضع خطوط فضل الداير لي ابن المهلبى [المهلبى or] رحمه الله.

The author of these glosses appears to be one Ibn al-Muhalabī.

Volume contents: Folio 44a contains miscellaneous notes, including a recipe and a poem; for the latter, see Part II below ('Incidental Arabic Poetry', item VI). For the other items in the volume, as well as the binding and provenance, see Entry No. 1.

References

Coxe, 57 entry CLXXV, item 2 (described as *Mahumed B. Mahumed de longitudine et latitudine locorum aliquot*).

Entry No. 8

MS 186

TITLE: *Rasā'il fī 'ilm al-mīqāt*

Discourses on Timekeeping

رسايل في علم الميقات

AUTHOR: Sibṭ al-Māridīnī, Badr al-Dīn Muḥammad (d. 912/1506)

CONTENTS: The volume contains five treatises on various types of quadrants and other topics relating to timekeeping, composed by the Mamluk astronomer Sibṭ al-Māridīnī, who was *muwaqqit* at al-Azhar mosque in Cairo. His writings on *mīqāt* (timekeeping) and various types of quadrants were very popular, and, according to the Egyptian historian al-Jabartī (d. 1237/1822), they were still being used as texts at al-Azhar in 1800 (see M. Plessner and J. Samsó, 'Māridīnī', in EI^2, vi. 542–3).

The five treatises are copied by the same scribe, with the last item in the volume dated 993/1584. This copy appears to be amongst the earliest recorded copies.

For al-Māridīnī's writing on quadrants, see the study by P. Schmalzl, *Zur Geschichte des Quadranten bei den Arabern* (Munich: Druck der Salesianischen Offizin, 1929), 33–5, 63, 68, 72, 84.

Each of the five treatises will be described separately, since they often circulated independently, and references to other copies will be given at that time.

The title page for the volume lists four of the five treatises and reads as follows (fo. 1a), illustrated in Colour Plate I:

كتاب يشتمل
على عدة رسايل في علم الميقات
وهى اظهار السر المودوع في
العمل بالربع المقطوع وهدايه السايل
والرسالة الفتحية ولقط الجواهر
كل ذلك تاليف الشيخ العلامة
بدر الدين محمد سبط المارديني
تغمده الله برحمته واسكنه
فسبح الجنان بمحمد واله
والحمد لله وحده امين

First Treatise

TITLE: *Iẓhār al-sirr al-mawdū' fī al-'amal bi-l-rub' al-maqṭū'*

رسالة اظهار السر المودوع في العمل بالربع المقطوع

CONTENTS: A treatise on the use of the almucantar quadrant, divided into a *muqaddimah* and 20 *bābs*.

For other copies: see King, *Survey*, 80 entry C97 and King, *Catalogue*, 441 entry 4.4.12 (two copies, one dated 1095/1683 and one dated 1118/1706); Brockelmann, *GAL* S i. 216 no. 8; Suter, *Die Mathematiker*, 184 no. 445.11.

18 leaves (fos. 1b–17a and fo. 29)

Beginning (fo. $1b_{1-10}$):

بسم الله ....:. **قال** الشيخ الامام العالم العلامه ، المحقق المدقق الفهامه رحلة الطالبين ، لسان المتكلمين ، عمدة الحساب والمؤقتين ، شيخ الفرضيين ، ابو عبد الله شمس الدين محمد سبط المارديني نفع الله ببركته ، وفسح في اجله ، امين ، الحمد لله رب العالمين ، حمدا دايما الي يوم الدين ، وصلي الله علي سيدنا محمد وعلي اله وصحبه اجمعين ، **وبعد** فهذه رسالة مختصرة جامعة لاحكام الربع الشمالي المقطوع وما يمكن استخراجه منه من المسايل مما يمكن وضعه فيه من الرسوم **وسميتها** اظهار السر المودوع في العمل بالربع المقطوع ...

Ending (fos. $16b_{15}$–$17a_6$):

... غربى ان كان الفضل للباقي وشرقي ان كان لنصف القوس ،
وليكن هذا اخر ما اردنا ايراده
، هنا والله سبحانه وتعالي ،
، اعلم بالصواب واليه ،
، المرجع والمأب ،
، تمت ،
، بحمد لله ،

The title *Iẓhār al-sirr al-mawdū' fī al-'amal bi-l-rub' al-maqṭū'* is given at the beginning of the text and on the volume title page (fo. 1a). The author is given as Badr al-Dīn Muḥammad Sibṭ al-Māridīnī on the title page (fo. $1a_7$) and as Abū ʿAbd Allāh Shams al-Dīn Muḥammad Sibṭ al-Māridīnī at the beginning of the first treatise.

There is a break in the text between fos. 9 and 10 (with the beginning of the 10th *bāb* missing). The missing folio has been mis-bound in with the third treatise in the volume. Consequently fo. 29 should be placed between fos. 9 and 10.

Second Treatise

TITLE: *Risālah mubārakah nāfi'ah fī ṭarīq al-'amal bi-l-khayṭ* | *Risālah fī naṣb al-khayṭ*

رساله مباركة نافعة في طريق العمل بالخيط | رسالة فى نصب الخيط

CONTENTS: A treatise on another type of quadrant.

No other copy has been identified.

4 leaves (fos. $17a_7$–19b)

Beginning (fo. $17b_{1-10}$):

بسم الله ... **رساله مباركة نافعة في طريق العمل بالخيط قال** الشيخ الامام العالم العلامه ، امام المؤقتين ، وشيخ الحساب والفرضيين ، الشيخ بدر الدين سبط المارديني لطف الله به في الدنيا والاخره **اعلم** ان الخيط نوعان **جنوبي** وهو الذي يكون في الحايط اعني الذي اذا استقبلته كان المشرق عن يمينك **شمالي** وهو بعكس ذلك والمستعمل غالبا هو الجنوبي لان الكواكب الظاهره عليه اكثر من الظاهره على الشمالي **ومن طرق استخراجه** ان تعلق ...

Ending (fo. $19b_{11-16}$):

... فعلم في ظل الخيط ايضا علامه كما مد واجمع تلك النقط بخطوط فهو
∴خطوط فضل الداير الشرقي والله ∴
∴تعالي اعلم بالصواب واليه ∴
∴المرجع والمأب والحمد لله رب العالمين ∴
، تمت الرساله ،
، بحمد الله ،

The title is given as *Risālah fī naṣb al-khayṭ* on the title page for this treatise (on lower half of fo. 17a), while the longer title is given at the beginning of the essay. It is not listed on the title page of the volume. The author is given on fo. 17a as Badr al-Dīn Sibṭ al-Māridīnī.

Third Treatise

TITLE: *Hidāyat al-sā'il fī al-'amal bi-l-rub' al-kāmil* | *Risālah fī al-rub' al-kāmil*

هداية السايل فى العمل بالربع الكامل | رسالة فى الربع الكامل

CONTENTS: A treatise on the 'complete' quadrant. Two versions circulated, one in 20 *bābs* and one in 15 *bābs*. The copy at St John's is that in 15 *bābs*.

For other copies: see King, *Survey*, 80 no. C97, and King, *Catalogue*, 446 entry 4.4.12 (where there are three copies of the version with 20 *bābs* and eight copies of the version with 15 *bābs*); Suter, *Die Mathematiker*, 184 no. 445.14.

17 leaves (fos. 20a–28b, 30a–37b)

Beginning (fos. $20b_1$–$21a_6$):

بسم الله ... ∴ **قال** الشيخ الامام ، العالم العلامة ، فريد دهره ، ووحيد عصره ، بدر الدين محمد سبط المارديني ، نفع الله ببركته وبركة علومه فى الدنيا والاخرة ورضي الله تعالي عنه وعن مشايخه وعن جميع المسلمين **الحمد لله رب** [*sic*] الذي رسم فى صفحات مصنوعات [fo. $21a_2$] ... **وبعد** هذه رسالة لخصت فيها احسن الرسايل ، وخصصتها بالاهم مما يتعلق بالربع الكامل من المسايل وسميتها هداية السايل الى الربع الكامل ورتبتها على مقدمة وخمسة عشر بابا ...

Ending (fo. $37b_{9-16}$):

... وان شيت فاجمع غايته السفلي لتمام بعده كما سبق او تمام غايته العليا لبعده يحصل العرض فيهما وفى هذا القدر كفاية لمن وقفه الله تعالى والحمد لله اولا واخرا وظاهرا وباطنا وصلى الله علي سيدنا محمد واله وصحبه وسلم

• تسليما كثيرا دايما ابدا الي يوم •
• الدين وسلم •
• تسليما •
• امين •

On the title page (fo. 20a) the title is given as *Hidāyat al-sā'il fī al-'amal bi-l-rub' al-kāmil*, and the author is given there as Badr al-Dīn Sibṭ al-Māridīnī. On the volume title page (fo. 1a), the title is given as *Hidāyat al-sā'il*.

Folio 29 is misplaced and belongs between fos. 9 and 10, in the first treatise.

Fourth Treatise

TITLE: *al-Risālah al-Fatḥīyah fī al-a'māl al-jaybīyah* | *al-Risālah fī al-'amal bi-l-rub' al-mujayyab* | *al-Risālah al-mukhtaṣarah fī al-'amal bi-l-rub' al-mujayyab*

الرسالة الفتحية فى الاعمال الجيبية | الرسالة فى العمل بالربع المجيب | الرسالة المختصرة فى العمل بالربع المجيب

CONTENTS: A treatise on the use of the sine quadrant, in twenty chapters (*bābs*) and an introduction (*muqaddimah*). It is preserved today in numerous copies, and was the subject of many commentaries.

For other copies: see King, *Survey*, 81 no. C97, and King, *Catalogue*, entry 4.5.12 (47 copies); Brockelmann, *GAL* S i. 216 no. 7; and Suter, *Die Mathematiker*, 183 no. 445.1; Quiring-Zoche, *VOHD*, 350–1 entry 372; and Sobieroj, *VOHD*, 250–2 no. 129.

9 leaves (fos. 38a–46b)

Beginning (fo. $38b_{1-8}$):

بسم الله ... **قال** الشيخ الامام العالم العلامة ، فريد دهره ووحيد عصره بدر الدين سبط المارديني ... **وبعد** فهذه رسالة في العمل بالربع المجيب مشتملة على مقدمة وعشرين بابا ...

Ending (fo. $46b_{3-9}$):

... وان القيت مطالعه من مطالع الشروق وبقى الباقى من الليل عند توسطه فان ساوى الباقى حصة الفجر ، توسط وقت الفجر والله اعلم

• وصلى الله علي سيدنا محمد وعلى •
• اله وصحبه وسلم تسليما •
• كثيرا دايما •
• ابدا •
• امين •

On the title page for the item (fo. 38a) the title is given as *al-Risālah al-Fatḥīyah fī al-a'māl al-jaybīyah*, with the author given simply as Sibṭ al-Māridīnī. On the volume title page (fo. 1a) the title is given as *al-Risālah al-Fatḥīyah.*

Fifth Treatise

TITLE: *Laqṭ al-jawāhir fī ma'rifat al-dawā'ir*

لقط الجواهر في معرفة الدواير

CONTENTS: An essay on the definition of terms relating to spherical astronomy. The treatise has 13 unnumbered *faṣl*s followed by an unnumbered *bāb.*

For other copies: see King, *Survey*, 80 no. C97, and King, *Catalogue*, entry 3.2.14; Suter, *Die Mathematiker*, 183 no. 445.6; and Brockelmann, *GAL* S ii. 216 no. 5.

12 leaves (fos. 47a–56b)

Beginning (fo. $47b_{1-5}$):

بسم الله ... **اما بعد** فهذه مقدمة اوردت فيها ما يجب استخصاره لمن يتبدي في علم الميقات **فاقول** النقطة شيء من ذوات الاوضاع ...

Ending (fo. $56b_{3-12}$):

... واعلم اني قد اطلقت لقط الافق هنا ومرادي به الافق الحقيقي لا المرئي وفيه بحب [*sic*] ذكرته في رسالتي المسماة بالمطلب ، والله اعلم بالصوا[ب] واليه المرجع والمأب وصلي الله

• علي سيدنا محمد وعلي اله وصحبه وسلم •
• تسليما كثيرا دايما ابدا الي يوم •

الدين • وحسبنا الله ونعم الوكيل •
ولا حول ولا قوة الا بالله •
• العلي العظيم •
• والحمد لله رب العا •
لمين

Colophon (fo. 56b$_{13-14}$):

سنه ∴ ٩٩٣
من كتابه العبد الفقير الراجي كرم العالي علي نور الدين الازميرى المعنافي

It is not certain whether the person whose name appears here (ʿAlī Nūr al-Dīn al-Izmīrī) with the date 993 [= 1584] is the copyist or merely the owner. The script and ink are quite similar to that employed on the title page.

The title of the treatise is given on the title page for this item (fo. 47a), where the author is given as Muḥammad Sibṭ al-Māridīnī. On the volume title page (fo. 1a) the title is given as *Laqṭ al-jawāhir*.

PHYSICAL DESCRIPTION OF ENTIRE VOLUME:

Arabic. Dimensions: 17.9 × 13.2 (text area 13.2 × 9.2) cm; 15 lines per page. The texts on the first two folios of each treatise (i.e. fos. 1b–2a, 17b–18a, 20b–21a, 38a–39b, and 47b–48a) are written within frames formed of blue, black, and gilt fillets. The remaining text is written in frames formed of two red fillets. It is written in a widely spaced medium-large Naskh with some ligatures; occasionally the final *kāf* looks like a *lām* with a dot in it. It is written in black ink with headings in red-brown and text-stops marked by red-brown teardrops. Occasionally the ends of words extend past the text frames. There are catchwords.

The volume is composed of six ten-leaf quires which have been numbered in large black script, using standard Arabic numerals, and on the first two quires also giving the numerals in words (e.g. *al-awwal*). Because one leaf (fo. 29) was misplaced when last bound, the first quire has only nine leaves and the third has eleven.

The stiff, glossy, ivory paper has a thickness of 0.10–0.15 mm and an opaqueness factor of 4 or 5. It has rather evident small inclusions and wavy vertical laid lines with single chain lines, and it is watermarked (initials W [?] and small flower-head). The edges have been trimmed from their original size.

Volume contents: The volume consists of 60 folios, with two front and two back endpapers (i–ii + 60 + iii–iv). The recent foliation has numbered fos. 57–60 as endpapers (fos. iii–vi), but they are blank but ruled leaves of the same paper as the rest of the manuscript. The two later endpapers (currently foliated vii–viii) are blank except for a foliation note. At the bottom of fo. 1a there is the usual signature of Archbishop Laud and the date 1640. At the top is a Latin annotation stating that it consists of *Quinq^{ue} opuscula*

Astronomica Muhammedis Subti Elmardini. This latter note is asterisked, and on the facing preliminary leaf (fo. iib), there is another asterisk and a Latin note (*Vid. D'Herbelot. Bibliothec. Orient. p. 556, 794. ubi hic auctor vocatur Sabth, & Sebth.*), referring to Barthélemy d'Herbelot's *Bibliothèque orientale*, and also stating that this copy was written in 993 which the writer converts to 1584. The two preliminary leaves are otherwise blank. The front pastedown has, in addition to a handwritten *ex libris* for St John's College, an earlier shelfmark *Abac:ij.N.38*; there is also attached to the front pastedown a small slip of paper giving in Latin the entry printed in Coxe's catalogue.

Binding: The volume is bound in pasteboards covered with a mottled brown leather. Each cover has a frame formed of two gilt fillets. The spine has five cords between which there are stamped gilt floral designs. The paper pastedowns and endpapers are probably 17th-century.

Provenance: The volume came to the College through the donation of Archbishop William Laud (d. 1645). On fo. 1a there is at the bottom the usual signature of Laud and the date 1640.

In the copy of Coxe's catalogue kept in the College library, there is the following handwritten annotation:

This book was recognised by Mohammed Arif Bey Effendi, who came with his highness Osman Pasha, grandson of Mehemet Ali, as having been written by an ancestor of his, from his native town
الفقير الله ... السيد محمد عارف ابن يوسف صدقى مصى راده والسرر بالاغازاده الحسينى المنفى الماروسى
[؟] غفر لهما فى ٩ شعبان المعظم سنه ١٢٩٩ *June 27, 1882*

References

Coxe, 63 entry CLXXXVI.
Bernard, *Catalogi*, E.38 (*in abaco secundo*).

Entry No. 9

MS 175 (item 1)

TITLE: *Risālat al-jāmi'ah lil-'urūḍ kullihā*

The essay [on] the universal [instrument] for all latitudes

رسالة الجامعة للعروض كلها

AUTHOR: [not given]

CONTENTS: This is an anonymous treatise on a universal instrument, probably a quadrant (*rub'*) though it may be a universal plate (*ṣafīḥah*), useful at all latitudes. The treatise is structured in unnumbered *bāb*s and *faṣl*s).

After the colophon there is a note on the zodiacal houses, written in the same hand, titled: قاعدة الميل فى البروج الشمالية . This note extends onto fo. 10b.

It is possible that the copyist of this treatise is also the author. The copy was completed by Abū al-Qāsim ibn Muḥammad ibn ʿAlī al-Khaddām al-Andalusī on 23 Rabīʿ II 915 [= 8 Aug. 1509].

No other copy has been identified.

PHYSICAL DESCRIPTION:

10 leaves (fos. 1b–10a)

Beginning (fo. $1b_{1-7}$):

الحمد لله وصلى الله على مولانا محمد واله وصحبه وسلم تسليما
هذه رسالة الجامعة للعروض كلها اول ذالك الخط المستقيم المعروف بخط وسط السما يسما يسما [*sic*]
قوس وسط السما ويسمى ايضا افق الاستوا ((افق القسي in margin)) وخط نصف النهار والخط الذي
قاطعه على المركز المسمى بخط المشرق والمغرب ويسمى ايضا افق الاستوا . . .

Ending (fo. $10a_{6-9}$):

. . . ويكون حرفها على تلك العلامة ثم انظر على اي درجة من منطقة البروج وقع الحرف من العضادة في
جهة العلامة فتلك الدرجة هى التي يتوسط السماء معها ذلك الكوكب .

Colophon (fo. $10a_{10-15}$):

وقد يكتفي بما ذكرنا من هذا التاليف عن ما تركناه والحمد لله كثيرا وصلي الله على سيدنا محمد واله وصحبه
وسلم تسليما كمل بحمد الله وحسن عونه على يدي العبد الفقير الي ربه الخايف من ذنبه ابي القاسم ابن محمد
بن على الخدام الاندلسي غفر الله له ولوالديه ولمن قرا فيها ولجميع المسلمين وكان الفراغ منها في الثالث
والعشرين لشهر ربيع الثانى عام خمسة عشر وتسعمايه . . . [؟] .

Copied (and composed?) by Abū al-Qāsim ibn Muḥammad ibn ʿAlī al-Khaddām al-Andalusī on 23 Rabīʿ II 915 [= 8 Aug. 1509].

Arabic. Dimensions: 19.9 × 14.8 (text area 14.8 × 9.5) cm; 20 lines per page. The title is given at the beginning (fo. $2b_3$). No author is named, though it is possible that the copyist in this instance was also the author.

The medium-small script is superficially Maghribī, but the dotting of the letter *fā'* is almost always above the letter rather than beneath. The text is written in dark-brown ink with headings written in larger, extended script. The last word or two on the verso is repeated at the beginning of the next folio.

Folio 10b has the continuation of the note on zodiacal houses that begins on fo. $10a_{16}$ after the colophon, written in the same hand as the main text.

The beige, stiff paper has a thickness of 0.12–0.14 mm and an opaqueness factor of 5. There are fine vertical laid lines, single chain lines, and watermarks (a thin hand with a flower at the end of the index finger). The paper is water damaged around the edges, particularly at the bottom. The outer margins of fos. 7–16 have one or two columns of small indentations or prickings; their purpose is unknown, but they were not apparently for ruling the text.

Marginalia and owners' notes: The copy has been collated; a collation note occurs at the bottom of fo. 10b. There are marginalia in different hands, marked ظ صح خ لعله . For later owners' notes, see Entry No. 1.

Volume contents: The volume consists of 74 leaves. Folio 1a, in addition to two lines giving the Basmala, has five owners' notes. Folio 10b has the continuation of the note on zodiacal houses written in the same hand as item 1. For the other items in the volume, as well as the binding and provenance, see Entry No. 1.

References

Coxe, 57 entry CLXXV (this item is not mentioned).

Entry No. 10

MS 155 (item 2)

TITLE: [not given]

AUTHOR: [not given]

CONTENTS: This is an anonymous set of Arabic calendric conversion tables for dates in the years 1022 to 1121 [= 1613–1709], followed by tables for the position of the sun in the zodiac for the latitude of Aleppo for the year 1028 [= 1618] 'according to recent observations' (على اصول الرصد الجديد).

This set of tables is annotated with notes apparently written by John Greaves (d. 1652).

PHYSICAL DESCRIPTION:

7 leaves (fos. 11b–17a; old pp. 22–33)

The copy is unsigned and undated. The nature of the paper, ink, and script suggest a date of the 17th century. In addition, a table for the position of the sun at the latitude of Aleppo for the year 1028/1618, as well as conversion tables covering the years 1613 to 1709, imply that the copy was made in the mid-17th century.

Arabic. Dimensions: 21.3 × 13.9 (text area 17 × 10.2) cm; lines per page vary. No compiler or author is given.

The text is written in a variable (small to medium), somewhat awkward, but consistent Naskh using black and red inks. The same hand transcribed both items in the volume. The text area has not been ruled, but the tables are divided into rows and columns. The texts are written in tables whose cells are delineated by red and black inked lines; occasionally there is writing around the perimeter of the table. There are no catchwords. The volume has been recently foliated; there are penciled pagination numerals enclosed by parentheses.

The paper is the same as that used in the first item in the volume (see Entry No. 4).

Marginalia and owners' notes: There are Latin marginal annotations throughout this item (e.g. fo. 11b). According to a note on the third preliminary leaf, these annotations were written by John Greaves, Savilian Professor of Astronomy (d. 1652). Folio iii consists of a piece of paper roughly contemporary with that used for the treatise, onto which has been pasted a piece of paper similar to that used for the more recent endpapers, having the following Latin notation:

MSS. 155. Collatio Mensium Arabicorum, Cophticorum, Græcorum, & Judaicorum. Vide pag. 1. ubi habes hunc titulum doctissimi ipsius Pocockij [a later hand has crossed out the last two words, and written in pencil: Gul. Laudi manuscriptum]. Nec non Tabulæ quædam Astronomicæ. Omnia imperfecta. In margine passim occurrunt Notæ Viri eruditissimi Joan. Grauij, Prof. Astronom. Sauil.

Volume contents: For the other item in this volume, and the binding and provenance, see Entry No. 4.

References

Coxe, 48 entry CLV (this item is not mentioned).

Entry No. 11

MS 175 (item 2)

TITLE: [not given]

AUTHOR: [not given]

CONTENTS: This item consists of anonymous astronomical and calendrical tables, concerned with the determination of the altitude of the sun at different latitudes and at different times of the year, followed by a short illustrated discourse on the geometric construction of the astrolabe. The tables and the essay on the design of an astrolabe appear to have been written by the same person, but were apparently added later to the volume, after the first and third items in the volume were copied in 1509.

PHYSICAL DESCRIPTION:

2 leaves (fos. 11a–12a)

Arabic. Dimensions: 19.9 × 14.8 (text area on fo. 11a: 15.1 × 10.4, on fo. 11b: 16.5 × 12) cm. On fo. 12a the text extends to the margins. No author or title is given.

The material is unsigned and undated. The hand and ink are quite different from the surrounding items in the volume, which were transcribed in 915/1509.

Fo. 11a: A table titled: نصف قطر دايرة اول السموط لكل عرض

Fo. 11b: An untitled table. The columns are labelled, reading right to left:

شهور | ايام | اسبع | دقيق | ارتفاع | دقيق

The horizontal ranks are labelled with the names of the months, using Egyptian/North African/Western Christian names (e.g. مارس | ابريل).

Fo.1 2a: A diagram demonstrating the principles of stereographic projection used in constructing an astrolabe, illustrated in Plate 6. There is a text written above and around, beginning: صفت وضع الاسطرلاب بالهندسه .

Though the script has many Maghribī characteristics, the diacritical dot on the letter *fā'* is placed over the letter. The brown ink fades to a lighter shade, and headings are in red.

The paper of fo. 11 is different from the rest of the volume in that it has chain lines in groups of groups of threes and no watermarks. Presumably fo. 12a was blank, and a later owner added a folio of paper on which he added new material, completing his addition on fo. 12a. For the paper of fo. 12, which is that of most of the volume, see Entry No. 1.

Marginalia and owners' notes: There are no collation notes or marginalia.

Volume contents: For the other items in the volume, as well as the paper of the main text, the binding, and the provenance, see Entry No. 1.

References

Coxe, 57 entry CLXXV (this item not mentioned).

Entry No. 12

MS 175 (item 4)

TITLE: [not given]

AUTHOR: [not given]

CONTENTS: These folios contain a collection of anonymous miscellaneous notes and tables concerned with astronomy, trigonometry, and calendrical problems.

They are written in several hands, beginning with the same copyist as transcribed the first and third items in this volume, which were copied in 915/1509 by Abū al-Qāsim ibn Muḥammad ibn ʿAlī al-Khaddām al-Andalusī.

Two of the folios, 40b and 41a, have circular diagrams with the names of the North African/Western Christian months to which are assigned numerals, surrounding a pious phrase. These folios are dated Rabīʿ II 917 [= June–July 1511] 'during the reign of Sultan Bayezid' and signed Muḥammad ibn Abī al-Qāsim, called Abū ʿUmar, known as al-Andalusī—apparently the son of the copyist of items 1 and 3 in the volume and one of the owners of the volume (an owner's entry in his name occurs on fo. 1a); see Entry No. 1 and No. 9. Some of the subsequent tables and charts were possibly written by the unnamed copyist of item 2 in the volume (see Entry No. 11).

PHYSICAL DESCRIPTION:

5 leaves (fos. 40a–43b)

Arabic. Dimensions: 19.9 × 14.8 (text area variable) cm; lines per page vary. No author or title is given.

The circular diagrams on fos. 40b and 41a were drawn by Abū ʿUmar al-Andalusī in 917/1511. The remaining components of this section of the manuscript are unsigned and undated.

The first sixteen lines of fo. 40a were apparently written by the same copyist as transcribed the preceding item, which was apparently copied by the same copyist as transcribed the first item in the volume (Entry No. 9), completed by Abū al-Qāsim ibn Muḥammad ibn ʿAlī al-Khaddām al-Andalusī on 23 Rabīʿ II 915 [= 8 Aug. 1509]. Thereafter the hand changes, with several different hands evident.

Maghribī script is used throughout, though in some of the hands the dotting of the letter *fāʾ* is above the letter rather than beneath. The ink varies from black to light brown, with some headings or tabular columns in red.

Individual components:

Fo. 40a: A 16-line note on converting between calendars, written by the same copyist as transcribed the preceding item, beginning (fo. $40a_{1-3}$):

الحمد لله مسئله اذا اردت بأي يوم يدخل ينير فخذ ما معك من سنى الهجرة بالسنة التي تريد دخول ينير فيها

...

Fos. 40b–41a: Circular diagrams with the names of the North African/Western Christian months written on an inner ring with concentric rings containing numerals; at the centre of each circular diagram is a pious phrase. At the bottom of fo. 41a there is the following statement:

صانعه محمد بن ابي القاسم المكنى بابي عمر المعروف بالاندلسي لطف الله به في شهر ربيع الثانى عام سبعة عشر وتسعمايه ه ((في دولت السلطان بايزيد نصره الله)) .

'Drawn by Muḥammad ibn Abī al-Qāsim, called Abū 'Umar, known as al-Andalusī, in Rabī' II 917 [June–July 1511].' A later hand as added 'during the reign of Sultan Bayezid [II, reg. 886–918/1481–1512]'.

Fos. 41b–42b: Conversion tables (not completed) between the Hijrah calendar and the 'Alexandrian' (Seleucid) calendar for the year 910 H and 1816 Seleucid [= 1504].

Fos. 42b–43a: More calendric tables for the years 912–94 [= 1506–85], based, according to the unnamed compiler, on the *zīj* of Ulugh Beg. It is written in a smaller hand than the preceding tables, and begins:

وطريقه ان تدخل بالايام الماضيه من شهر الرومى تمت فما وجدت باريه [؟] زد عليه دقايق الامين [؟] ابدا يخفر [؟ n.d.] مقوم الشمس لنصف نهار ذلك اليوم وقد حسبت هذا الجدول من زيج الغ بيك

Fo. 43b: A trigonometric sine table.

The paper is the same as that used for items 1 and 3 in the volume; see Entry No. 1.

Marginalia and owners' notes: There are some marginalia, for example on fo. 42b.

Volume contents: For the other items in the volume, as well as the binding and provenance, see Entry No. 1.

References

Coxe, 57 entry CLXXV (this item not mentioned).

Entry No. 13

MS 175 (item 6)

TITLE: [not given]

AUTHOR: [not given]

CONTENTS: This is a collection of various calendric and astronomical tables and diagrams, transcribed in many different hands. Virtually with every item the hand seems to change.

PHYSICAL DESCRIPTION:

19 leaves (fos. 56b–74a)

Arabic. Dimensions: 19.9 × 14.8 cm; text areas vary greatly. Many different hands are involved, most of them Maghribī. The ink varies from dense black to brown, and various headings and tabular columns are in a warm-red ink.

None of the components of this section of the manuscript is signed or dated. The general appearance of the paper, ink, and script, as well as other items in the volume, suggest the first half of the 16th century.

Individual components:

Fo. 56b: Two shadow tables for latitude 30° [north].

Fo. 57a: A table giving the longitude, latitude, and azimuth of the *qiblah* for 9 localities: ʿAmūrīyah, Rūmīyah [emended by a later hand to al-Isṭanbūl], Adirnah [Edirne], Maqdūnyā [Macedonia], Baṭalyūs [Bitlis, in Turkey], Bruṣah [Bursa], Sarukhān [a region in Turkey], Qusṭanṭīnīyah [Istanbul], and Hiraqlah [Ereğli]. It is transcribed in a much larger hand than the preceding table. There is a marginal note in Turkish.

Fo. 57b: A chapter (*bāb*) on the determination of the diameter of the shadow from the sine of the azimuth of the pole, illustrated with trigonometric tables. It is transcribed in yet a different hand, and it begins: باب معرفت قطر الظل من جيب ارتفاع القطب .

Fo. 58a: A crudely rendered circular diagram with the North African/Western Christian names of the months written in the two outmost concentric circles and *abjad* numeral-letters in the inner segments. Yet a different hand produced it.

Fo. 58b: Two medicinal recipes written in two different hands.

Fo. 59a: Trigonometric tables.

Fo. 59b: A carefully drawn design for a sundial with accompanying text, by a different hand from the previous item.

Fos. 60a–63b: Tables of almucantars with trigonometric functions, quite casually executed. Those on fos. 60b–63a specify a latitude of 41°. The table on 63b provided data specific to Bruṣah [Bursa, in Turkey] and Qusṭanṭānīyah [= Istanbul].

Fo. 64a: Another chapter (*bāb*) on the determination of various trigonometric relationships. It is a casually written text, partially covered by arcs drawn with a compass.

Fo. 64b: A paragraph on the determination of the altitude of the azimuth (في معرفت ارتفاع السمت). The discourse occupies 15 lines of text, written in black ink with headings in red; portions have been crossed out, and there is a marginal correction.

Fo. 65a: A drawing of a horizontal sundial, with annotations in two hands giving instructions for its use. It is drawn in red and black ink, and it was at one time part of a larger diagram of which only a small portion remains after the edges of the paper were trimmed.

Fo. 65b: A very casually made table giving the latitudes, longitudes, and *inḥirāf* for the following cities: Qayṣarīyah [Caesarea, either in Palestine or Turkey], Damascus [crossed out and Ḥalab written over], Ḥalab [Aleppo, crossed out and Damascus overwritten], Bruṣah [Bursa], Consṭanṭinīyah [Istanbul], Maghnīsah [Magnesia, in Turkey], Ṣūfīyah [Sofia], Askūb [Skopje], Sirās [? = Siwas], and Miṣr [Cairo, with Iskandarīyah overwritten].

Fo. 66a: A table giving the visibilities of the zodiacal constellations, beginning with Capricorn, for latitude 41° north.

Fo. 66b: A carefully written table of azimuths, with instructions. The table is titled: جدول السموت لكل عرض.

Fo. 67a: A table giving values for the shadows and azimuths for the zodiacal houses Cancer, Capricorn, Aries, Pisces, and Taurus. Over, around, and under this table there are many annotations and notes written in different hands. One provides the azimuth for Istanbul.

Fos. 67b–68b: Almucantar tables for latitude 41°.

Fo. 69a: Astronomical chart or *zīj*.

Fo. 69b: An unfinished table labelled '*inḥirāf* 35° South at latitude 41° North'.

Fo. 70a: A table of observational values for the Tropic of Cancer and Tropic of Capricorn and other astronomically defined phenomena.

Fo. 70b: Table labelled:

جدول قوسى الشفق والفجر الشفق مكتوب بالاحمر والفجر مكتوب بالاسود فى عرض ما

Fo. 71a–71b: Two tables, labelled:

[1] جدول الميل | عصر افاقى [2] جدول قوس العصر افاقى | جدول قوس الميل

Fo. 72a–72b: Trigonometric tables. Damp stained.

Fo. 73a: Blank except for two lines of a miscellaneous note that was then crossed out.

Fo. 73b: Three rows of alphanumerical symbols (often called *zimāmī* or *rūmī* ciphers) with their equivalent value in standard Arabic numerals given above. The bottom half of the page is blank. For *zimāmī* letter-numerals, see Rosa Comes, 'Arabic, *Rūmī*, Coptic, or Merely Greek Alphanumerical Notation? The Case of a Mozarabic 10th-Century Andalusī Manuscript', *Suhayl*, 3 (2002–3), 157–85; David A. King, *The Ciphers of the Monks: A Forgotten Number-Notation of the Middle Ages*, Boethius 44 (Stuttgart: Steiner, 2001).

Fo. 74a: The upper half of the page has a carefully written magical/medical procedure for toothache, written in a large Naskh script in dense black ink, reading:

باب لوجع الضرس : يكتب هذه الاحرف علي لوح من خشب ويدق في راس اول حرف منهم وهو يتلوا هذه الاية الكريمة هى الم ترا الي ربك كيف مد الظل ولو شا لجعله ساكنا [*Qur'ān* 25:45] وله ما سكن في الليل والنهار وهو السميع العليم [*Qur'ān* 6:13] فان سكن والا فانقل المسمار الي الحرف الذي يليه والاحرف هذه ح ب ر ص لا و ع م لا والله اعلم .

Above, below, and alongside this prescription, two other hands (Maghribī script) have written notes regarding the determination of the azimuth and a table for latitude 41° north.

Fo. 74b: Five pieces of Arabic poetry. See Part II below ('Incidental Arabic Poetry', items VII–XI).

The paper of fos. 56–62 is that comprising most of the volume; see Entry No. 1.

Volume contents: For the other items in this volume, as well as the binding and provenance, see Entry No. 1.

References

Coxe, 57 entry CLXXV (this item not mentioned).

Entry No. 14

MS 151 (item 2)

TITLE: [not given]

AUTHOR: [not given]

CONTENTS: An anonymous Persian (with some Arabic) miscellany on nativities.

There are various tables and a horoscope made for Ramaḍān 942 [= Feb.–Mar. 1536].

PHYSICAL DESCRIPTION:

17 leaves (fos. 132a–148a)

Beginning (fo. $132a_{1-2}$):

وقت طلوع شعرآء يمانيه يقال لها العبود تسقط التاريخ الاسكندريه اربعة اربعة ان سقطت ...

Ending (fo. 148a), a table titled:

المركز **يا يح** ح يؤخذ من هنا اذا كان المركز **يا يد** ح بالخاصة ويزاد على الوسط يكون منقوصة [؟]

Persian and Arabic. Dimensions: 21.5 ×14.6 (text area 16.8 × 9.8, tables 16 × 13.5) cm; 22 lines per page. The script is slightly different from that in item 1 (Entry No. 5), with the Naskh written in dense black ink using a slightly broader nib.

The horoscope occurs on fo. 133a.

The paper of the second item is essentially the same as that for the first (see Entry No. 5), though with fo. 133 the paper becomes slightly stiffer and thicker and the laid and chain lines even more indistinct. Similar watermarks, however, can still be distinguished (e.g. fos. 151, 152). The glossy, ivory paper has occasional thin patches and creasing. There are indistinct vertical laid lines, with single chain lines (slightly varying spacing), and watermarks (several designs, including a circle with double perimeter and two small circles inside, a vase (?), and a hand). The edges have been trimmed from their original size; fo. 139 has an edge turned in where it was not trimmed. There is some foxing and a few wormholes.

Marginalia and owners' notes: There are considerable marginalia at the beginning of the tract, in several hands.

Volume contents: Folio 148b is blank except for a quotation from the *Qur'ān* 41: 29–30, added by a later hand. For the other items in the volume, as well as the binding and provenance, see Entry No. 5.

References

Coxe, 46 entry CLI, item 2.

Entry No. 15

MS 151 (item 3)

TITLE: [not given]

AUTHOR: [not given]

CONTENTS: A collection of Persian astronomical and calendric tables.

It is possible that these tables relate to Ulugh Beg's *zīj*, which forms the first part of the volume (Entry No. 5), though this relationship has not been established.

PHYSICAL DESCRIPTION:

32 leaves (fos. 149a–180b)

Beginning (fo. 149a), a table titled:

جدول ساعات لعرض **م** ط درجه | جدول ساعات لعرض **ما** ط

Ending (fo. 180b, in lower left cell of an untitled table):

تاريخ يزدجرد اوله يوم الثلثاء سنوه فارسية

A possibly later hand has then written six lines of text diagonally alongside the table, ending with وتنـــزل باصبع اليد اليمنى حتى محاذى بها اليسرى فتجد فى البيت المشترك ما بين التاريخين .

The copyist appears to be the same as transcribed item 1 in the volume—an unnamed copyist who completed it in 938/1532 (see Entry No. 5). No author or title is given.

Persian. Dimensions: 21.5 × 14.6 (text area 16.8 × 10.5) cm; 22 lines per page, varying. The script is slightly different from that in items 1 or 2, with the medium-large Naskh written more casually. The text is written in dense black ink with headings in red and portions of the tables in red. There is little trace of the frame ruling. The folios are numbered in Arabic numerals with a later foliation in pencilled Western numerals. When the earlier Arabic foliation was made one leaf was skipped, in consequence of which the recent foliation is off by a factor of 1 beginning at fo. 156.

The paper is essentially identical to that of item 1 (see Entry No. 5). The edges have been trimmed from their original size. There is some foxing and a few wormholes.

Marginalia and owners' notes: A few corrections have been made by the copyist. At the top of fo. 149a a later hand has written the symbols for the zodiacal signs. On fo. 180b a horoscope has been added by a later hand.

Volume contents: For the other items in the volume, as well as the binding and provenance, see Entry No. 5.

References

Coxe, 46 entry CLI, item 3.

Entry No. 16

MS 156B (item 2)

TITLE: [not given]

AUTHOR: [not given]

CONTENTS: This is an anonymous and miscellaneous collection of astronomical tables and notes scattered throughout the volume, apparently written by one later owner. They have been inserted into the midst of another astronomical compilation (see Entry No. 3).

PHYSICAL DESCRIPTION:

20 leaves (fos. 18b, 28b, 84–6, $90a_6$-91b, 92b–93a, 94a–103a)

Beginning (fo. 18b):

جدول حركه الاصول للكواكب السبعه والجوزهر | الاصول لسنة ٨٠٠ | الاصول لسنة ٩٠٠ | الاصول لسنة ١٠٠٠

Ending (fo. 103a): [illegible words written in a few cells of an unfinished table]

The table on fo. 28b is titled: جدول حركة الشمس في السنين والشهور والايام .

The tables on fos. 84–86a are so poorly executed that their titles are unclear.

On fo. 86b, the same poorly formed hand has copied the text from a folio of item 1, that is fo. 23b, lines 2–24, ending with the same catchword that is on fo. 23b and that aligns with the start of fo. 87a.

The same crude hand also copied fols. $90a_6$–103a. The script is so poorly formed as to be at times nearly illegible.

$90a_6$: جدول تعرف اعياد اليهود وشهور

90b: جدول في عروضات [؟] البلدان والاطوال والانحرافات

91a: **باب** في رموز التقويم

91b: [table] متاعد النهار

92b: وهو ان تد[؟] فى الايام الماضى من الشهر العربى فى الطول وفى الشهر القبطى [...] في العرض

93a: جدول لمعرفة العمل فى [؟] البروج ادخل بالايام الماضى من الشهر العربى وبالشهر الرومى تحد [=تجد] العمد وبرجه

94a: جدول لمعرفة ساعات عروض البلدان تدخل ان العرض [؟]

94b: جدول يعرف به اولا [؟] السنين العربيه استعدال [؟] تاريخ ٢١٠٢١٠ وتدخل ان [؟] الباقى

95a: جدول لمعرفة اوايل شهر الرم [*sic*] تسقط التاريخ ٢١٠٢١٠ و ... وتدخل بما بقارحه [؟]

95b: جدول تعرف به اوايل شهور الروم تسقط التاريخ ٢٨٢٨ التنه [؟] الناقعه وادحل بالباقى ...

96a: جدول لمعرفة اوايل الشهر القبط وهو ان تسقط التاريخ ٢٨٢٨...

The tables occupying fos. 96b–98a are so poorly written as to be illegible. The table on fo. 98b in unfinished and untitled.

The tables on fos. 99a–103a are also essentially illegible. That on fo. 103a is untitled.

Arabic. Dimensions: 20.8 × 15.2 (text areas 16.7 × 12 and 16 × 11.7) cm; 23 and 24 lines per page. No author is given.

The text is written by a different hand from those in items 1, 3, and 4 in the volume. It is written in a very awkward and poorly formed medium-small cramped, compact Naskh script using black ink. The text is written in frames of doubled black lines. The paper appears to be identical to that in the main item in the volume (see Entry No. 3).

Folios 18a, 92a and 93b are blank except for red frames and a mutilated small Arabic note in the upper corner of 18a. Folio 28a is entirely blank.

Volume contents: For the other items in the volume, and the binding and provenance, see Entry No. 3.

References

Coxe, 48 entry CLVI.B (this item not mentioned).

The volume is now designated as MS 156B to distinguish it from another manuscript which had inadvertently been given the same number in the catalogue by Coxe.

Entry No. 17

MS 156B (item 3)

TITLE: [not given]

AUTHOR: [not given]

CONTENTS: This is an anonymous collection of miscellaneous Arabic chapters and charts on various astronomical topics. It was apparently taken from another manuscript (along with item 4, Entry No. 18) and inserted into the midst of another astronomical compilation (see Entry No. 3).

PHYSICAL DESCRIPTION:

3 leaves (fos. 24b–26b)

On fo. 24b there is a table titled جدول الروية السادسة with an untitled table on fo. 25a. A short anonymous discourse in six sections (*bābs*) occupies fos. 25b–26b, beginning:

بسم الله ... **اما بعد** فهذه طرق في كيفيه استخراج حل الكواكب السبعه ومقوماتها مرتبه علي ستة ابواب **الباب الاول** ق معرفة تقويم الشمس من فلك البروج وطريق ذلك اعرف مركزها واوجها بالتاريخ الفارسي لذلك الوقت المفروض ...

Arabic. Dimensions: 20.8 × 15.2 (text area 16.2 × 12) cm; 20 lines per page. No author or title is given.

The text is written in a medium-large Naskh script using black ink, with headings in red. The *tā' marbuṭah* is nearly always ligatured to the preceding letter. The text throughout is written with frames of two thin red lines (black, on fo. 24), and the text area has been ruled in red ink. Occasionally the last letter or two of a word occurring at the end of a line is written outside the text frame. Folio 24a has the text area marked with a frame, but is otherwise blank. There are only six lines of text on fo. 26b. There are catchwords. This item (along with item 4) appears to have been extracted from another manuscript volume and inserted into this one, thus disturbing the proper sequence of the folios.

The paper differs slightly from that of the treatise surrounding it (see Entry No. 3). The beige semi-glossy paper is slightly lighter in hue and has thinner, fine horizontal laid lines with traces of chain lines. The edges have been trimmed from their original size.

Volume contents: For the other items in the volume, and the binding and provenance, see Entry No. 3.

References

Coxe, 48 entry CLVI.B (this item is not mentioned).

The volume is now designated as MS 156B to distinguish it from another manuscript which had inadvertently been given the same number in the catalogue by Coxe.

Entry No. 18

MS 156B (item 4)

TITLE: *Bāb fī ma'rifat kusūf al-shams bi-l-jadwal*

باب في معرفة كسوف الشمس بالجدول

Chapter on the Knowledge of the Eclipse of the Sun with a Chart

AUTHOR: [not given]

CONTENTS: This is an anonymous short essay on how to determine when an eclipse of the sun will occur. It was apparently taken from another manuscript (along with item 3, Entry No. 17) and inserted into the midst of another astronomical compilation (see Entry No. 3).

PHYSICAL DESCRIPTION:

1 leaf (fo. 27a–b)

Beginning (fo. $27a_{1-3}$):

بسم الله ... باب في معرفة كسوف الشمس بالجدول وهو ان تنظر الي اجتماع الشمس مع القمر ان كان الاجتماع قريبا من احدي العقدتين في الشمال **يح** درجة ...

Ending (fo. $27b_{24}$):

... طالع سنة العالم انقص منه **س** يبقى [؟] العاشر قومه بالفلك المستقيم يخرج طالع العاشر والحمد لله وحده.

Arabic. Dimensions: 20.8 × 15.2 (text areas 16.7 × 12 and 16 × 11.7) cm; 23 and 24 lines per page. No author is given.

The text is written by a different hand from those in items 1 and 2 in the volume. It is written in a medium-small, cramped, compact Naskh script using black ink, very crowded at the bottom of fo. 27b. The text is written in frames of doubled black lines. This item (along with item 2) appears to have been extracted from another manuscript volume and inserted into this one, thus disturbing the proper sequence of the folios.

The paper appears to be identical to that in item 3 (see Entry No. 17), which is different from that in the main item in the volume (Entry No. 3).

Volume contents: For the other items in the volume, and the binding and provenance, see Entry No. 3.

References

Coxe, 48 entry CLVI.B (the item is not mentioned).

The volume is now designated as MS 156B to distinguish it from another manuscript which had inadvertently been given the same number in the catalogue by Coxe.

MATHEMATICS

Entry No. 19

MS 145 (item 3)

TITLE: *Sharḥ muṣādarāt li-kitāb Uqlīdis*

Commentary on the Postulates in the book of Euclid

شرح مصادرات لكتاب اقليدس

AUTHOR: Ibn al-Haytham (d. 431/1041 or 430/1039)

CONTENTS: This item consists of excerpts from Ibn al-Haytham's commentary on the Postulates in Euclid's *Elements*. It was composed before Ibn al-Haytham wrote his treatise on doubts about various points in Euclid's *Elements* (*Fī ḥall shukūk Kitāb Uqlīdis fī al-uṣūl*).

For other copies: see Sezgin, *GAS* V, 370 no. 28, 107 no. 26b, and 404; King, *Survey*, 47 no. B77; King, *Catalogue*, 812 entry 6.1.3; and Rudolf Mach and Eric L. Ormsby,

Handlist of Arabic Manuscripts (New Series) in the Princeton University Library (Princeton: Princeton University Library, 1987), entry 4499.

Though numerous copies are preserved today, the text has not been edited or published.

PHYSICAL DESCRIPTION:

8 leaves (fos. $208a_5$–213b, 214b–215a)

Beginning (fo. $208a_{5-10}$, with some diacritical dots missing):

قال ابن الهيثم فى شرح مصادراته لكتاب اقليدس فى المقالة الخامسة فى حد المقادير المتحدة النسب ومختلفتها هذا حد بالخاصة محتاج الى بيان وانا ابينه ولم استعمل فى بيانه شيا مما يتعلق بهاتين المصادرتين واستعمل فى بيانه ثلث مقدمات هى هذه **الاولى** اذا كان ...

Ending (fo. $215a_{5-6}$, with most diacritical dots missing):

... وحد ر مربع تمام ء **ح** من القاعدة مع مربع العمود مقدار ا **ب** الساق الاخر وذلك ما اردناه .

The copy is unsigned and undated. The appearance of the paper, script, and ink suggest a date of the 16th century.

Arabic. Dimensions: 21.4 × 12.4 (text area 13.5 × 6.1) cm; 19 lines per page. Ibn al-Haytham is mentioned in the first line of the text. The title is given also in the first two lines of text as well as on fo. $212b_7$ where the copyist quotes a passage from the sixth *maqālah*.

The text is written in a small Naskh script with some Ta'līq characteristics, using dense black ink with headings in red. Space was left for three diagrams which have not been drawn. For some reason fo. 214a was skipped, with the text continuing from the bottom of 213b to the top of 214b. The text area has been frame ruled. There are catchwords, some partially cut off when the paper was trimmed.

The paper is the same as that used for items 1 and 2 in the volume. See Entry No. 20.

Marginalia and owners' notes: There are no marginalia.

Volume contents: The volume consists of 216 leaves, with single front and back blank endpapers (i + 216 + ii). Folio 216 (old foliation ii), though blank, is the same paper as the manuscript itself. Folios 1b–203a (item 1, Entry No. 20) are the redaction of Euclid's *Elements* by Naṣīr al-Dīn al-Ṭūsī; fos. 204a–$208a_4$ (item 2, Entry No. 21) are the addendum by Naṣīr al-Dīn al-Ṭūsī following the 15th book of Euclid; and fos. $208a_5$–213b and 214b–215a (item 3) have the excerpts here catalogued from a commentary on Euclid by Ibn al-Haytham. Folio 203b is blank except for a note in the upper corner reading *awrāq 200*. Folio 214a is blank; fo. 215b is blank except for a bookplate from St John's College, a note in Arabic in the upper corner reading *awrāq 12*, and the pencilled European numeral *214*; fo. 216 (old ii) is blank. On fo. 1a there are three owners' stamps or annotations, and near the centre of the folio someone has transcribed a short poem titled للشيخ الرئيس قدس سره while a Latin hand has written nearby: *Carmen Abu Ali Geometri Ægyptii, Abulfaraj. p. 253*; beneath the latter there is written in slightly darker ink: *Arab. 385*. For the poem on fo. 1a, an epigram in praise of Euclid, and the identity of its author, see Part II below ('Incidental Arabic Poetry', item V).

Binding: The volume is bound in vellum over pasteboards. The spine has a gold-stamped numeral *145*. The paper pastedowns and endpapers were placed at the time of the last binding. On the inside front cover there is pasted at the top a Latin note (partially defaced) reading: *Euclidis Elementa Geometrica. Cum Commentariolis.*; there is also a small slip of paper pasted in the middle on which there is a Latin description of the volume as *Euclidis Elementa geometrica; adjectis commentariolis marginalibus: cum figuris. Arabice*, along with the new and old shelfmarks (the latter shelfmark given as *ol.96.Abac.iii.1928*). The numeral *145* has been inked on the fore-edge of the manuscript.

Provenance: The volume came to the College through the donation of Archbishop William Laud (d. 1645), and prior to that it was in the collection of Sir Kenelm Digby (d. 1665).

On fo. 1a, near the bottom, there is an undated owner's ovate stamp of ʿAbd al-Karīm ..?.. ibn Muḥammad … [?]. At the top is the *ex libris* of Digby, crossed out, while at the bottom there is the *ex libris* of Archbishop Laud dated 1639.

References

Coxe, 43 entry CXLV (this item is not mentioned).

Bernard, *Catalogi*, assigns number 96 to the volume (see Hanna, *St John's Catalogue*, 338).

Entry No. 20

MS 145 (item 1)

TITLE: [*Taḥrīr Kitāb Uṣūl al-handasah li-Uqlīdis*]

[*A Revision of the 'Principles of Geometry' by Euclid*]

[تحرير كتاب اصول الهندسة لاقليدس]

AUTHOR: Naṣīr al-Dīn al-Ṭūsī (d. 672/1274)]

CONTENTS: A complete copy, in fifteen *maqālah*s or chapters, of a redaction composed in 646/1248 by Naṣīr al-Dīn al-Ṭūsī of Euclid's treatise on geometry. The latter's treatise was written originally in Greek in the 1st century AD, and was translated into Arabic in the second half of the 8th century by al-Ḥajjāj ibn Yūsuf and again in the 9th century by Isḥaq ibn Ḥunayn, whose translation was then revised by Thābit ibn Qurrah.

Many copies of Naṣīr al-Dīn al-Ṭūsī's reworking of this important treatise are preserved today. This particular copy is undated and probably originated in the 16th century.

For other copies: see Sezgin, *GAS* V, 111–13 no. 49a; and King, *Survey*, 24 no. A5.

The text has not been edited or published.

PHYSICAL DESCRIPTION:

203 leaves (fos. 1b–203a)

Beginning (fo. $1b_{1-14}$):

بسم الله ... **الحمد لله الذى منه الابتداء** ... **وبعد** فلما فرغت عن [*sic*] تحرير المجسطى رايت ان احرر كتاب اصول الهندسة والحساب المنسوب الى اقليدس الصورى بايجاز غير مخل ، واستقصى فى ثبت مقاصده استقصاء غير ممل ، واضيف اليه ما يليق به مما استفدته من كتب اهل هذا العلم واستنبطته بقريحتى وافرز ما يوجد من اصل الكتاب ... **اقول** الكتاب يشتمل على خمس عشرة مقالة ...

Ending (fo. $203a_{4-11}$):

... **اقول** ولنا ان نرسم ذا عشرين قاعدة فى ذى اثنتى
عشرة قاعدة بهذا الوجه بعينه فان زوايا كل واحد
منها بعدة قواعد الاخر والبيان قريب من بيانه
واذ وفقنى الله تعالى من تحرير هذا الكتاب حسب ما
قصدته فلاختم الكلام بحمده انه خير موفق ومعين
والحمد لله ولى الحمد وصلوته على سيد
الاولين والاخرين اشرف الانبياء والمرسلين
محمد النبى وعلى آله الطاهرين

The copy is unsigned and undated. The appearance of the paper, script, and ink suggest a date of the 16th century.

Arabic. Dimensions: 21.4 × 12.4 (text area 13.5 × 6.1) cm; 19 lines per page. Euclid is mentioned on fo. $1b_6$ and elsewhere. No title is given, and the name of the commentator is not given. It opens by referring to Ptolemy's *Almagest* (*al-Majisṭī*) and its dependence upon Euclidean geometry. Identification has been made by comparison with other copies (for example, that quoted extensively in King, *Catalogue*, 813–14, entry 6.1.3).

The text is written in a small Naskh script with some Taʿlīq characteristics, using dense black ink and headings and diagrams in red. There are also red over-linings, some added later, and red-dot text-stops. The text area has been frame ruled. There are catchwords, some partially cut off when the paper was trimmed. Not all the diagrams are drawn in the body of the text, though space was allotted for them; often there is an annotation by the scribe in the space to the effect that it was blank in the exemplar.

The beige, glossy paper has a thickness of 0.08–0.1 mm and an opaqueness factor of 5, with very indistinct, sagging, horizontal laid lines. The edges have been trimmed from their original size, with occasional pieces folded over to conserve marginal material. There are occasional ink blotches and thumbprints. The edges and corners of fos. 1 and 2 have been repaired. The paper is slightly worm-eaten.

Marginalia and owners' notes: There are considerable marginalia and interlinear annotations up to fo. 100a, after which they stop. Some of the longer annotations, often written upside down, are designated by the letters س or ن at the end (an example is illustrated in Plate 7). There are also simple marginal corrections, designated ص or صح .
One marginal note has been erased on fo. 24a.

Volume contents: For other items in the volume as well as the binding and provenance, see Entry No. 19.

References

Coxe, 43 entry CXLV.

Entry No. 21

MS 145 (item 2)

TITLE: [not given]

AUTHOR: Naṣīr al-Dīn al-Ṭūsī (d. 672/1274)

CONTENTS: This is a copy of an addendum, called a *dhayl*, by Naṣīr al-Dīn al-Ṭūsī which is found also in some other copies of Naṣīr al-Dīn al-Ṭūsī's revision (*Taḥrīr*) of Euclid's *Elements*.

The copyist of the preceding item in this volume (see Entry No. 20) states that in some copies of Euclid this addendum is found following the 15th *maqālah*.

For other copies: see King, *Survey*, 24 no. A5.

The text has not been edited or printed.

PHYSICAL DESCRIPTION:

5 leaves (fos. 204a–$208a_4$)

Beginning (fo. $204a_{1-4}$, with many diacritical dots missing):

وجد فى بعض نسخ اقليدس بعد تمام المقالة الخامسه عشر ما هذه نسختته وفى نسخه اخرى زيادة هذا الشكل كل مخمس متساوى الاضلاع والزوايا فى دايرة مربع نصف قطرها خمس مربع خط منطق فان ...

Ending (fo. $208a_{1-4}$, with many diacritical dots missing):

... وذلك ما اردناه فهذا ما قصدته وانما لم اورده
فى الكتاب لكونه مبنيا على ما هو خارج منه
فمن شاء فليلحقه به والله الموفق
والمعين

The copy is unsigned and undated. The appearance of the paper, script, and ink suggest a date of the 16th century.

Arabic. Dimensions: 21.4 × 12.4 (text area 13.5 × 6.1) cm; 19 lines per page. The text corresponds with the *dhayl* found in Cairo, Dār al-Kutub, Ṭaʿlat *riyāḍah* MS 107 fos. 135a–137b, copied in 789/1387 (see King, *Catalogue*, 814 entry 6.1.3).

The text was transcribed by the same unnamed copyist as transcribed the first item in the volume (see Entry No. 20). It is written in a small Naskh script with some Taʿlīq characteristics, using dense black ink with diagrams labelled in red. The text area has been frame ruled. There are catchwords, some partially cut off when the paper was trimmed.

The paper is the same as that used in item 1 (see Entry No. 20).

Marginalia and owners' notes: There are no marginalia.

Volume contents: For the other items in the volume, as well as the binding and provenance, see Entry No. 19.

References

Coxe, 43 entry CXLV (this item not mentioned).

MILITARY ARTS

Entry No. 22

MS 83

TITLE: *Kitāb al-Ḥiyal fī al-ḥurūb wa-fatḥ al-madā'in wa-ḥifẓ al-durūb*

The Book of Devices for Wars, Conquest of Cities, and Protecting Mountain Passes

كتاب الحيل في الحروب وفتح المداين وحفظ الدروب

AUTHOR: [Muḥammad ibn Manglī, *fl.* 778/1376–7], attributed in manuscript to Alexander the Great

CONTENTS: This is a highly illustrated treatise on military devices in 39 chapters (*bābs*), attributed in this copy to Alexander the Great. It is in fact a treatise written by Ibn

Manglī, a Mamluk officer of the guard (*ḥalqah*) to Sultan al-Malik al-Ashraf Shaʿbān (reg. 764–78/1362–77) and author of several treatises on the military arts and on hunting.

For Ibn Manglī, see *EI²* supplement, 392–3, art. F. Viré, 'Ibn Manglī' (where it is erroneously stated that his military treatises are known only through citations).

The St John's College manuscript is an illuminated and illustrated Mamluk copy completed in 757 H [= 1356], the same year as the earliest of the other recorded copies. The copy now at St John's is, however, a much finer copy than the one produced in the same year and now in Istanbul.

For other copies: Five additional copies are recorded, all of them attributing the treatise to Alexander the Great:

(1) Istanbul Ahmet III, MS 3469, fos. 127a–181b, copied in Jumādá II 757 (1356). See F. E. Karatay, *Topkapı Sarayı Müzesi Kütübhanesi Arapça yazmalar kataloğu*, Cilt III (Topkapı Sarayı Müzesi Yayınları, 15, Istanbul: Topkapı Sarayı Müzesi, 1966), 878 no. 7418, and H. Ritter, 'Kleine Mitteilungen und Anzeigen: La Parure des Cavaliers und die Literatur über die ritterlichen Kunste', *Der Islam*, 18 (1929), 116–54, esp. 150–2.

(2 and 3) Leiden, MS Or. 499 Warn. (undated) and MS Or. 92 Gol. (copied from exemplar dated 622/1225). See Pieter De Jong, and Michael Jan de Goeje, *Catalogus codicum orientalium Bibliothecae Academiae Lugduno Batavae*, 4 vols. (Leiden: E.J. Brill, 1851–77), iii. 288–92 nos. 1414–15.

(4 and 5) Rabat, al-Khazānah al-Malakīyah, MS 43/*jīm* (copied 763/1361) and MS 85 (undated).

These five copies were employed in the recent edition of the text by Sulaymān al-Ruḥaylī, *Kitāb al-Ḥiyal fī al-ḥurūb wa-fatḥ al-madā'in wa-ḥifẓ al-durūb mansūb li-Ibn Manglī* (Riyāḍ, 1998). See pp. 38–40 and 52–64 for a discussion of the copies and sample pages; see also Sezgin, *GAS* VII, 64 (Alexander der Grosse, 2). The copy at St John's College was not used in the edition nor was it referred to by the editor.

PHYSICAL DESCRIPTION:

192 leaves (fos. 1b–47a, 48b–192a)

Beginning (fo. $1b_1$–$2b_1$):

بسم الله ... الحمد لله الواسع ذى النعم .: خالق البرايا ... [fo. $2a_6$] فوجب علينا من ذلك ان يذهب عدو الله ونخدعه لقول نبينا عليه السلام الحرب خديعة **كتاب الحيل** في الحروب وفتح المداين وحفظ الدروب من حكيم ذي القرنين ابن اميليس اليوناني وجد في دمياس بالاسكندرية بين حجرين مطبقين احدهما علي الاخر باليونانية مترجم بالعربية وهذا الكتاب في جميع ابوابه يحتاج اليه في انواع الحرب من الحيل والمكر والخديعة ومخادعة العدوّ والاختراص [؟] [fo. 2b] من كيد العدو وعمل الالات والسلاح وهو مبوب ابواباً نوعتها منه علي تسعة انواع فمن ذلك ...

Ending (fo. $192a_{4-11}$):

... وان لم يمكن السفن والزواريق وامكن اتخاذ الاطواف عمل ذلك على ما قلنا من اتخاذها على الشط من قبل ثم تجر بالحبال او بالقلوس حتى تشد الى الجانب الاخر فان اراد ان يسكر الخندق القى على هذا الطوف الطوب والقصب او سائر الحطب بعضها فوق بعض حتى يرسب الاول فالاول ويعلو منه الماء ثم يلاحق بالردم <بالتراب>حتى يعلوا التراب على الماء ويحمل المشي فيمشي عليه بالاقدام ثم بالخيل فيعبر عليه الى ناحية العدو ان شا[ء] الله تعالى.

The copy is a Mamluk Egyptian product completed in 757 H [= 1356] by an unnamed copyist.

Colophon (fo. $192a_{12-13}$ continued in margins):

تم الكتاب بعون الله تعالى وحسن توفيقه فى
شهور سنة سبع وخمسين وسبعمايه هجريه
[in right margin] عضر[= غفر] الله لكاتبه ومالكه ولمن طالع فيه ودها لها بالمغفره ولجميع المسلمين
[in left margin] وصلى الله على سيدنا محمد واله وصحبه وسلم تسليماً كثيراً

Arabic. Dimensions: 26.7 × 18.4 (text area 19.5 × 13.5) cm; 13 lines per page. The title and the attribution to Alexander the Great (*ḥakīm Dhī al-Qarnayn*) are given at the beginning of the text. The attribution to Ibn Manglī is made on the basis of comparison with the edited and published text.

The text on fos. 1b–2a is written within frames of gold, blue, and black fillets. The text throughout is written in a large Naskh with considerable vocalization. The headings are in gold, outlined with fine black-inked lines (except for the table of contents on fos. 2b–3b, where the gold headings are not outlined). Carons sometimes occur on ر and س, with occasional minuscule letters under ح especially in headings. The ends of some of the last words on a line are occasionally (e.g. fo. 14a) written outside the text area. There are text-stops of three gold dots. Except on the replacement leaves (fos. 1–3), the ruling of the text area is not very evident. There are catchwords. There is an earlier foliation in European numerals, beginning with the third of the four front preliminary leaves.

On fo. 1b, a replacement leaf (old fo. 4b), there is an illuminated opening, rather crudely executed and now damaged through adhesion to facing folio; the gilt evident on fo. 2a (old 5) is an offset from the facing illuminated opening.

The contents of the 39 *bāb*s are given on fos. 2b–3b (old 5–6), followed immediately by the beginning of the first *bāb*. Within the text itself the *bāb*s are not numbered and the divisions are not always evident.

There are illustrations of devices on the following folios (using the most recent foliation). The pages in the edition by Sulaymān al-Ruḥaylī are given in square brackets. In general the illustrations in the St John MS 83 carry more labels and are more detailed and more carefully executed than those reproduced in the printed edition of the text (which did not employ the St John's manuscript):

103a	[p. 214 edition]
104a	[p. 216 edition]
105a	[p. 217 edition]
106a	[p. 218 edition]
107b	[p. 220 edition]
108b	[p. 221 edition]
109b	[p. 223 edition]
111a	[p. 224 edition]
112a (see Colour Plate II)	[p. 226 edition]
113a	[p. 228 edition]
114b (see Colour Plate III)	[p. 230 edition]
115b	[p. 232 edition]
116b	[p. 233 edition]
117b (damaged)	[p. 234 edition]
119a	[p. 236 edition]

The strong, thick, lightly burnished ivory-biscuit paper has a thickness of 0.20–0.25 mm and an opaqueness factor of 3–4. There are vertical laid lines, slightly curved, but only occasional traces of chain lines (e.g. fos. 7, 10, 14). The leaves toward the centre of the volume are creamier. The paper is worm-eaten in places and damp stained near the edges; fos. 96, 126, and 187 have had large wormholes repaired, though smaller ones have been left. There is some soiling and occasional smudges. Folios 1–3 are replacement leaves of the same paper as the last two of the four front preliminary leaves; they are of thick, brown, very fibrous paper with horizontal laid lines and chain lines in groups of threes.

Marginalia and owners' notes: There are no marginalia.

Volume contents: The volume consists of 193 folios with four preliminary leaves and two endpapers (i–iv + 193 + v–vi). Folio 1a is blank except for the *ex libris* of Archbishop Laud dated 1638 at the bottom of the page, and a Latin note at the top identifying the author as Alexander the Great. Folio 47b is blank; fo. 192b is blank except for a later owner's note (no longer legible due to water damage). Folio 193 (old 196) is very different paper (no laid or chain lines) and very water damaged; the verso of the folio has a talismanic design, while on the recto there is an offset from the owner's inscriptions on the facing folio (fo. 192b). Two of the preliminary leaves (fos. iii–iv) are of the same paper as fos. 1–3; they are blank except for a note in later hand on fo. iii reading:

كتاب الحيل فى الحروب وفتح المداين وحفظ الدروب واعمال عجيبه وغرايب بديعه وغير ذلك.

The first two preliminary leaves (fos. i–ii) are of the same paper type as the endleaves (fos. v–vi) and are also blank.

The front pastedown has the annotation *No. 83* and the St John's College bookplate, while a second College bookplate is on the back pastedown.

Binding: The volume is bound in a European binding with covers of dark-brown leather over boards, having a gold-stamped coat of arms in the centre of each cover. The spine is a lighter tan leather, with five cords and a gilt-stamped *83* at the top. The fore-edge has an inked number *83*. The pastedowns and endpapers are contemporary with the last binding.

Provenance: The volume came to the College through the donation of Archbishop William Laud (d. 1645).

References

Coxe, 24 entry LXXXIII, where title is given as *Liber de arte mechanica in rebus belllicosis, ex disciplina Alexandri Magni.*

Bernard, *Catalogi*, A.18 (*in abaco secundo*).

ENCYCLOPEDIAS AND COMPENDIA

Entry No. 23

MS 122

TITLE: *Miftāḥ al-'ulūm*

The Key to the Sciences

مفتاح العلوم

AUTHOR: al-Sakkākī, Yūsuf ibn Abī Bakr ibn Muḥammad (d. 626/1229)

CONTENTS: This is a heavily annotated copy of the influential compendium on all the linguistic sciences written in the 13th century by al-Sakkākī. The copy at St John's was made in Khwārazm and completed on 23 Rajab 732 [= 20 Apr. 1332].

After opening with a brief section on phonetics (*makhārij al-ḥurūf*), the compendium is divided into three major sections (*qism*s): on *'ilm al-ṣarf* (morphology), *'ilm al-naḥw* (syntax), and *'ilm al-ma'ānī wa-al-bayān* (stylistics and theory of imagery). There are also two appendices concerned with poetry. All these sections are then subdivided into many subsections (*faṣl*, *qānūn*, *bāb*, etc.). For full details of the structure of the treatise, see Ahlwardt, *Berlin*, vii. 363–4.

Al-Sakkākī was an influential rhetorician who was born in Khwārazm in 555/1160 and spent the last three years of his life in prison on the order of Chaghatay, son of Chinghiz Khan. Numerous commentaries and glosses were composed on his *Miftāḥ al-'ulūm*, especially on the third part (*qism*). For al-Sakkākī, see W. P. Heinrichs, 'Sakkākī', in *EI²*, viii. 893–4.

For other copies: see Brockelmann, *GAL* i. 294 (352–3) and S i. 515; Ahlwardt, *Berlin*, vii. nos. 7184, 7185, 7186; and Sellheim, *VOHD*, 229–324. The text has been printed many times in Cairo (e.g. 1317/1899, 1318/1900, 1356/1937). A faulty text was edited by Nuʿaym Zarzūr, *Miftāḥ al-'ulūm* (Beirut: Dār al-Kutub al-ʿIlmīyah, 1983; 2nd edn., 1987). No definitive modern edition has been issued.

The third part (*qism*) of the treatise has been translated into German: U. G. Simon, *Mittelalterliche arabische Sprachbetrachtung zwischen Grammatik und Rhetorik — 'ilm al-ma'ānī bei as-Sakkākī* (Heidelberg: Heidelberger Orientverlag, 1993).

PHYSICAL DESCRIPTION:

253 leaves (fos. 1b–70b, 71b–187b, 188a–253a)

Beginning (fo. $1b_1$–$3a_1$):

بسم الله ... احق كلام ان تلهج به الالسنة ، وان لا يطوى منشوره على توالي الازمنة ، ... **وبعد** فان نوع الادب نوع يتفاوت كثرة شعب وقلة ، وصعوبة فنون وسهولة ، وتباعد طرفين وتدانيا بحسب حظ متوليه من ساير العلوم كمالا ...[fo. $2a_8$] وقد ضمنت كتابي هذا من انواع الادب دون نوع اللغة ... [fo. $2b_{20}$] وسميته مفتاح العلوم وجعلت هذا الكتاب ثلاثة اقسام القسم الاول فى علم الصرف القسم الثانى فى علم النحو القسم الثالث فى علم المعانى والبيان ...

Ending (fo. $253a_{15-20}$):

... فيقال بناءً على مقتضى البلاغة وما علمناه الشعر وعلى هذا المحمل كيف يلزم شيء مما ذكرتم ... ختم الكلام حامدين الله تعالى ومصلين على الاخيار ، ولنشح الذيل لاملاء حواشٍ عرى عن فوايدها المتن لقصد الاختصار ، والسلام .

Colophon (fo. $253a_{20-24}$, many diacritics missing), illustrated in Plate 8:

قد وقع الفراغ من تنميقه بعون الله وحسن توفيقه
على يد بدر السرايي [n.d.] فى بلدة خوارزم حفظها الله
عن الازمً يوم الاثنين الثالث والعشرين من شهر لله
الاصم رجب سنه اثنتين وثلاثين وسبعمائه

The copy was made in Khwārazm by Badr al-Sarāyī and completed on 23 Rajab 732 [= 20 Apr. 1332].

Arabic. Dimensions: 22.8 × 14.2 (text area 15.5 × 9.1) cm; 21 lines per page. The title is given on fo. $2b_{20-21}$. The author is not named.

A complete copy. The first *qism* begins on fo. $3a_{16}$, the second *qism* on fo. 33b and ends on fo. 70b, and the third occupies fos. 71b–219a. The first appendix begins on fos. 219b and the second appendix begins on fo. $242b_{19}$.

On fo. 4b there is a carefully rendered diagram, in red and black ink, of the throat, teeth, and tongue, illustrated in Colour Plate IV. On fos. 222a and 222b there are circular diagrams illustrating stress in various metres (i.e. the Khalīlian circles).

The text (except for the replacement folios) is written in a careful, medium-small Naskh script with some ligatures (e.g. *alif-lām-alif*, the *tā' marbūṭah* joined with letters not customarily attached). It is written in black ink with headings in a warm red, red teardrop text-stops, and red over-linings. Occasional catchwords are visible, but most have been lost in the gutter or cut off when rebinding. Vocalization appears to have been added later. The beginning of the treatise is fully vocalized. The text area is frame ruled. Folios 74 and 77 (guarded), 83–8, 113–32, 156–63 are replacement folios (watermarked paper). There are no rubrications on the replacement pages, which are written in a dense black ink and generally have 16 to 18 lines per page, sometimes fewer (fos. 153–163 have 21 lines per page). Folio 144 is an older replacement leaf.

Folio 188a has the Arabic numeral ٢ in the upper corner, indicating that it is the beginning of the second quire; similarly, fo. 196 is labelled ٣, fo. 204 ٤. Thus a new enumeration of the eight-leaf quires was undertaken beginning with fo. 179, where there is also a clear section break in the third *qism* (fo. 187 is a small modern piece of paper with unrelated text). These three folios (188, 196, and 204) are the only ones in the volume with quire numerations still evident.

The beige paper of the original copy has a thickness of 0.11–0.16 mm and an opaqueness factor of 4 or 5. It is quite fibrous with occasional thin patches and occasional creasing; the thickness is variable. It has broad horizontal laid lines with traces of chain lines visible on some leaves, possibly in groups of threes (fos. 71, 72, 80, etc.). Modern paper (17th century) similar to that of fos. iii and iv, has been pasted onto the recto of fo. 1; in the middle of fo. 1b there is a hole, at which point the text has been overwritten on the 'modern' paper pasted onto its recto. There are large unrepaired holes in fos. 70, 79, and 193. The older paper is slightly worm-eaten. The edges of the paper have been trimmed, with the loss of some marginalia. The paper is damp stained.

Marginalia and owners' notes: The volume is heavily annotated in the margins and interlinearly in several hands, written in a very small script in a light-brown ink and also a black ink. Much of the marginalia appears to consist of extracts from an unspecified commentary. The annotations in the lightest brown ink are usually designated by the letter *sīn*. Those in darker ink are often, but not always, marked ه or ط ه ; there are also textual corrections (usually designated صح). Next to the Basmala on fo. 1b, one of the annotators has written:

قال الاستاذ الامام البادع العلامة سراج الملة والدين ابو يعقوب يوسف بن ابى بكر بن محمد بن على جزاه الله ...

There are fewer marginalia in the second *qism* than in the first and third. Some of the marginalia are now lost in the gutter.

Volume contents: The volume consists of 253 leaves (i–iv + 253 + v–vi). Folio 71a is blank. Folio 187 is a small piece of modern paper (*c.*10 × 6.5 cm) torn from a large sheet and bound into the volume at this point; it has a casually written Persian note on it concerned with geometry. Folio 253b is blank except for a later note recording the death of one Yūsuf ibn ʿAbd Allāh Muʿtiq Ilyās ibn Ṭūrah ibn al-Ḥājāt known as Shams al-Dīn al-Ashʿarī, dated 773 [= 1371–2], with the day specified in the margin as 14 Ṣafar, which was 29 August 1371:

بسم الله ... توفي المعصوم المرحوم السعيد الشهيد المحتاج الى رحمه ... الرحمن الغفور يوسف بن عبد الله معتق الياس بن طوره بن الحاجات المعروف بشمس الدين الاشعرى ... فى تاريخ سنه ثلث وسبعين وسبعمايه

((فى يوم الثلثآء الرابع عشر من الشهر المبارك صفر تغمده الله بغفرانه واسكنه بخير فى [؟] جنانه صح))

Folio 1a has pasted over it a leaf of modern (17th-century) paper like that of fos. iii and iv; it is blank except for the *ex libris* (crossed out) of Digby at the top, and at the bottom the *ex libris* of Archbishop Laud, dated 1639. Preliminary fos. i and ii are of the same paper as the pastedowns; fos. iii and iv are of different, watermarked paper (17th century?), blank except for, on fo. iiib, a short miscellaneous note and an old shelfmark (no. C.34), on fo. iva the Arabic annotations ١٤٩٥ مط, and, on folio ivb, a Latin annotation *Commentarius Grammaticus et Rhetoricus* and the St John's College bookplate. Folios v and vi are blank endpapers of the same paper type as the pastedowns.

Binding: The volume is bound in a European binding, identical to that of MS 103 (Entry No. 2), made of pasteboards covered with a light-brown suede leather; the spine has five cords. The covers have blind-stamped rectangular designs of acanthus leaves on one side of two fillets, and repetitive flower-heads and leaves on the other side, with a large tulip at each corner. The same design can be seen in MS 107 (Entry No. 32), but impressed in a brown, mottled, shiny leather rather than suede leather. The modern paper endpapers are blank. The back paper pastedown has the bookplate of St John's College, and the front pastedown has a handwritten *ex libris* for St John's College and, pasted beneath, another piece of paper having the following Latin annotation:

Liber Arabicus dictus مفتح العلوم [*sic*] Meftah Al-olûm, i.e. Clavis Scientiarum.
Est Introductio ad Grammaticam, Rhetoricam, & Poeticam: Auctore Seraj'eddîn Abu Jacob Joseph Ben Abubekr Ben Mohammed, Ben Ali, cognomento Sakkâki; aliàs dicto Seraj'eddîn Chorasmiano, à patriâ Chorasmiâ: qui natus est An. Hejrae 555. i.e. X^{ti}. 1160; mortuus an. Hej. 626. i.c. X^{ti}. 1228.

Hic Liber dicitur, alio nomine, Encyclopaedia Sakkâki, estque magnae apud Arabas existimationis.

Hoc Exemplar exaratum est, in Urbe Chorasmiâ, An Hej. 732, i.e. X^{ti}. 1331.

Vid. D'Herbelot Bibliothec. Orient. p. 727. Col. 2. p. 794. Col. 2. Vid. & p. 549. Col. 2 & p. 921. col. 1.

Provenance: The volume came to the college through the donation of Archbishop William Laud (d. 1645), and prior to that it was in the collection of Sir Kenelm Digby (d. 1665).

References

Coxe, 36 entry CXXII; according to a typescript list appended at the back of the Coxe catalogue kept in the College library, there may have been a lithographed printing of this text at one time in the library.

Bernard, *Catalogi*, C.34 (*in abaco tertio*).

Entry No. 24

MS 33

TITLE: *Kitāb Durrat al-tāj li-ghurrat al-Dubāj / Unmūdhaj al-'ulūm*

The Pearl of the Crown for the noble Dubāj / The Model of the Sciences

كتاب درة التاج لغرة الدباج / انموزج العلوم

AUTHOR: Quṭb al-Dīn Maḥmūd ibn Masʿūd al-Shīrāzī (d. 710/1311)

CONTENTS: This is a complete copy of a Persian encyclopedia of the sciences that was also known as *Unmūdhaj al-'ulūm*, according to the Ottoman historian and bibliographer Kātib Çelebi (Ḥājjī Khalīfah) (ḤKh, iii. 201 no. 4926, where the editor Flügel vocalized the title as *Inmúzej*). The encyclopedia was completed in 705 (= 1305) and dedicated to Dubāj ibn Ḥusām al-Dīn Fīl-Shāh ibn Sayf al-Dīn Rustam ibn Dubāj Isḥāqāwand, prince of Bayah Pas, of the western Gīlān province of Iran.

The treatise is divided into a prologue (*fātiḥah*) and five chapters (*jumlah*s). The prologue consists of three sections (*faṣl*s). The five chapters are on (1) logic, in seven subsections (*maqālah*s), (2) philosophy, in two parts (*fann*s), (3) physics, in two *fann*s, (4) mathematics, in four *fann*s (on Euclid's geometry, Ptolemy's *Almagest*, arithmetic, and music), and (5) metaphysics, in two *fann*s. The treatise also has an appendix (*khātimah*) in four subsections (*quṭb*s).

The copy now at St John's, though unsigned and undated, is an excellent manuscript with an illuminated title page and opening. It is unusual, though not unique, in providing at the end of the treatise the precise day upon which Quṭb al-Dīn al-Shīrāzī completed the work: 12 Rajab 705 (= 28 Jan. 1306). This date of completion is also given in one other copy, now in Mashhad; see Māhdukht Bānū Humā'ī (ed.), *Durrat al-tāj: bakhsh-i ḥikmat-i ʻamalī va sayr va sulūk*, Shirkat-i Intishārāt-i ʻIlmī va Farhangī 247 (Tehran, 1369/1991), 18 and photograph p. 25.

Quṭb al-Dīn Maḥmūd ibn Masʻūd al-Shīrāzī is perhaps better known for two comprehensive astronomical works (both composed in Arabic) and his Arabic-language commentary on the *Canon of Medicine* (*Kitāb al-Qānūn fī al-ṭibb*) by Ibn Sīnā. The latter commentary was titled *al-Tuḥfah al-Saʻdīyah* because Quṭb al-Dīn dedicated the work to Saʻd al-Dīn Sāvajī, vizier to Öljeytü, the Ilkhanid ruler of Iran 1304–17. See E. Wiedemann, 'Ḳuṭb al-Din Shīrāzī', in *EI²*, v. 547–8; and Maddison and Savage-Smith, *Science, Tools & Magic*, 32–5 no. 8.

Two partial editions of the Persian encyclopedia have been published (neither employing the St John's copy): *Durrat al-tāj li-ghurrat al-Dubāj*, ed. Sayyid Muḥammad Mishkāt, 5 parts (Tehran, 1317–20/1938–41), which is an edition of the five *jumlah*s only and not the *khātimah*; and *Durrat al-tāj: bakhsh-i ḥikmat-i 'amalī va sayr va sulūk*, ed. Māhdukht Bānū Humā'ī, Shirkat-i Intishārāt-i ʻIlmī va Farhangī 247 (Tehran, 1369/1991), an edition of the *khātimah* only. Extracts have also been published in German translation: *Forsetzung der Auszüge aus encyclopædischen Werken der Araber, Perser und Türken. Aus dem Durret-et-tadsch (Perle der Krone) Mahmud Schirasî's*, trans. Hammer-Purgstall (Vienna, 1857), previously published in *Denkschriften der philos.-hist. Klasse der Kaiserl. Academie der Wissenschaften*, VIII.

For other copies: see Storey, *PL* II₃, 354–5 no. 592; and *Durrat al-tāj: bakhsh-i ḥikmat-'amalī va sayr va sulūk*, ed. Māhdukht Bānū Humā'ī, Shirkat-i Intishārāt-i ʻIlmī va Farhangī 247 (Tehran, 1369/1991), 18–32.

PHYSICAL DESCRIPTION:

402 leaves (fos. 1a–226a, 227a–402a)

Beginning (fo. $1b_{1-2}$), illustrated in Colour Plate VI:

بسم الله ... رب انعمت فزد .·. اگرجه بر ضمیر ارباب کیاست ، وخاطر اصحاب فراست بوشیده [= پوشیده] نماند [*sic*] كي نعت جلال ربوبيت ، ...

Ending (fo. $402a_{30-33}$):

... و وصول بجناب عزت سرمدیت نباشد وذلك فضل الله يؤتيه من يشاء بفرحی و پیروزی تمام شد کتاب درة التاج لغرة الدباج در روز جمعه دوازدهم رجب سال بر [؟] هفتصد [؟] و پنج از هجرت نبوی مصطفوي صلى الله عليه وعلى آله واصحابه الطاهرين .

The copy is unsigned and undated. The general appearance of the illumination, script, and paper suggests a date of *c*.1550–80 in Iran or Sultanate India. It appears to have been copied by at least two different scribes, one of which uses the 'ancient' spelling of ذ in words such as باشاذ and گنذ.

Persian. Dimensions: 32.7 × 23.6 (text area 25.5 × 17.2) cm; 35 lines per page. The title occurs at the top of the illuminated title page (fo. 1a) and also at the end of the treatise.

At the bottom of the title page (illustrated in Colour Plate V), the author is given as Quṭb al-millah wa-al-ḥaqq wa-al-dīn; various honorifics occupy the central medallion of the title page. On fo. $2b_4$ the author is given as Maḥmūd ibn Mas'ūd ibn al-Muṣliḥ al-Shīrāzī. The patron Dubāj is named on fo. $2b_7$.

A complete copy. The first *jumlah* begins on fo. 22b, the second on fo. 50a, the third on 69a, the fourth on 91a, and the fifth on fo. 236b. The concluding section (*khātimah*) begins on fo. 255b.

The text is written in a calligraphic and elegant medium-large Naskh script in dense black ink. The headings are in large Thulth script in black ink as well as in red, blue, and green, as well as occasionally gilt outlined in black. There are text-stops of red dots or teardrops, occasionally in groups of threes. The title page (fo. 1a) and opening page (fo. 1b) are illuminated with gilt and opaque watercolours (see Colour Plates V and VI). On fo. 1a the title, author's name, and honorifics are written in cloudbands inside frames of gilt with red, blue, and black ink, with the grounds behind the cloudbands filled with red ink hatching or gilt paint decorated with leaves. On fo. 1b the Basmala is written in gilt, outlined in black, in a cartouche set within an illuminated rectangle with a nearly triangular illuminated design on top; gilt with opaque watercolours. The text on fos. 1b–2a is written within frames of gilt, black, red, and blue fillets, while the remaining text is written within frames of two narrow red fillets. There are catchwords. Folios 348a–367b appear to be written by a slightly different hand, using a broader nib to the pen.

There are diagrams and tables (in red and black ink) on fos. 41a, 92a–151a, 153b–170b, 171b, 173b–174a, 175b, 178ab, 179b–186b, 187b–188a, 189a, 190a–192b, 194a, 195b–199a, 210a–211a, 212b–215b, 216b–219b, 220b–221b, 222b–226a, 227b, 228b, 230ab, 232a, 233ab, 235a–236a. The diagram on fo. 217a is illustrated in Colour Plate VII.

The glossy cream paper has a thickness of 0.07–0.09 mm and an opaqueness factor of 6–7. There are indistinct laid lines, sometimes horizontal and sometimes vertical, with only traces of single chain lines (e.g. fo. 296). There are occasional streaks and rib shadows. The small fibres are lightly dispersed. There are a few wormholes and some damp staining near the lower outside corner. Folio 4 has some unrepaired tears; there are unrepaired holes in fos. 20, 21, 32, 345.

Marginalia and owners' notes: There are some marginal corrections and numbering of diagrams by the copyist, but no other marginalia. On fo. 1a, the signature of Kenelm Digby has been marked out at the top and, at the bottom, the *ex libris* of Archbishop Laud and the date 1639 have been inscribed (see Colour Plate V).

Volume contents: The volume consists of 402 leaves, four preliminary leaves (one a flyleaf placed at last binding), and one endpaper (i–iv + 402 + i). Folios 226b and 402b are blank; the top half of fo. 227a is blank. The preliminary leaves are blank except for a few annotations. On fo. ib there is a Latin note denoting it as MS 33 at St John's College. On fo. iia: پاشا خضرتلرینکدر 'it belongs to his honour the Pasha'. On preliminary fo. ivb :

Liber Gemma Diadematis dictus.
Sive
Systema rerum et Artium Universarum.
Arabico-Persice.

Binding: The volume is bound in a European library binding of dark-brown leather over pasteboards. The covers have narrow frames of two gilt fillets and the spine has six cords with pairs of gilt fillets either side. There are modern pastedowns. Staining from the envelope flap of an earlier Islamic binding can be seen on the three older preliminary leaves (fos. ii–iv). The numeral *33* has been inked on the fore-edge of the manuscript.

Provenance: The volume came to the College through the donation of Archbishop William Laud (d. 1645). Prior to that it was in the collection of Sir Kenelm Digby (d. 1665).

References

Coxe, 11 entry XXXIII.
Bernard, *Catalogi*, G.45 (*in abaco secundo*).

BELLES-LETTRES/LITERATURE

Entry No. 25

MS 370

TITLE: [*Maqāmāt al-Ḥarīrī*]

The Maqāmāt of al-Ḥarīrī

[مقامات الحريري]

AUTHOR: al-Ḥarīrī (d. 516/1122)

CONTENTS: This is a complete copy of all 50 *maqāmāt* by al-Ḥarīrī.

A literary genre that had developed by the 10th century was called *maqāmah* (or in the plural, *maqāmāt*). It usually consisted of a collection of stories written in rhymed prose (called *saj'* in Arabic) having verse insertions, with the stories sharing a common plot-scheme and two constant figures: the narrator and the hero/trickster. The *Maqāmāt* of al-Ḥarīrī, a collection of 50 such rhymed-prose narrations, were an immediate success, and there are testimonies to people coming from as far away as Spain to hear al-Ḥarīrī recite his *Maqāmāt* in his home in Baghdad. Al-Ḥarīrī's *Maqāmāt* became a symbol of Arabic eloquence and literary style. The adventures of its unscrupulous hero were a favourite subject matter for illustrators, and extant copies of al-Ḥarīrī's *Maqāmāt* are amongst the finest examples of Arab painting.

There are no illustrations in this copy. The opening, however, has an illuminated head-piece in brown and blue opaque watercolours and gilt, rather crudely executed (illustrated in Colour Plate VIII).

This copy is also notable for having been collated and vocalized by Jarmānūs Farḥāt (1670–1732), a Syrian lexicographer, grammarian, and poet who was also Maronite archbishop of Aleppo from 1725 (see I. Kratschkowsky and A. G. Karam, 'Farḥāt', in *EI*[2], ii. 795–6).

The undated and unsigned copy was apparently made for the Maronite Christian Arab community in Syria. There are a series of notes, the earliest dated 1715, for a number of Maronite Christian owners in Aleppo. The flower scrolls and other features of the illuminated head-piece (see Colour Plate VIII) are reminiscent of the illumination on a *Qur'ān* made in Aleppo in 895/1489; see James, *After Timur*, 66–7 no. 16.

For other copies: see Brockelmann, *GAL*, i. 276–8 (325–9); *GAL* S i. 486–9; Wagner, *VOHD*, 361–2 no. 426; Schoeler, *VOHD*, 334–6 no. 295; and Sobieroj, *VOHD*, 260–1 no. 134. An uncatalogued copy, incomplete and unillustrated, is at Palto Alto, Calif., Stanford University, Lane Medical Library, MS Z 310 (145 folios). For illustrated copies, see Oleg Grabar, *The Illustrations of the 'Maqamat'* (Chicago: University of Chicago Press, 1989).

PHYSICAL DESCRIPTION:

143 leaves (fos. 1b–143a)

Beginning (fo. $1b_{1-4}$ and fo. $2a_{17}$–$2b_2$), illustrated in Colour Plate VIII:

بسم الله ... اللهم انا نحمدك * علي ما علمت من البيان * والهمت من التبيان * كما نحمدك علي ما اسبلت من الغطاء * واسبغت من العطاء * ونعوذ بك من شرة اللسن ... * [fo. 2a] **وبعد** فانه جرى [fo. 2b] ببعض اندية الادب * الذى ركدت في هذا العصر ريحه * وخبت مصابيحه ذكر المقامات التي ابتدعها بديع الزمان * وعلامة همدان * رحمه الله وعزا الي ابي الفتح الاسكندري نشأتها * والي عيسي بن هشام ...

Ending (fo. $143a_{1-5}$):

الذي لم يزل مستورا ولكن كان ذلك فى الكتاب مسطورا وانا
استغفر الله العظيم مما اودعتها من اباطيل اللغو واضاليل اللهو
واشترشده الي ما يعصم من السهو ويحظي
بالعفو انه اهل التقوي والمغفره
وولي الخيرات في الدنيا
والآخرة
تم

The copy is undated and unsigned. It must have been produced before 1715, the earliest dated owner's entry.

Arabic. Dimensions: 21.6 × 13.8 (text area 15.5 × 8.3) cm; 17 lines per page. The text area has been frame ruled.

A complete copy containing all 50 *maqāmāt.*

Text is written throughout in a careful medium-small Naskh within frames formed of red, black, and gilt fillets, using dense black ink with headings in magenta and red-dot text-stops. There is full vocalization. There are catchwords. Poetry and section headings are framed by thin gilt and black fillets.

On fo. 1b there is an illuminated head-piece (*'unwān*) painted in dark-blue and brown opaque watercolours, highlighted with gilt (Colour Plate VIII).

The volume has been paginated using Arabic standard numerals beginning with fo. 1b having the illuminated *'unwān*. A table of contents has been written, probably by the same hand, on preliminary fo. vib giving the titles of the 50 *maqāmāt* and the corresponding page numbers. The volume has recently been foliated using European numerals, and it is the latter designation that has been used here.

The thin ivory paper has a thickness of 0.06–0.08 mm and an opaqueness factor of 7. There are fine vertical laid lines, single chain lines, and watermarks (not identified; see fos. 121 and 143). The paper is now somewhat brittle and lightly soiled near the edges.

Marginalia and owners' notes: There are marginal corrections and annotations as well as occasional interlinear additions. The volume was collated (collation marks occur on fo. 15a and other leaves). On fo. 143a there is poetry written on the bottom half, in two different hands, one of which has added the following:

قد حركتها بيدي الفانيه من الاول الي الاخر الفقير اليه تعالي جرمانوس فرحات المطران علي طائفة المارونيه
بحلب المحميه وهي برسم ولدنا الشماس انطون فرنجيه

Jirmānūs Farḥāt (d. 1732) is also referred to in a pencilled note on the last endpaper in the volume, reading *Collated and vocalized by Germanos Farhat / £2-00.*

Folios 143 and 144 also have poetry written by various owners; see Part II, below ('Incidental Arabic Poetry', items XII–XXIII).

Volume contents: The volume consists of 144 leaves, with six preliminary leaves and four back endpapers (i–vi + 144 + vii–x). Folio 1a is blank except for four owners' notes. Folios 143 and 144 have poetry written by several different later hands; see Part II, below ('Incidental Arabic Poetry', items XII–XXIII). Of the preliminary leaves, fos. v and vi are of paper similar to that of the main text; they are blank except for the table of contents on fo. vib. Folios ii–iv are blank except for a carefully written entry signed *G.C.R.* on fo. iia, reading:

The Makamat or Discourses of Harīrī—very neatly and correctly written. The earliest date is 1715. It belonged to the Franjiyyeh family at Aleppo. Of this celebrated work no less than three editions have been printed, two nearly at the same time at Paris, and one, with an English preface by Mr. Thomasson, at Calcutta. The best is that of M. De Sacy. The students in Asia often learn the whole of Hariri by heart. Les Cinquantes Fiances di Hariri en Arabe par M. Coussin de Perceual. Paris. 1820. 4to. Dauce un Commentaire choisi par M. le Baron Silvestre de Sacy. Paris. 1822. in folio.

The first preliminary leaf (fo. i) has been pasted to the marbled endpaper, and has the annotation: *G.C.R.| N°.97 | New Cat | N°. 52.* Folios vii–x are blank except for a pencilled note on the last one reading: *Collated and vocalized by Germanos Farhat | £2-00.*

Binding: The volume is bound in a European binding of pasteboards covered in brown leather. The covers (now loose) have borders of two thin gilt fillets. The doublures and endpapers are of European marbled paper. There is a green silk place-marker.

Provenance: The volume was in the collection of St John's College in 1932, when it was given the shelfmark MS 126F. The volume has an *ex libris* plate of John Trott (BA, St John's College, Cambridge), dated 1806, who was, presumably, the donor.

Prior to that, the volume was in Aleppo. Folio 1a has one defaced owner's note and three legible ones providing the following information: (1) Ghafūr ibn al-Qadīr Aghūsṭīn [Augustine] ibn Yūsuf ibn al-Hindī al-Ḥalabī al-Mārūnī [the Maronite of Aleppo], dated 1715 AD; (2) it then transferred to al-Shammās Anṭūn son of (*walad*) Maqdisī Ḥannā Franjīyah in 1729 in Aleppo (Ḥalab); (3) and thereafter it transferred to al-Shammās Dīrkus son of al-Shammās Anṭūn ibn Maqdisī Ḥannā Franjīyah.

On the last endpaper in the volume there is a note reading *Collated and vocalized by Germanos Farhat / £2-00.*

Former shelfmark 126F

References

Unpublished.

Coxe-supplement-2 (unpublished typescript) has a short entry in the handwritten list kept at the back of the volume in the College library.

ḤADĪTH and *FIQH*

Entry No. 26

MS 369

TITLE: *Kitāb al-Jāmi' al-ṣaḥīḥ / Kitāb al-Ṣaḥīḥ / Kitāb Ṣaḥīḥ al-Bukhārī*

The Correct Collection / Book of the Correct [Traditions] / al-Bukhārī's Book of Correct [Traditions]

كتاب الجامع الصحيح / كتاب الصحيح / كتاب صحيح البخارى

AUTHOR: Muḥammad ibn Ismāʿīl al-Bukhārī (d. 256/870)

CONTENTS: This is a collection of *ḥadīth* that took sixteen years to compile. Al-Bukhārī collected the *ḥadīth* into 97 books containing 3,450 chapters (*bāb*s).

The St John's College manuscript is a fine illuminated, highly annotated, copy completed in 901 [= 1496]. It was probably made in Iran, judging from the names (*nisbah*s) of the copyist, though the illumination also has similarities with illuminated manuscripts produced in Istanbul at the end of the 15th century. The table of contents has an illuminated head-piece (*'unwān*), while the text itself begins on two facing illuminated folios (Colour Plate IX). There are copious Arabic and Persian marginal glosses and interlinear notes in several hands.

For other copies: see Brockelmann, *GAL* S i. 261–4; and Sezgin, *GAS* I, 116–32.

There have been numerous printings of this text, for example: *Le Recueil des traditions mahométanes par Abou Abdallah Mohammad ibn Ismaîl el-Bokhâri*, ed. M. Ludolf Krehl and Th. W. Juynboll, 4 vols. (Leiden: Brill, 1864–1908). The St John's copy has not been used in any edition or printing.

PHYSICAL DESCRIPTION:

512 leaves (fos. 1a–2a, 3b– 512b)

Beginning (fo. $1b_{1-3}$ and fo. $3b_{1-4}$):

فهرست كتاب صحيح البخاري . بسم ... عدد جميع حديث الكتاب الجامع الصحيح من تاليف ابى عبد الله محمد بن اسمعيل البخارى رحمة الله عليه [fo. 3b] ... **كتاب صحيح البخاري** : بسم الله ... **باب** كيف كان بدو الوحى الى رسول الله صلى الله عليه وسلم وقول الله جل ثناؤه ... حدثنا الحميدى قال حدثنا سفين ...

Ending (fo. $512b_{20-21}$):

... **حديثنا** احمد بن اشكاب حدثنا محمد بن فضيل عن عمارة بن القعقاع عن ابي زرعة عن ابي هريرة قال قال النبى صلى الله عليه وسلم كلمتان حبيبتان الى الرحمن خفيفتان على اللسان ثقيلتان فى الميزان سبحان الله وبحمده سبحان العظيم .

Colophon (fo. $512b_{22-27}$), illustrated in Colour Plate X:

فرغ من تنميق هذا الكتاب المبارك الميمون المشهور بجامع البخارى احد الكتابين
المعرفين بأنهما اصح الكتب المصنفة يوم الثلاثاء الثالث
والعشرين من شوال سنة احدى وتسعمائه من الهجرة اقل عباد الله
السيد احمد بن شمس الدين بن فخر الدين الجهرمى
مولدا والجويمى اصلا رضى الله عن مصنفه وغفر لكاتبه
ولمستكتبه ولوالديهما ولمن نظر فيه .

The copy was completed on 23 Shawwāl 901 [= 5 July 1496] by Aḥmad ibn Shams al-Dīn ibn Fakhr al-Dīn al-Jahramī *mawlidan* al-Juwaymī *aṣlan.* Jahram and Juwaym are both towns in the Iranian province of Fārs.

The title is given as *al-Kitāb al-Jāmi' al-ṣaḥīḥ* at the beginning of the table of contents (fo. $1b_3$), where the author is given as Abū ʿAbd Allāh Muḥammad ibn Ismāʿīl al-Bukhārī. In the colophon, the title is given as *Jāmi' al-Bukhārī* (fo. 512b, illustrated in Colour Plate X). The title is given as *Kitāb Ṣaḥīḥ al-Bukhārī* in the illuminated head-piece opening the table of contents and the illuminated opening of the first page of text (fo. 3b, illustrated in Colour Plate IX). On the title page (fo. 1a) it is given in Persian as *Kitāb-i Ṣaḥīḥ-i Bukhārī dar ḥadīth.*

A complete copy. The table of contents occupies fos. 1b–2a. The text proper begins on fo. 3b.

Arabic. Dimensions 21.4 × 14.5 (text area 14.3 × 8.4) cm; 27 lines per page. There is no evidence of ruling.

The text is written in a very small and compact Naskh script with nearly full vocalization, using black ink with headings in gilt or blue (only occasionally in red). There are some red over-linings and red interlinear symbols indicating related marginalia, added later. The text throughout, including the table of contents, is written within frames formed of a blue fillet and three narrow black fillets filled with gilt. A small illuminated head-piece (in black ink and gilt) opens the table of contents on fo. 1b. The first two folios of text proper (fos. 3b–4a) are richly illuminated (illustrated in Colour Plate IX).

There are catchwords, though many have been cut off when the leaves were trimmed. The volume has been recently foliated in pencilled Western numerals, replacing an earlier foliation using Arabic numerals that began with the first folio at what is now the third folio in the recent foliation.

The thin biscuit-brown paper has a thickness of 0.07–0.09 mm and an opaqueness factor of 4. There are slightly sagging laid lines with only occasional, indistinct chain lines. The laid lines run horizontally on all the leaves except fos. 3–170 where they run vertically. Almost all the leaves are guarded. There are numerous small wormholes and extensive, but careful, repairs have been made to the corners, edges, and tears on most of the folios. There is substantial water staining at the bottom and lower outside edges. The edges have been trimmed from their original size.

Marginalia and owners' notes: There are copious Arabic and Persian marginal annotations and interlinear notes in several hands, written in a very small but precise and careful script. There are also occasional sectional headings written in the margins in a large and later hand.

Volume contents: The volume consists of 512 folios, with two front and two back endpapers (i–ii + 512 + iii–iv). Folios 2b and 3a are blank, except for a Persian note on fo. 8a mentioning a price of 500 rupees (?). There are also two blank preliminary leaves. The two endpapers are blank except for pencilled annotations on the last endpaper stating that the foliation was done in 1993 and the price of the volume was £5.00. Folio 485b has attached at the top a piece of rather modern paper (17.3 × 10 cm) on which there are written 20 lines of Persian annotations.

Binding: The volume is bound in a European binding of leather over pasteboards. The covers have a central panel of red leather framed by wide gilt-stamped borders formed of an acanthus leaf design surrounded on the outside by two simple fillets enclosing a twisted vine. The outer edges of the covers are dark-brown leather. There are maroon leather doublures and modern endpapers.

Provenance: The volume has been in the library since 1932, when it was given the shelfmark MS 126E. No further information is available on its immediate provenance, though on the last endpaper there is an annotation that the volume was foliated in 1993 and also a note of the price of £5. This price is presumably that paid for the volume when it was acquired either by St John's Library or by the unknown donor, rather than the price paid for foliation.

On the title page (fo. 1a) there are seven obliterated owners' notes, one six-line note written diagonally and partially cut off when the folio was trimmed, and an undated octagonal reverse owner's stamp which is impressed twice. On fo. 3b there are two other owners' stamps: an oval one in the side margin, of which only the name Ibrāhīm can be read, and a Persian circular one at the bottom, partially cut off. The latter stamp is repeated (now defaced) to the right of the colophon on fo. 512b, and to the left of the colophon a yet different circular owner's stamp appears, also defaced (see Colour Plate X).

The former shelfmark was MS 126E.

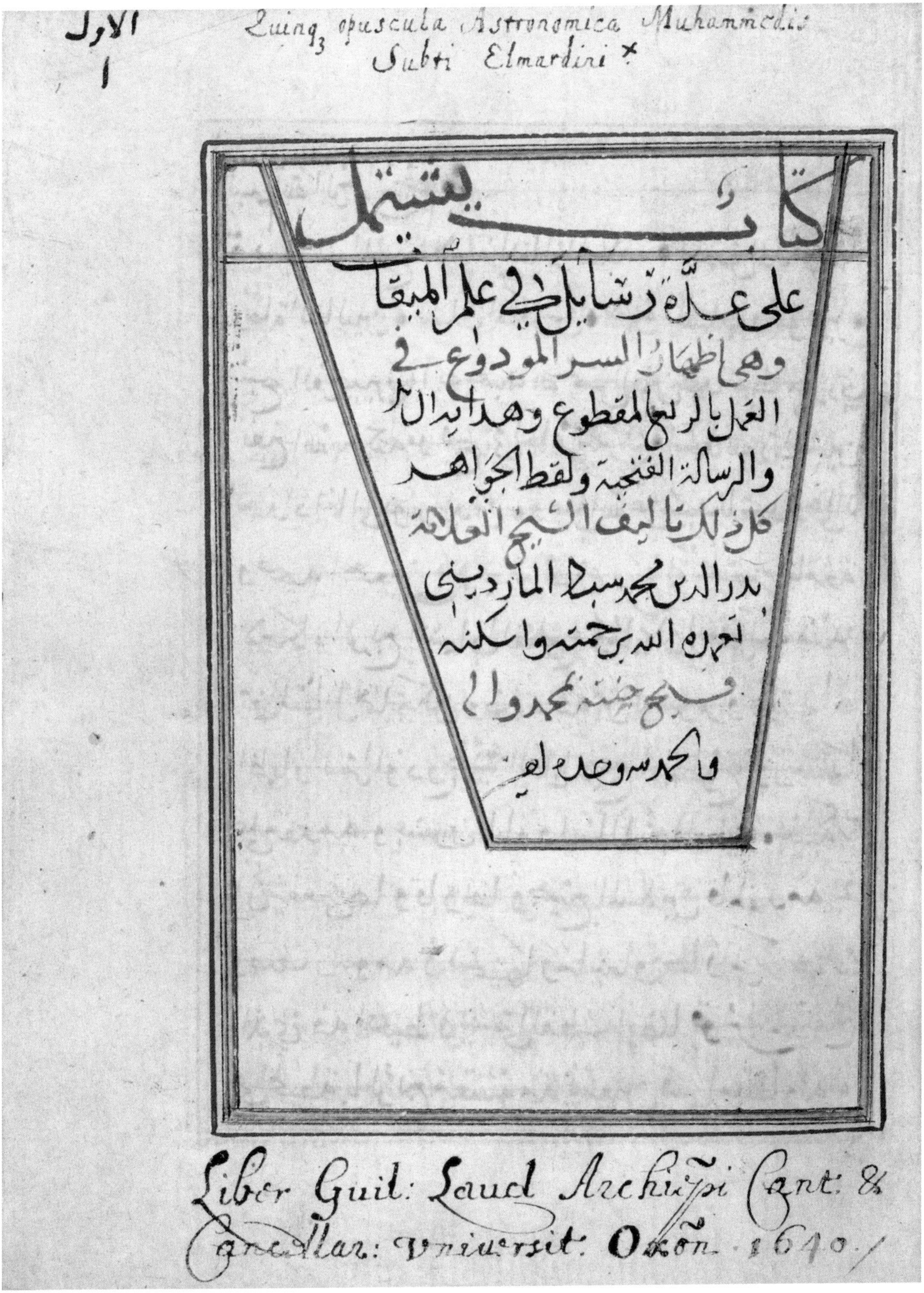
الاول
١
Quinq3 opuscula Astronomica Muhammedis Subti Elmardini ×
كتاب يشتمل
على عدة رسايل في علم الميقات
وهي اظهار السر الموضوع في
العمل بالربع المقطوع وهداية الرسالة الفتحية ولقط الجواهر
كل ذلك تاليف الشيخ العلامة
بدر الدين محمد سبط المارديني
رحمه الله برحمته واسكنه
فسيح جنته بمحمد واله
والحمد لله وحده
Liber Guil: Laud Archiepi Cant: &
Cancellar: Universit. Oxon. 1640.

Plate I. MS 186, fo. 1a: title page, Sibṭ al-Māridīnī, *Rasā'il fī 'ilm al-mīqāt* (16th cent.)

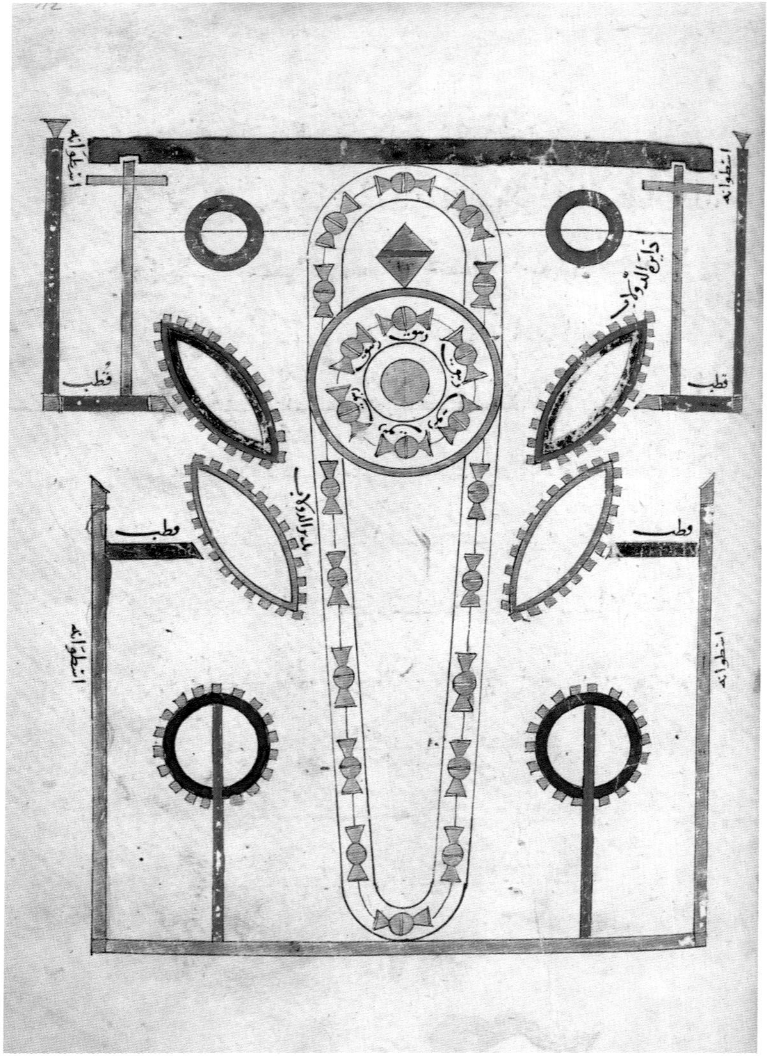

Plate II. MS 83, fo. 112a: mechanical device from *Kitāb al-Ḥiyal fī ḥurūb wa-fatḥ* by Ibn Manglī (Egypt, 1356/757 H)

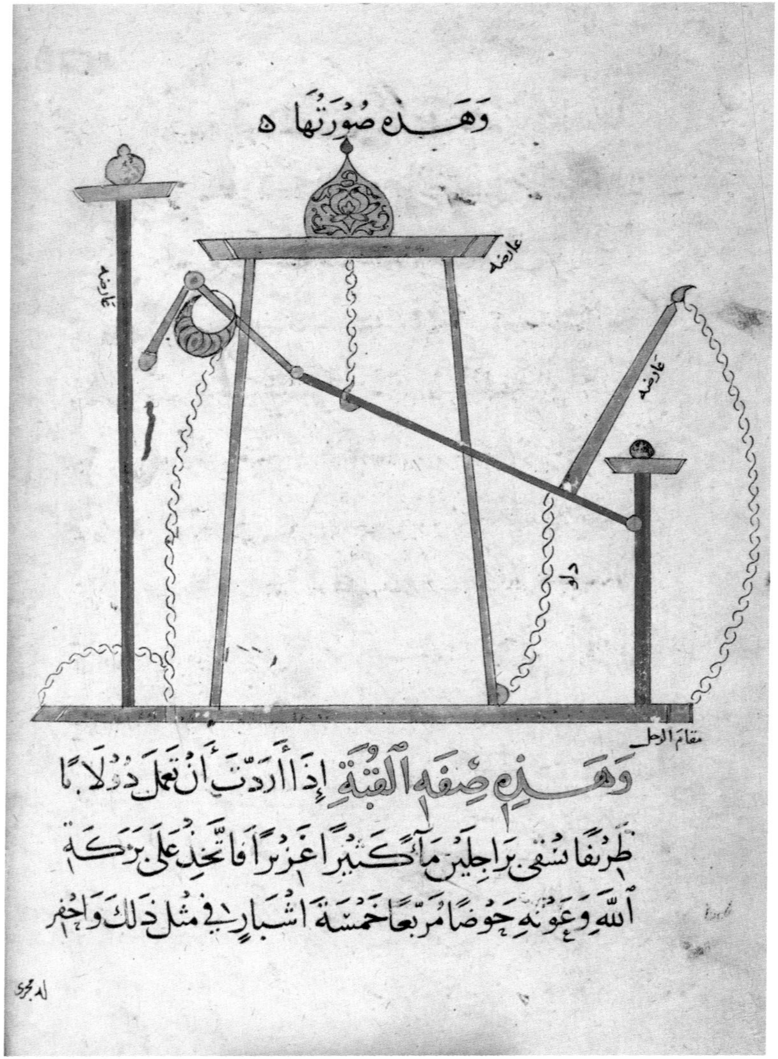

Plate III. MS 83, fo. 114b: trebuchet from *Kitāb al-Ḥiyal fī ḥurūb wa-fatḥ* by Ibn Manglī (Egypt, 1356/757 H)

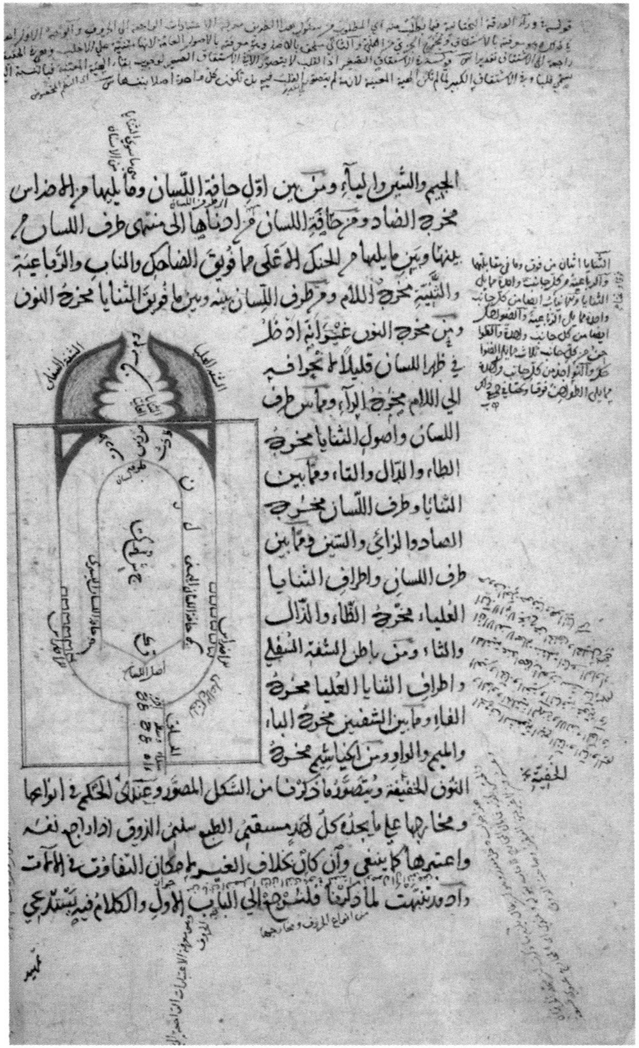

Plate IV. MS 122, fo. 4b: diagram of throat, teeth, and tongue in *Miftāḥ al-ʿulūm* by al-Sakkākī (Khwārazm, 1332/732 H)

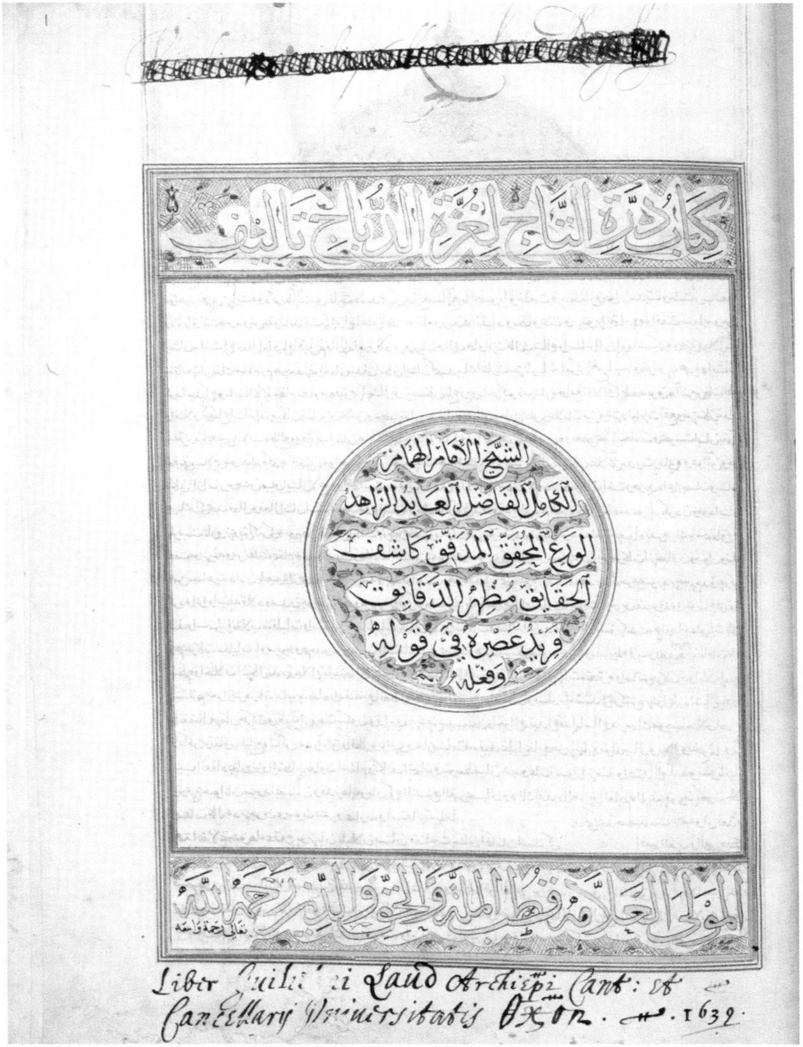

Plate V. MS 33, fo. 1a: title page, Quṭb al-Dīn al-Shīrāzī, *Kitāb Durrat al-tāj li-ghurrat al-Dubāj* (Iran or Sultanate India, *c.*1550–80)

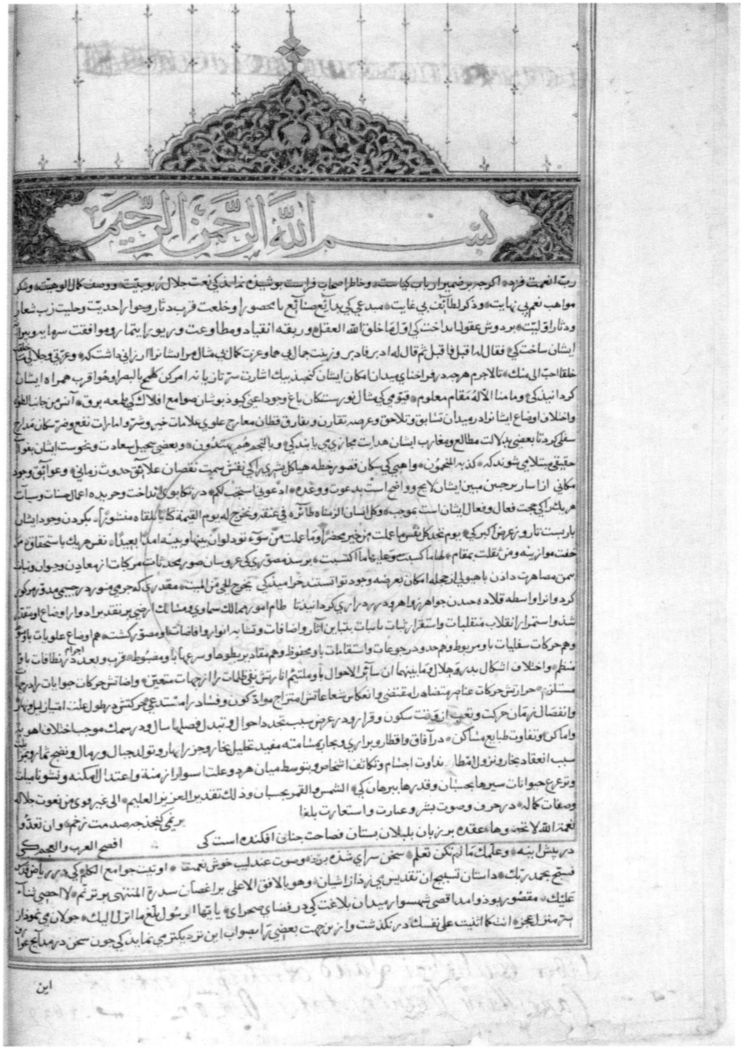

Plate VI. MS 33, fo. 1b: the opening of *Kitāb Durrat al-tāj li-ghurrat al-Dubāj* by Quṭb al-Dīn al-Shīrāzī (Iran or Sultanate India, *c.*1550–80)

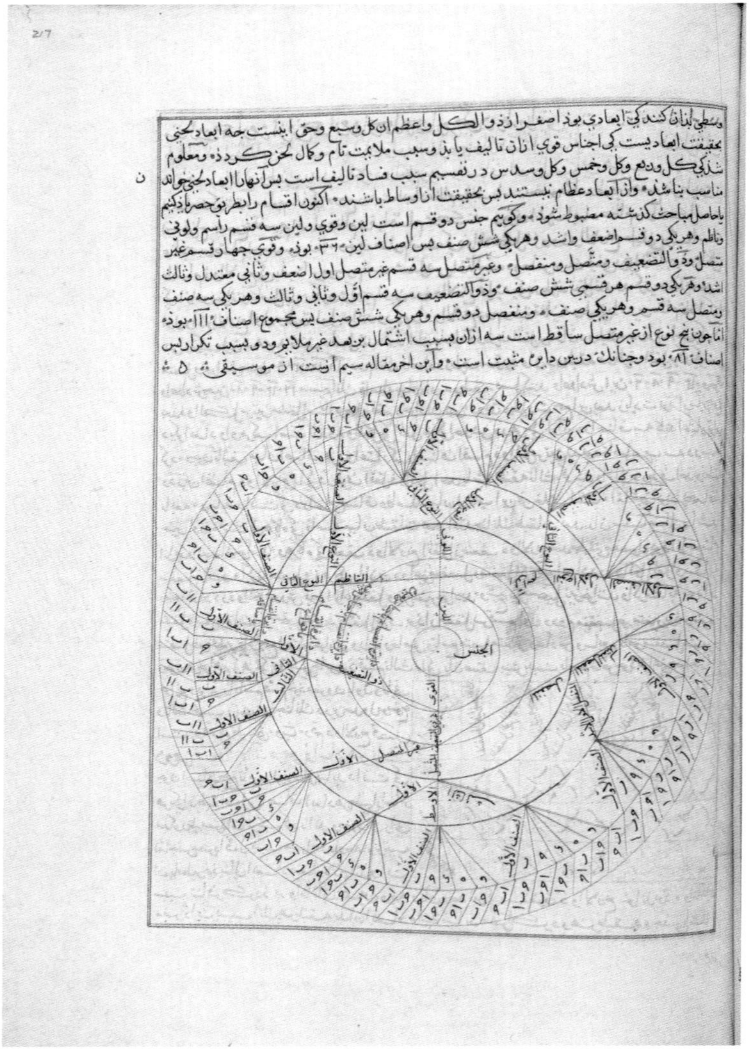

Plate VII. MS 33, fo. 217a: diagram in *Kitāb Durrat al-tāj li-ghurrat al-Dubāj* by Quṭb al-Dīn al-Shīrāzī (Iran or Sultanate India, *c.*1550–80)

بسم الله الرحمن الرحيم

اللهم لك الحمد • على ما علمت من البيان • والمخبر من التبيان • كما

نحمدك على ما اسبلت من العظا • واسبغت من العطا •

ونعوذ بك من شرة اللسن • وفضول الهذر • كما نعوذ بك من

معرة اللكن • وفضوح الحصر • ونستكفيك الافتنان باطرا

المادح • واغضا المسامح • كما نستكفيك الانصاب لازرا

القادح • وهتك الفاضح • ونستغفرك من سوق الشهوات

الى سوف الشبهة • كما نستغفرك من نقل الخطوات الى خطط

الخطيات • ونستوهب منك توفيقا فايدا الى الرشد • وخلسا

منقلبا مع الحق • ولسانا متحليا بالصدق • ونطقا مويدا

بالحجة

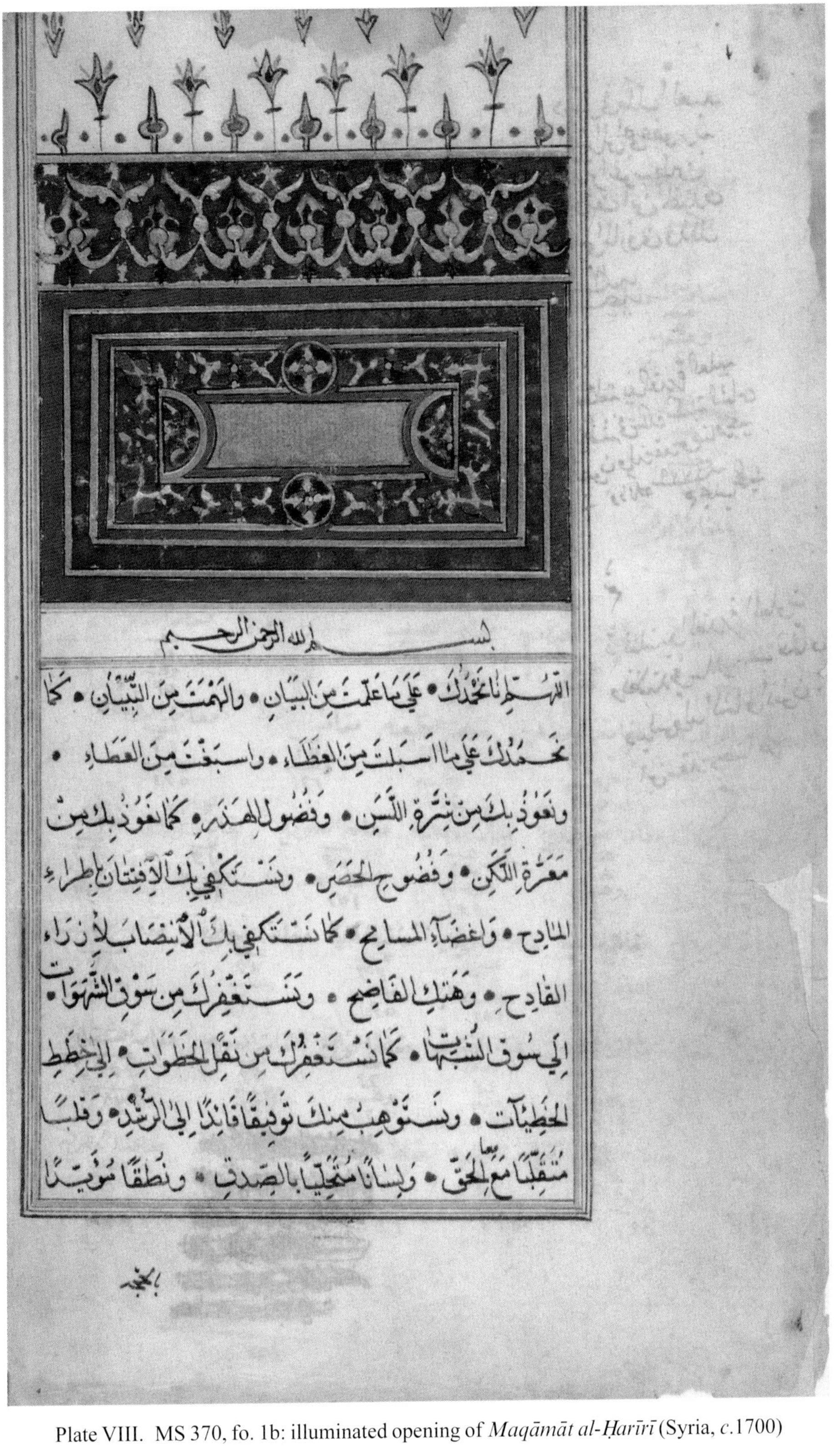

Plate VIII. MS 370, fo. 1b: illuminated opening of *Maqāmāt al-Ḥarīrī* (Syria, *c.*1700)

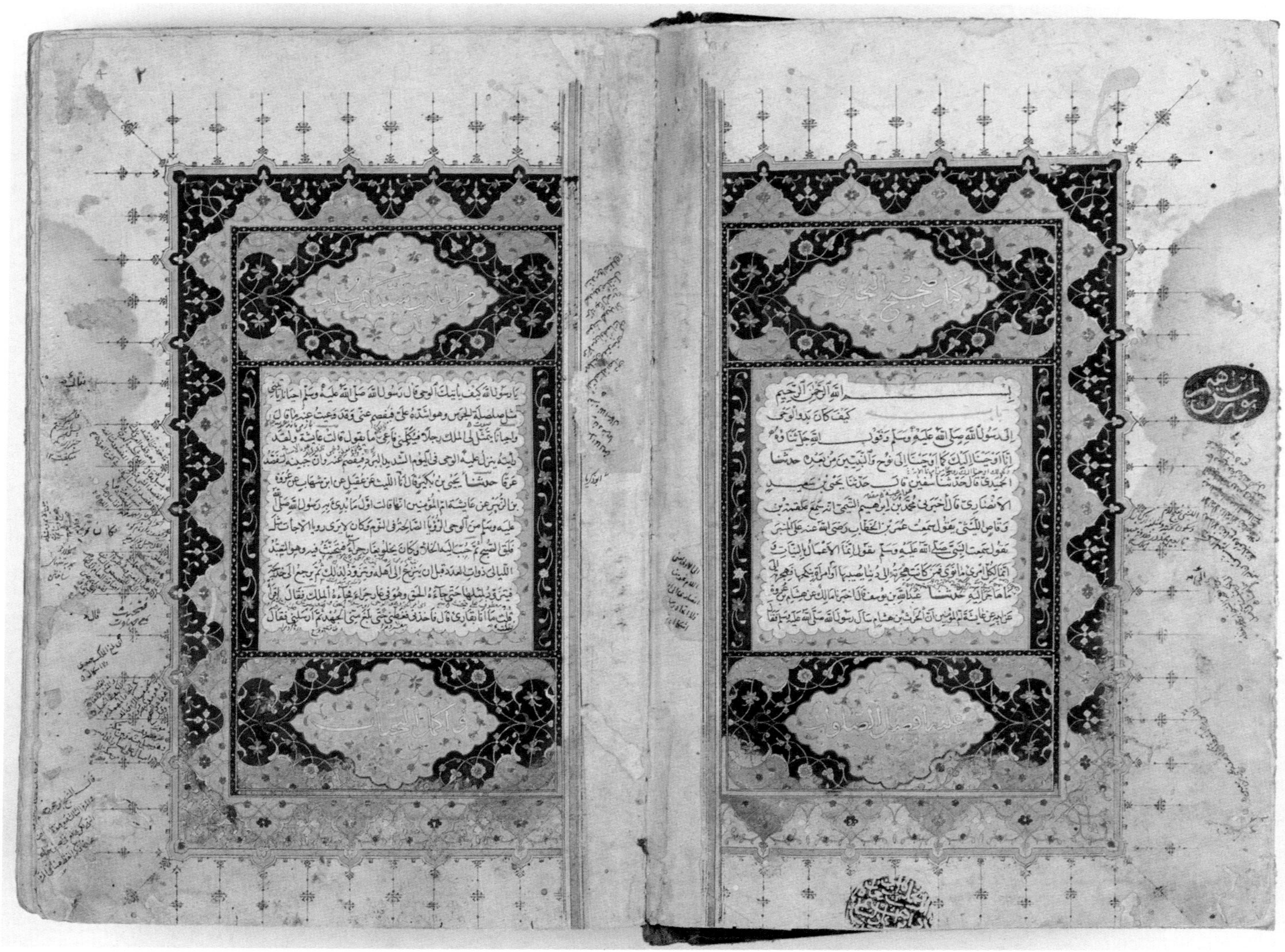

Plate IX. MS 369, fos. 3b–4a: illuminated opening of the collection of *ḥadīth* by al-Bukhārī (Iran, 1496/901 H)

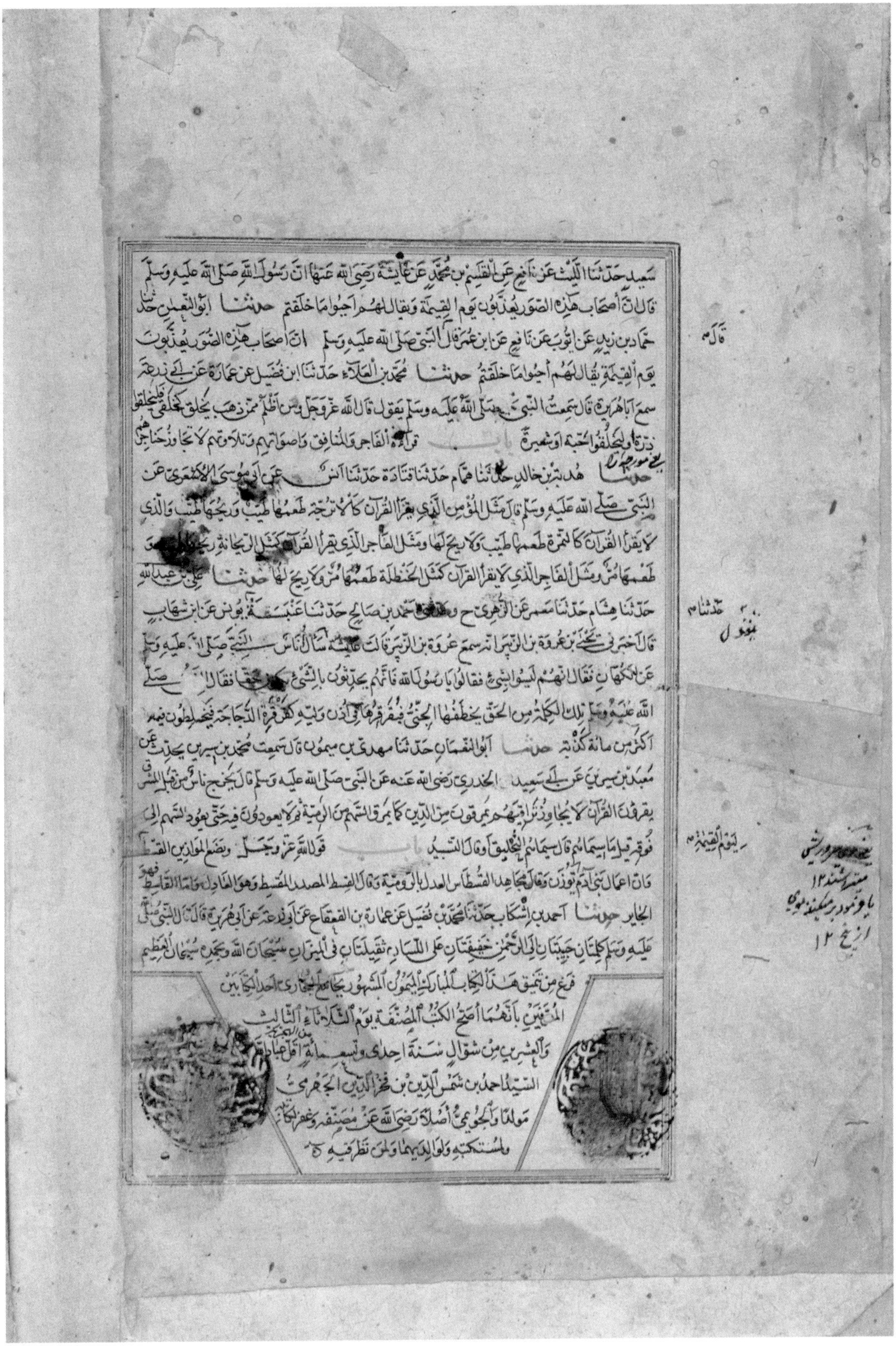

Plate X. MS 369, fo. 512b: colophon dated 23 Shawwāl 901 [5 July 1496] of the collection of *ḥadīth* by al-Bukhārī

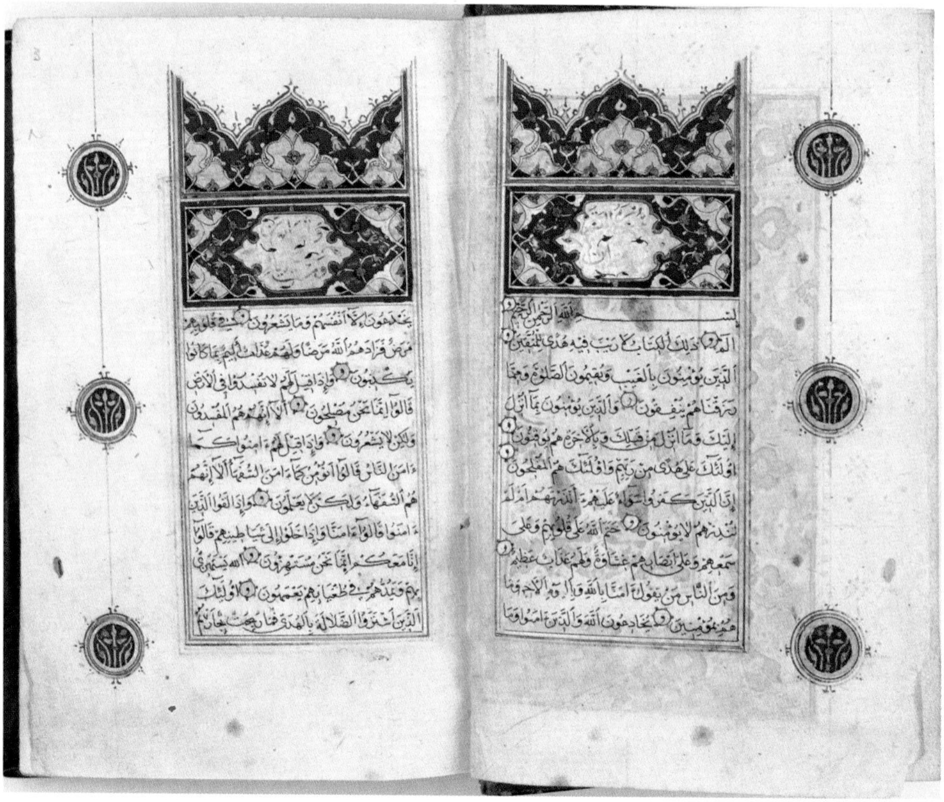

Plate XIII. MS 201, fos. 331b–332a: the final two *sūrahs*, *Qur'ān* (Iran, first half 16th cent.)

Plate XI (*above left*). MS 201, fos. 1b–2a: opening of *Qur'ān, Sūrah* 1 (Iran, first half 16th cent.)

Plate XII (*below left*). MS 201, fos. 2b–3a: illuminated head-pieces, *Qur'ān, Sūrah* 2 (Iran, first half 16th cent.)

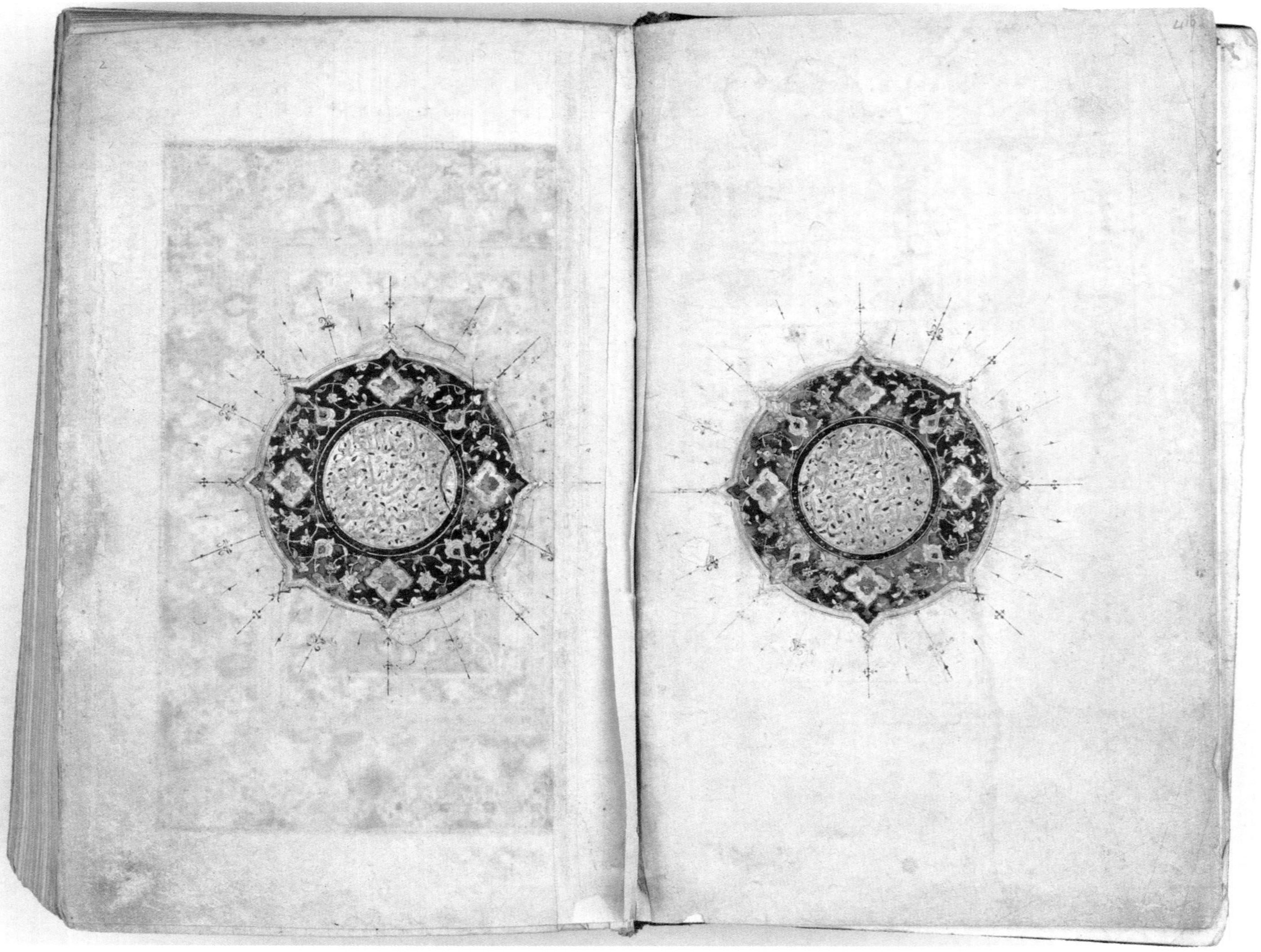

Plate XIV. MS 304, fos. 1b–2a: illuminated *shamsah* panels, *Qur'ān* (Iran, mid-16th cent.)

Plate XV. MS 304, fos. 2b–3a: illuminated opening, *Sūrah* 1, *Qur'ān* (Iran, mid-16th cent.)

Plate XVI. MS 304, fos. 3b–4a: beginning of *Sūrah* 2, *Qur'ān* (Iran, mid-16th cent.)

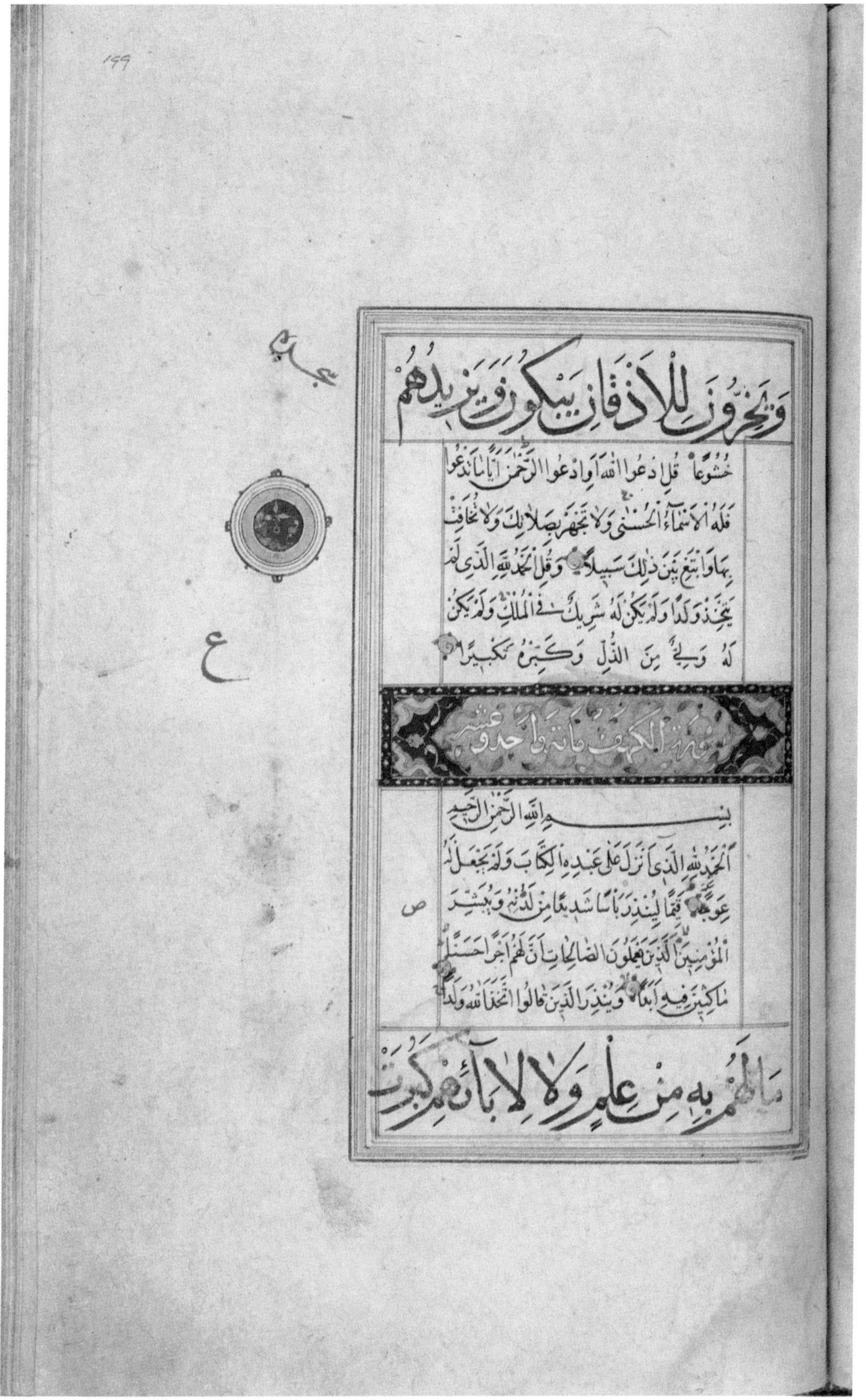
ويخرون للاذقان يبكون ويزيدهم
خشوعا قل ادعوا الله او ادعوا الرحمن ايا ما تدعوا
فله الاسماء الحسنى ولا تجهر بصلاتك ولا تخافت
بها وابتغ بين ذلك سبيلا وقل الحمد لله الذي لم
يتخذ ولدا ولم يكن له شريك في الملك ولم يكن
له ولي من الذل وكبره تكبيرا
سورة الكهف مائة واحدى عشرة
بسم الله الرحمن الرحيم
الحمد لله الذي انزل على عبده الكتاب ولم يجعل له
عوجا قيما لينذر باسا شديدا من لدنه ويبشر
المؤمنين الذين يعملون الصالحات ان لهم اجرا حسنا
ماكثين فيه ابدا وينذر الذين قالوا اتخذ الله ولدا
ما لهم به من علم ولا لابائهم كبرت

Plate XVII. MS 304, fo. 149a: typical *sūrah* heading, *Qur'ān* (Iran, mid-16th cent.)

Plate XVIII. MS 215, fos. 1b–2a: *Sūrah* 1, *Qur'ān* (Safavid Iran or Mughal India, 17th cent.)

Plate XIX. MS 215, fos. 352b–353a: margins filled with gold-painted foliage, *Qur'ān* (Safavid Iran or Mughal India, 17th cent.)

Plate XX. MS 107, fo. 1b: opening of *Qur'ān* (North Africa, 16th–17th cent.)

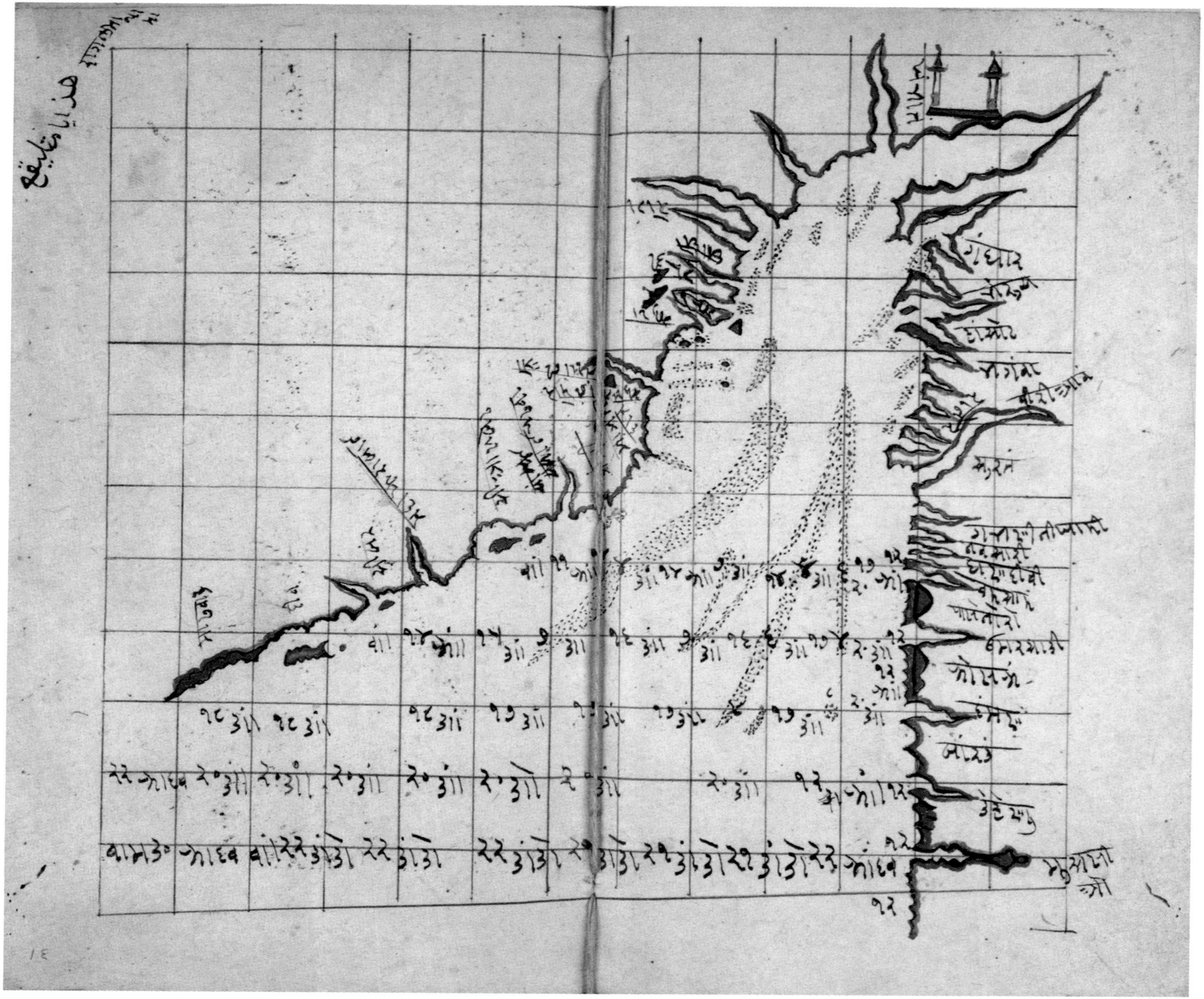

Plate XXI. MS 254, item 45, fos. 30b-31a: Gujarati coastal map showing the Gulf of Khambhat, drawn on a grid (Gujarat, 17th–18th cent.)

References

Unpublished.

Coxe-supplement-2 (unpublished typescript) has a short entry in the handwritten list at the back of the volume kept in the College library.

Entry No. 27

MS 367

TITLE: [*al-Muqaddimah al-Ghaznawīyah fī furū' al-Ḥanafīyah*]

The Ghaznawian Introduction to the Islamic law of the Ḥanafite school

[المقدمة الغزنوية فى فروع الحنفية]

AUTHOR: al-Ghaznawī, Jamāl al-Dīn Aḥmad ibn Muḥammad ibn Maḥmūd ibn Sayyid (d. 593/1197)

CONTENTS: This is a treatise on Islamic law (*fiqh*) written by the Ḥanafite scholar al-Ghaznawī, who died in Aleppo at the end of the 12th century. This copy, made in 1186 [= 1773], has numerous marginalia and interlinear glosses.

The treatise is composed of eight chapters, called *faṣl*s in this copy (Ḥajji Khalīfah, who described the work in some detail, called the chapters *bāb*s; ḤKh, vi. 84 no. 12772). The chapter headings are:

فصل فى طلب العلم

فصل فى مناقب ابي حنيفة . . .

فصل فى السواك

فصل فى الوضوء

فصل فى الصلوة المكتوبة

فصل فى الزكوة

فصل فى شهر رمضان

فصل فى العمل بالعلم

For other copies: see Brockelmann, *GAL*, i. 378 (470) and S i. 649; Bodleian Library, Oriental Collections, MS Arab. e. 219; and Berlin MS Min. 187, fos. 419b–435b (for the latter, which has a different beginning and ending from the present manuscript, see Ahlwardt, *Berlin*, ii. no. 1883).

PHYSICAL DESCRIPTION:

170 leaves (fos. 1b–170a)

Beginning (fo. $1b_{1-4}$–$2b_8$):

بسم الله ... **الحمد** لله الذي عم البلاد بنعمته وارفاده وخص العباد بهدايته وارشاده • وخلق النهار بأنواره والليل بسواده ... [fo. $2b_7$] • **اما بعد** فاني لما رايت قصور همم الناس في طلب العلم • واشتغالهم ...

Ending (fos. $169b_8$–$170a_5$ Plate 9):

... وصلي
الله علي سيدنا محمد وعلي
اله وصحبه وازواجه وذريته
الطيبين الطاهرين والحمد لله
رب العالمين ∴ تم كتاب ∴
الغزنوي رحمه
الله تعالي
امين امين
امين

Colophon (fo. $170a_{6-12}$), illustrated in Plate 9:

تحريرا في ٧ ذي حجة الحرام سنة ١١٨٦
بعد هجرته
عليه افضل
الصلاة
والسلام
امين
م

The copy is stated to have been finished on 7 Dhū al-Ḥijjah 1186 [= 1 Mar 1773]. The copyist is not named.

Arabic. Dimensions: *c.*23.8 × *c.*16.5 (text area 13.6 × 7.7) cm; 11 lines per page. The text area is frame ruled. The author is given as al-Ghaznawī at the end of the text (fo. $170a_2$). The title is not given. The beginning of the treatise agrees with the quotation given by Ḥajjī Khalīfah, and the title supplied here is that given by Ḥajjī Khalīfah (ḤKh, vi. 84 no. 12772).

A complete copy. The text is written in a large, widely spaced Naskh with full vocalization. Folios 1–12 are written in a different hand from the rest of the volume, slightly shakier and less fluid, and lacking the distinctive palaeographical features evident in the second hand. In the hand (or hands) copying the remainder of the volume, the letter *kāf* usually (especially in initial and final positions) has an unusual hook toward the left at the top of the top stroke. Occasionally (as on fo. $49b_8$) the *tā' marbūṭah* is formed by an everlasting knot, while on fo. $130a_6$ the attached pronoun is formed by an everlasting knot. Black ink, fading to a lighter shade, with warm-red headings and teardrop line-fillers and text-stops. There are catchwords.

The stiff, thick, glossy, ivory paper has a thickness of 0.12–0.22 mm and an opaqueness factor of 5. Its edges are irregular and crinkly (especially the front and bottom edges), and there is some creasing and areas of uneven thickness. The paper has broad, slightly wavy, vertical laid lines, single chain lines, and watermarks (three nested lunar crescents; initials L V G (?).

Marginalia and owners' notes: There are numerous marginalia, glosses, and interlinear annotations. There are also some marginal corrections by the copyist(s).

Volume contents: The volume consists of 170 folios, with two recent, blank, preliminary leaves and two back endpapers that are also blank except for a recent foliation note (i–ii + 170 + iii–iv). On the back pastedown there is a small blue and white hexagonal paper label with the entry *E.r.vi* written in pencil. Folio 170b is blank, and fo. 1a is blank except for the later annotation: *A Commentary on the Alcoran in Arabick. No. 69.*

Binding: The volume is bound in pasteboards covered with Islamic (Turkish?) marbled papers in pink, grey, and yellow. The spine is of light-tan leather, and the corners of the covers have been reinforced with the same type of leather. Marbled paper was placed over the leather sides of the spine and the corners, though now the paper is damaged, revealing the underlying structure. There are paper pastedowns of the same type of paper as the preliminary and back endleaves.

Provenance: The volume was in the collections of St John's College in 1932, when it was assigned the shelfmark '126B'. No further information is available on its provenance.

Former shelfmark: 126B.

References

Unpublished.

Coxe-supplement-2 (unpublished typescript) has a short entry in a handwritten list at the back of the volume in the College Library.

QUR'ĀNS

Entry No. 28

MS 201

CONTENTS: A richly illuminated copy of the *Qur'ān*, probably made in Iran in the first half of the 16th century.

The copy is undated, but came into the collections of St John's College in the donation of Archbishop William Laud (d. 1645), who entered the date of 1638 in his *ex libris* placed in the volume.

The first *sūrah* is written on two facing illuminated folios, while the final two *sūrahs* also occupy two facing illuminated folios. The beginning of the second *sūrah* is written on two facing folios each of which has an illuminated head-piece.

The style of illumination and decoration suggests that the volume was produced in Iran in the early to mid-16th century, possibly in Herat or Tabriz. See James, *After Timur.*

PHYSICAL DESCRIPTION:

332 leaves (fols. 1b–332a)

Beginning (fo. $1b_{1-6}$), illustrated in Colour Plate XI:

سورة [الفاتحة facing page]
بسم الله الرحمن الرحيم
الحمد لله رب
العالمين * الرحمن الرحيم * مالك
يوم الدين * اياك
نعبد واياك نستعين

Ending (fo. $332a_{1-9}$), illustrated in Colour Plate XIII:

سورة الناس
بسم الله الرحمن الرحيم*
قل اعوذ برب الناس*
ملك الناس* اله الناس*
من شر الوسواس الخناس*
الذي يوسوس في
صدور الناس* من

الجنة والناس*
ست ايات

Dimensions: 15.1 × 9.5 (text area 9.0 × 4.8) cm; 15 lines per page. The text area has been frame ruled. The first *sūrah* is written on two facing illuminated folios (1b–2a, illustrated in Colour Plate XI). The title of the *sūrah* is written in white opaque watercolour and the text with a small Naskh script in black ink; the text-stops are blue opaque watercolour. The text is written in a small rectangular area with a scallop on each side, on a gilt ground. These texts areas are then enclosed by intertwined gilt bands (decorated with black dots) that divide a rectangular area into 18 compartments with dark-blue, red-brown, or gilt grounds decorated with foliate vines. The rectangular area is enclosed in a frame of gilt plait work which is in turn enclosed by a wider frame decorated with intertwined vines and palmettes worked in gilt and blue.

Both fos. 2b and 3a (illustrated in Colour Plate XII) have illuminated head-pieces (*'unwāns*) at the top of each text panel which contains the second *sūrah* (*al-Baqarah*).

The final two *sūrah*s (*al-Falaq* and *al-Nās*) are also on two facing illuminated folios (fos. 331b–332a, illustrated in Colour Plate XIII), executed in a similar style to fos. 1b–2a, but apparently by a different artisan. The headings and statement of the number of verses are written in opaque white watercolour on gilt grounds in lozenges within rectangular frames at the top and bottom of each folio. The texts themselves are written in black ink on gilt rectangular grounds. Each rectangular area is separated from the next by a gilt and black plaited design, while the entire rectangular design on each folio is enclosed by a similar gilt plaited frame. The margins have similar inked devices to those on fos. 1b–2a.

With the exception of the illuminated fos. 1b–2a and 331b–332a, the text is written with frames formed of blue, red, black, and gilt fillets; occasionally a line of text breaks through the decorative frame. The text-stops are gilt-filled circles with a black central dot and three red and three blue dots around its perimeter. There are circular medallions and pendants in the margins at various intervals; these are drawn in blue ink filled with blue, red, and gilt paint. The headings of *sūrah*s are written in white opaque watercolour on gilt ground with black ink vocalization, enclosed in rectangular frames of black, gilt, and dark-blue fillets.

The thin, ivory paper has a thickness of 0.08–0.09 mm and an opaqueness factor of 7. There are sagging, rather indistinct, laid lines running horizontally on fos. 1–29 and 190–332, and vertically on the other folios. The paper has some scattered inclusions. There is some foxing and wormholes. Folios 177, 178, and 329 are bound upside down in the volume.

Binding: The volume is bound in a European 17th-century binding of mottled brown leather over boards. The covers have frames of two gilt fillets, and the spine has a gilt-stamped floral and leaf design between and either side of the five cords.

Volume contents: The volume consists of 333 folios, with two front endpapers. Folios 332b and 333a are blank. On fo. 333b a later hand has carefully written a pious procedure for prayer: اذا اراد ان يفتح المصحف الكريم ليتعادل .بما يريده من المبهمات الدنيوية والاخروية فتوضا اولا ثم يستغفر الله ثلاث مرات ... . Folio 1a is blank except for the *ex libris* of Archbishop Laud, dated 1638, and a carefully inscribed Latin note *Alchoranus. MS. Arab.* The two front endpapers are blank.

Provenance: The volume came to the College through the donation of Archbishop William Laud (d. 1645). His *ex libris* on fo. 1a is dated 1638.

References

Coxe, 69 entry CCI.

Pearson, *Oriental Collections Great Britain*, 49 (no description given).

Pearson, *Oriental Manuscripts Europe*, 308 (no description given).

Hanna, *St John's Catalogue*, appendix 1, 336 states '[another such MS 201]' alongside MS 72 given the number A.6 (*in abaco secundo*) in Bernard, *Catalogi*. The significance of this statement is unclear.

Entry No. 29

MS 304

CONTENTS: A fine illuminated copy of the *Qur'ān,* probably made in Safavid Iran in the mid-16th century.

The copy is undated and unsigned. It came into the collections of St John's College through the donation of Charles Stafford Playdell [or Pleydell] in 1769, thus providing a date before which it must have been produced.

The volume opens with two facing folios each decorated with an illuminated *shamsah* panel (Colour Plate XIV). The first *sūrah* is written on two facing illuminated folios (Colour Plate XV), and the beginning of the second *sūrah* has an illuminated head-piece (Colour Plate XVI). The style of illumination and decoration suggests that the volume was produced in Iran in the mid-16th century.

PHYSICAL DESCRIPTION:

417 leaves (fos. 1b–417a)

Beginning (fo. $2b_{1-5}$), illustrated in Colour Plate XV:

سورة الفاتحة

بسم الله الرحمن الرحيم

الحمد لله رب العالمين

الرحمن الرحيم مالك يوم الدين
اياك نعبد واياك نستعين

Ending (fo. 417a$_{4-9}$):

سورة الناس ست ايآت
بسم الله الرحمن الرحيم
قل اعوذ برب الناس * ملك
الناس * اله الناس * من شر الوسواس الخناس
الذي يوسوس في صدور الناس * من الجنة و
الناس
وتمت كلمة ربك صدقا وعدلا لا مبدل
لكلماته وهو السميع العليم

Dimensions: 21.5 × 13.4 (text area 12.3 × 6.5) cm; 13 lines per page.

A richly illuminated copy, using coloured inks, opaque watercolours, and gilt. The first *sūrah* (*al-Fātiḥah*) is written on facing folios (fos. 2b and 3a, illustrated in Colour Plate XV) in very small Naskh script within a central scalloped lozenge of gilt ground. The lozenge is framed by a white strapping highlighted with black dots that wraps around the lozenge and twists around other decorative lozenges (gilt ground with minute floral designs in pink, red, blue, and white; or dark-blue ground with floral designs). This small panel (9.5 × 4.1 cm) is then framed by three concentric rectangular panels, the first of a floral design on a dark-blue ground, the second of gilt in a plaited design, and the third having a ground of gilt or dark blue decorated with intertwined vines and floral designs. The margins are decorated with geometric pendants in blue ink.

The beginning of the second *sūrah* (*al-Baqarah*) on fo. 3b (see Colour Plate XVI) has an illuminated head-piece (*'unwān*), with the title written in a lozenge set in a rectangular frame. Dark-blue, light-blue, red, and white opaque watercolours are used as well as gilt.

Other *sūrah* headings and accentuated lines are written in panels extending across the text area using either gilt ink for the Thulth script, on a light-blue ground decorated with minute leaves, or a Thulth script in white opaque watercolour outlined by fine black lines on a gilt ground decorated with a small floral design highlighted in red and blue. See Colour Plate XVII.

Folios 1b and 2a (see Colour Plate XIV) each have an illuminated *shamsah* panel, circular with a gilt central ground decorated with black leaves containing text written in white outlined in black; the central circle is surrounded by a decorative ring of dark-blue ground covered with gilt arabesques and floral sprays highlighted with light blue and red. Blue-inked pendants radiate from the edges of the medallions. Verse 88 of *Sūrah* 17 is inscribed in the two *shamsah*s.

On the folios without illuminated headings, the text is written in five panels within a text area defined by fine black and gilt lines. The first, third, and fifth panels are as wide as the text area and are written in a large Thulth script using dark-blue ink (first panel), gold ink (third panel), and dark-blue ink (fifth panel). Between the first and third panels there are five lines of a medium-small Naskh script written in an area narrower than the text area frame; the same pattern is repeated between the third and fifth panels. There are verse-stops of gilt-filled circles decorated with small black dots, and in the margins dark-blue and gilt medallions and pendants.

There are catchwords and occasional (as at the top of fo. 109b) annotations in a small script indicating what text was to be written in the three panels containing Thulth script. This provides evidence that a different person perhaps wrote the Thulth panels. Such instructions were probably intended to be cut off when the leaves were trimmed before binding, and these were most likely left only by mistake.

The volume has been foliated with pencilled European numerals both in the proper Arabic sequence and as a European volume (from left to right). As a result, every leaf has two sets of pencilled numbers, the European sequence at the upper corner in the right-hand opening and the Islamic sequence at the upper corner in the left-hand opening.

Several types of beige paper were used for the volume. Most of the paper has a thickness of 0.12–0.14 mm, an opaqueness factor of 3, fairly evenly distributed fibres, occasional thin patches and vertical, sagging laid lines, but no chain lines,. The paper is soiled through thumbing and there is some damp staining. Folios 223–30 and 302–9 have no laid or chain lines. On a few folios (e.g. 231, 238) there are clear, widely spaced, single chain lines. No watermarks have been detected. All the papers appear to be contemporaneous.

Volume contents: The volume consists of 417 leaves, with three preliminary endpapers and six at the back (i–iii + 417 + iv–ix). Folio 1a is blank. Folio 417b has quotations of a prayer of the Prophet ('it is transmitted from one of the Companions that when the Apostle of God recited … he would recite after it this prayer …'). The three modern preliminary leaves (fos. i–iii) are blank except for two ownership annotations. Preliminary fo. i has been pasted onto the front endpaper of marbled paper. All six back endpapers are blank; folio ix has been pasted onto the final endpaper of marbled paper.

Binding: The volume is bound with pasteboards decorated with lacquered paper (now quite damaged). Each cover has a central scalloped medallion and two related pendants, decorated in the centre with maroon flowers and having edges painted in white and light blue; the ground is a diaper design of dark-brown leaves on a gilt ground. Near the edges of the covers there are broad bands of bright-red flowers on a gilt ground framed by narrow white and blue fillets. The brown leather spine is a European replacement. There are doublures and endpapers of marbled paper (red, pink, and grey).

Provenance: Presented to the library in 1769 by Charles Stafford Playdell (as noted on fo. iiib: *Dono dedit Carolus Stafford Playdell Arm: 1769*). On fo. iia there is a small ownership note in the corner: بخط عبد الله طاق .

References
Unpublished.
Coxe-supplement-1, 32 (unpublished typescript).

Entry No. 30

MS 72

CONTENTS: An Ottoman copy of the *Qur'ān* made in 1626–7 (1036 H), only slightly more than a decade before it came into the collections of St. John's College.

PHYSICAL DESCRIPTION:

382 leaves (fos. 1b–382a)

Beginning (fo. $1b_{1-6}$):

سورة الفاتحة سبع ايات مكية
بسم الله الرحمن الرحيم
الحمد لله رب العالمين • الرحمن الرحيم _ مالك
يوم الدين • اياك نعبد واياك نستعين
اهدنا الصراط المستقيم • صراط الذين انعمت
عليهم • غير المغضوب عليهم ولا الضالين •

Ending and colophon: (fo. $382a_{1-7}$ with *Sūrat al-Nās*):

قل اعوذ برب الناس ملك الناس اله الناس
من شر الوسواس الخناس الذي يوسوس في
صدور الناس من
الجنة والناس
سنه
١٠٣٦
تم

It was copied in 1036 [= AD 1626–7]. The copyist is not named. The appearance of the script and paper suggests that it is an Ottoman copy, made possibly in Egypt or Syria.

Arabic. Dimensions: 29.0 × 18.0 (text area 18.6 × 9.8) cm; 11 lines per page. There is no evidence of frame ruling.

A complete copy.

The text is written in a large Naskh script, fully vocalized. It is written in dense black ink with red teardrop text-stops and *sūrah* headings in red. The text is written within frames formed of a single red line. On fos. 1b and 2a the frames are formed of doubled red lines, and, above and below the text, space was allotted for an illuminated opening which was never inserted. There are catchwords.

The ivory, very glossy paper has a thickness of 0.11–0.14 mm, with an opaqueness factor of 4. It has fine horizontal laid lines and single vertical chain lines with watermarks (a large, four-lobed shield with a human-headed (?) four-legged animal carrying a flag; a small trefoil above the letter 'B').

Marginalia and owners' notes: There are occasional marginal corrections by the copyist and also some ink smudges, especially in the red-inked frames.

Volume contents: The volume consists of 382 folios plus three preliminary leaves and three back endpapers (i–iii + 1–382 + iv–vi). Folios 1a and 382b are blank, except for an obliterated Latin note on fo. 1a indicating that it was formerly in the collection of Sir Kenelm Digby. Two of the preliminary leaves are blank folios of different paper from the main manuscript and probably placed there during a rebinding or restitching. The third preliminary leaf (fo. iii) has the Latin label *Alcoranus* on the verso, with two cataloguing notes (*Abac.ij. N°. 6*; *MSS.72*) on the recto; it also has stains from the envelope flap, which are not evident on the other preliminary leaves. Similarly, the first of the endpapers (fo. iv) is of the same paper as the manuscript, and it also has the same catalogue annotations as the third preliminary leaf (fo. iii). The last two endpapers (fos. v, vi) are blank. The numeral *72* has been inked on the fore-edge of the manuscript.

Binding: The volume is bound in a Middle Eastern binding that has been restored, with a recent spine replacement. The covers and envelope flap are pasteboards covered with red leather. The covers have a blind-stamped almond-shaped, scalloped, central medallion filled with a floral design; there are two pendants with a wreath design. The medallions and pendants are enclosed in blind frames of single fillets. The envelope flap has a scalloped circular stamped medallion with central design similar to that in the pendants. The fore-edge flap has two blind-stamped cartouches in which there are two Arabic phrases impressed: لا يمسه الا المطهرون ('None but the purified shall touch', *Qur'ān* 56: 79) and تنزيل من رب العالمين ('A revelation from the Lord of the worlds', *Qur'ān* 56: 80). There is a grey cloth lining to the envelope flap and fore-edge flap. The pastedowns are recent white paper placed over earlier pastedowns of multicoloured marbled paper.

On the front pastedown there is the following Latin note:

MSS, 72.
Alcoranus,
manu satis eleganti, sed recenti
scriptum enim est hoc Exemplar
an. Hej. 1036. i.e. A.D. 1626.
In eâ parte involucri, quæ Arabibus dicitur

Lingua Libri, legitur hæc sententia, (in elegantioribus
Alcorani Exemplaribus extrinseus scribi solita,)
لا يمسه الا المطهرون , i.e. Ne attingant eum, nisi
purificati. Mohammedani enim adeò pié et
reverenter Alcoranum suum tractant, ut nunquam
eum vel in manus sumant, nisi priús lotas.

Provenance: The volume came to the college through the donation of Archbishop William Laud (d.1645). At the bottom of fo. 1b there is the Latin annotation: *Liber Guilielmi Laud Archiepi Cant: et Cancillarij Universit: Oxon: 1639.* Prior to that it had been in the collection of Sir Kenelm Digby (d. 1665), whose obliterated *ex libris* is on fo. 1a.

References

Coxe, 20, entry LXXII.
Bernard, *Catalogi*, A.6 (*in abaco secundo*).
Pearson, *Oriental Collections Great Britain*, 49 (no description given).
Pearson, *Oriental Manuscripts Europe*, 308 (no description given).

Entry No. 31

MS 215

CONTENTS: A beautifully illuminated copy of the *Qur'ān*, probably made in Safavid Iran (or Mughal India) in the 17th century.

The copy is undated and unsigned. It came into the collections of St John's College through the donation of William Stoddart (or Stoddard), who died in 1856, thus producing a date before which it must have been produced.

The first *sūrah* is written on two facing illuminated folios, and the beginning of the second *sūrah* has an illuminated head-piece. The paper on which the text is written is gold sprinkled. The margins are filled with gold-painted designs of foliage (in addition to the decorative medallions indicating standard text divisions). The style of illumination and decoration suggests that the volume was produced in either Safavid Iran or Mughal India in the 17th century.

PHYSICAL DESCRIPTION:

392 leaves (fos. 1b–392b)

Beginning (fo. $1b_{1-4}$), illustrated in Colour Plate XVIII:

فاتحة [الكتاب facing page]
الحمد لله رب العالمين * الرحمن
الرحيم * مالك يوم الدين *
اياك نعبد واياك

Ending (fo. $392b_{4-9}$):

سورة الناس ست ايآت
بسم الله الرحمن الرحيم
قل اعوذ برب الناس * ملك الناس *
اله الناس * من شر الوسواس الخناس *
الذي يوسوس في صدور الناس * من
الجنة والناس *

Dimensions: 14.2 × 9.4 (text area 8.3 × 4.3) cm; 11 lines per page.

A richly illuminated copy, using coloured inks, opaque watercolours, and gilt. The first *sūrah* (*al-Fātiḥah*) is written on facing folios (fos. 1b and 2a, Colour Plate XVIII) within scalloped ogival lozenges of gilt ground which are encompassed by scalloped dark-blue bands filled with intertwined vines lying within gilt scalloped bands with similar vines; this arrangement is then enclosed by a narrow rectangular frame of black, gilt, and dark-blue fillets, the latter filled with white dots. The frame is then surrounded by a wide, scalloped design of gilt and dark blue, over-painted with intertwined vines; the margins are decorated with blue-inked geometrical pendants with the ground between filled with pale gold-painted small flower-heads. The text is written in black ink, except for the headings which are broad letters of fine black lines filled with white opaque watercolours. There are large circular text-stops with the number of the verses written in red ink in *abjad* letter-numerals; the ground between the lines is filled with small flower-heads and vines.

The beginning of the second *sūrah* (*al-Baqarah*) on fo. 2b has an illuminated head-piece (*'unwān*), with the title written in a lozenge set in a rectangular frame topped with a triangular decoration.

With the exception of the first *sūrah* (fos. 1b–2a), all the text is written within frames formed of fine black, gilt, and red fillets. The paper of the text area is gold sprinkled. The text-stops on all the folios that do not have a gilt ground are filled with gilt. The verses are numbered in red ink with *abjad* numerals. Throughout the volume, the titles of *sūrah*s, and occasionally the total number of verses, are written in white opaque watercolour (outlined in black ink) on a gilt ground, set in a panel surrounded by a dark-blue narrow frame.

There are circular gilt and dark-blue medallions in the margins at various intervals, and the margins are filled with gold-painted designs of foliage. See Colour Plate XIX.

The text is written in a very small Naskh script with full vocalization. In the headings, the letter *sīn* has three dots beneath. The folios are assigned numbers in red ink, using standard Arabic numerals, beginning with the numeral 3 (٣) on fo. 2a; the volume was recently refoliated in pencil using Western numerals which are off by a factor of 1 from the earlier Arabic numbers.

The very thin, biscuit paper has a thickness of 0.04–0.06 mm and an opaqueness factor of 7. There are indistinct vertical laid lines and no visible chain lines. The preliminary leaf fo. 1 is guarded and has been pasted onto a more recent piece of white (blank) paper. Folio 2 is guarded and the edges have been repaired. The edges of several of the leaves have been repaired, though there are some unrepaired tears on a few leaves.

Volume contents: The volume consists of 392 folios, with two later endpapers (i + 392 + ii). Folio 1a is blank. The verso of the front endpaper (fo. ib) has a Latin annotation stating that it was a donation of William Stoddart (or Stoddard), of St John's, and provides the manuscript number of 215 (*ex dono Gul: Stoddard, S.J.B. Socii. M.S.S. 215*).

Binding: The volume is bound in a Persian binding, with the spine replaced with maroon leather; envelope flap missing. The covers has gilt-stamped ogival scalloped medallions in the centre, filled with embossed intertwined vines. Gilt rays are painted around the periphery of the medallion. Each cover is framed by gilt fillets filled with a gilt plaited design. The doublures are silver-sprinked beige paper and the endpapers are of stiff, orange-dyed, gilt-sprinkled paper pasted onto white paper.

Provenance: The volume was presented to the College by William Stoddart [or Stoddard] (1809-56), a Fellow of St John's from 1828 to 1853 and vicar of Charlbury, Oxon., from 1853 until his death in 1856.

References

Unpublished.
Coxe-supplement-1, 1 (unpublished typescript).

Entry No. 32

MS 107

CONTENTS: An illuminated, North African (probably Moroccan) copy of the *Qur'ān*, probably made in the late 16th or early 17th century.

The copy is undated, but came into the collections of St John's College in the donation of Archbishop William Laud (d. 1645).

The style of illumination and decoration suggests that it was produced during the Saʿdid dynasty in Morocco (reg. 1511–1659). It has certain characteristics similar to (though not as professionally executed as) a *Qur'ān* made in 975/1568 for the Saʿdī ruler ʿAbd Allāh al-Ghālib (London, British Library, APAC, MS Or. 1405). See Tim Stanley, 'North Africa: The Maintenance of a Tradition', in Manijeh Bayani, Anna Contadini, and Tim Stanley, *The Decorated Word: Qur'ans of the 17th to 19th Centuries*, Khalili Collection of Islamic Art 4 (London: Azimuth Editions/Oxford: Oxford University Press, 1999), 42–53.

PHYSICAL DESCRIPTION:

204 leaves (fos. 1b–204a)

Beginning (fo. $1b_{1-6}$), illustrated in Colour Plate XX:

بسم الله الرحمن الرحيم صلى الله على سيدنا محمد وعلى اله وصحبه وسلم تسليما
سورة الفاتحة مكية
الحمد لله رب العالمين الرحمن الرحيم مالك يوم الدين
اياك نعبد واياك نستعين اهدنا الصراط المستقيم
صراط الذين انعمت عليهم • غير المغضوب عليهم
ولا الضالين

Ending (fo. $204a_{5-9}$ with *Sūrat al-Nās*):

سورة الناس مكية
بسم الله الرحمن الرحيم
قل اعوذ برب الناس ملك الناس اله الناس من شر
الوسواس الخناس الذي يوسوس في صدور الناس
من الجنة والناس

The copy is undated and unsigned. The appearance of script and paper suggests that it was made in North Africa, probably in Morocco, in the early 17th century.

Arabic. Dimensions: 24.3 × 17.2 (text area 16.8 × 11.4) cm, with medallions extending into margins an additional 3 cm; 21 lines per page (with variation when illuminated headings occur). There are traces of frame ruling of the text area.

The titles of the first two *sūrah*s (fo. 1b, see Colour Plate XX) are written in Kufic using gilt on red or blue opaque watercolour grounds and enclosed in frames of a plaited gilt design inside a blue-ink frame. There are illuminated medallions attached to the frames and extending into the margins. On fos. 50b, 102b, and 151b three other *sūrah* titles are written in Kufic (in white on red or green grounds) and surrounded by similar illuminated frames of plaited design with attached medallions. The titles of the remaining *sūrah*s are written in Kufic script and filled in with a yellow watercolour. The non-illuminated beginnings of the *sūrah*s and other important places, such as the fifth and tenth verses of a chapter and places at which ritual prostration is required, are also indicated by marginal medallions and decorative devices executed in coloured inks and opaque watercolours; each appears to be of a slightly different design. In the bottom half of fo. 204a there is a rectangular area, framed in a gilt plaited design with attached medallion, that has been left blank, apparently intended for the scribe's name and date.

The text is written in a medium-large Maghribī script, fully vocalized, using black ink (fading to a lighter shade) with magenta-red vocalization and overlinear green or yellow dots marking text-stops. The script and decoration are careful and consistent, but not the work of a professional calligrapher or illuminator. There are numerous erasures (scrapings) of lines with the text rewritten by the copyist. There are no catchwords.

The beige, lightly glossed, stiff paper has a thickness of 0.13–0.16 mm and an opaqueness factor of 5. It has vertical, nearly straight, laid lines and single, irregular chain lines, and watermarks (a circle with a fleur-de-lis (?), and other large elaborate designs). Different paper was used for fos. 21, 25, 99, and 190 The lower half is damp stained and some of the coloured inks have run slightly.

Marginalia and owners' notes: There are no marginalia or annotations.

Volume contents: The volume consists of 204 folios, with two preliminary and two back endpapers (i–ii + 204 + iii–iv). Folios 1a and 204b are blank except for the signature of Sir Kenelm Digby (now crossed out) on the former and the *ex libris* of Archbishop Laud on the latter. The preliminary endpapers are blank except for someone's handwritten note torn from a piece of scrap paper and pasted to fo. ia; the note simply records the manuscript number in the St John's collection, adding *Alcoranus charactere Mauritanico.*

On the front pastedown, another sheet of paper has been pasted onto it, on which is written:

MSS, 107.
Alcoranus,
Charactere Mauritanico.
Annus Hejræ,
quo hoc Exemplar scriptum est,
non apponitur.

The back pastedown has the annotations: *MSS, 107* and (crossed out) *Abac.ij. N°. 6.*

Binding: The volume is bound in a 17th- or 18th-century European binding (which has been restored) of mottled brown leather over pasteboards. The covers have an inner decorative blind-stamped frame composed of two rows of a scalloped design enclosing fans or palm leaves, with tulip heads at the four corners; the outer frames are formed of two thin blind fillets. The spine has five cords. The pastedowns and endpapers are modern (19th century?). The binding is very similar in design to the bindings of MS 103 (Entry No. 2) and MS 122 (Entry No. 23), but here it is embossed on a shiny leather rather than a suede leather.

Provenance: The volume came to the college through the donation of Archbishop William Laud (d. 1645). Prior to that it was in the collection of Sir Kenelm Digby (d. 1665). On fo. 1a, the signature of Sir Kenelm Digby has been marked out. At the bottom of fo. 1b there is the Latin annotation: *Liber Guilielmi Laude Archiepi Cant: et Cancellij Universit Oxon.*

References

Coxe, 31 entry CVII.

Bernard, *Catalogi*, assigns the number 105 to the volume (see also Hanna, *St John's Catalogue*, 338).

BIBLES/OLD TESTAMENT

Entry No. 33

MS 105

TITLE: *Kitāb-i Zabūr* [*-i Dā'ūd*]

The Book of the Psalms [*of David*]

کتاب زبور داود

CONTENTS: A Persian translation of the Book of Psalms by an unnamed translator.

It is the same anonymous translation that is preserved in MS 133 (Entry No. 34) of St John's College and also in two Bodleian Library manuscripts: MS Laud Or. 141 and MS S. Clarke 10. This anonymous translation was certainly made sometime before 1640—a date that appears with Archbishop Laud's ownership entry in Bodleian Library, Oriental Collections, MS Laud Or. 141. The ending of this particular copy (MS 105 at St John's College) differs slightly from St John's MS 133 and from Bodleian MS Laud Or. 141, though the translation in all three is substantially the same. The Bodleian Library MS S. Clarke 10 is an incomplete transcription, possibly of MS Laud Or. 141, made by Samuel Clarke, who died in 1669.

Two 17th-century Persian translations are known to have been made. In 1027/1618 Shah ʿAbbās I ordered that a translation of the Psalms be prepared, and this was done from the Hebrew by John Thaddeus, Carmelite bishop of Isfahan, whose name is given as assisted by three Muslim mullahs and one Jewish rabbi. Thaddeus' translation is preserved in three Bodleian Library manuscripts: MS Greaves 4, MS Bodl. Or. 130, and MS Bodl. Or. 439, where the Portuguese friar John Thaddeus is referred to as Padre Juan (پادری جوان); see SEB I, cols. 1050–1, nos. 1827, 1828, and 1829.

The second translation was made from the Vulgate Bible by Jeronimo Xavier during the reigns of the Mughal rulers Akbar I (reg. 1556–1605) and Jahāngīr (reg. 1605–27). No manuscript copies of this translation, however, are recorded as being preserved today.

The anonymous translation in two St John's copies (MS 105 and MS 133) is different from that made by John Thaddeus. Whether or not it might be the translation made by Jeronimo Xavier has not been determined.

For other copies: see St John's College, Oxford, MS 133 (Entry No. 34); Bodleian Library, Oriental Collections, MS Laud Or. 141, which ends with Psalm 150 (SEB I, col. 1052 no. 1830), and MS S. Clarke 10, which ends with Psalm 138 and is in Samuel Clarke's handwriting (SEB I, col. 1052, no. 1831).

For Persian translations in general, see J. Thomas, 'Bible.iii: Chronology of Translations of the Bible' and Kenneth J. Thomas and Fereydun Vahman, 'Bible.vii: Persian Translations of the Bible', in *EncIr*, iv. 203–6 and 209–13.

PHYSICAL DESCRIPTION:

103 leaves (fos. 1b [old iiib]–103b)

Beginning (fo. 1b [old iiib]$_{1-3}$):

كتاب زبور

فصل اول ١ سعادتمند مردي كه به تدبير ظالمان نرفت • وبراه خطا نايستاد • وبر تخت طاعون ننشت • ٢ ...

Ending (fo. 103b$_{6-8}$, Psalm 150):

٤بستائيد اورا بدهل و دف بستايد اورا بتار وچنك ٥ • بستايد اورا بدهل خوب آوازها و هنده بستايد اورا بدهل تسبيحرا • جميع روح خداوندرا ستايش كند • حال لويه .

Colophon (fo. 103b$_{9-13 \text{ and diagonals}}$), illustrated in Plate 10:

بدانكه از نصف فصل صد وچهل و دويم تا اينجا گم
شده بود پادريان پا برهنه متوجه
شده تصنيف نمودند
سنه ١٠٧١
بتاريخ هشتم شهر ذي حجه قلمی شد
العبد الفقير الحقير محمد كاتب
تم تم
تم

نوشتم خط ندانم تا كه خواند [diagonally on right]

كه بيشك من نمانم خط بماند [diagonally on left]

The copy was completed on 8 Dhū al-Ḥijjah 1071 [= 4 Aug 1661]. It was not copied in 1001 (1592) as has been previously recorded by Coxe (and as noted in Latin annotations on the final leaf), for the numeral for 'seven' is clearly written, and what was read as representing 'zero' is in fact the diacritical dot over the letter *nūn* in the word for 'year', *sanah*.

Persian. Dimensions: 25.7 × 18.9 (text area 18.2 × 12.2) cm; 12 lines per page. The text area has been frame ruled, and on every leaf two vertical impressed lines (possibly fold lines) can be seen 10 mm apart along the outer margin of the text area. The text is written in a very large Nastaʿlīq script in black ink, with headings in a warm red. There are occasional pages (e.g. fos. 21b, 61a, 67b) where either a silvery ink has been applied over the red ink, or some corrosion has occurred. The lines within each psalm are numbered over the text lines, and there are text-stops of small red circles. There are catchwords.

The thin, glossy beige paper has a thickness of 0.09 mm and an opaqueness factor of 5. It has unevenly distributed fibres, and there are globular inclusions and numerous thin patches. There are indistinct vertical laid lines and no visible chain lines. The paper is very similar to that in MS 133 (Entry No. 34). Water damage to the paper is evident at the front of the volume and also at the back.

Marginalia and owners' notes: There are no marginalia, but some leaves have large rust-brown sweeping pen strokes as if the pages were used for pen practice.

Volume contents: The volume consists of 104 leaves and two front and two back endpapers (i–ii + 104 + v–vi). Folios i and vi are blank endpapers of marbled paper. Folios ii and v are endpapers of different plain paper, blank except for an *ex libris* of St John's College. Folio 1a (foliated as iii) appears to have been blank; it currently has a leaf of modern paper pasted to the recto side. Folio 104 (foliated as iv) appears to have had some writing on it, but it is currently unreadable, for a modern piece of paper has been pasted over the verso, and the recto has pasted onto it another piece of modern paper, slightly smaller in size than the original leaf itself (20.5 × 15.5), which has the following annotation:

Psalterium Persicum,
manu satis eleganti.
Hoc Exemplar scriptum est an. Hejræ
1001, i.e. circiter an. X^ti 1592.

Pasted on top of this later paper with the Latin annotation is a second piece of modern paper, quite small (9.5 × 5.7), with yet another note: *MS. 105. Coll. D.J. Bapt.—Psalterium Pers. script. A.H. 1001 = C. 1592.* There is also a pencilled annotation: *II.16.*

Binding: The volume is bound in a European library binding of light-tan leather over pasteboards. The covers have frames of tulip heads alternating with leaf stalks. The pastedowns and endpapers are of European multicoloured marbled paper. There are additional blank endpapers of modern paper.

Provenance: No information is available on the provenance of this manuscript or when it came into the collections of St John's College.

References

Coxe, 31 entry CV, where it is said incorrectly to have been copied in 1001 H.

Bernard, *Catalogi*, A.16 (*in abaco secundo*).

Pearson, *Oriental Collections Great Britain*, 49 (no description given).

Pearson, *Oriental Manuscripts Europe*, 308 (no description given).

Entry No. 34

MS 133

TITLE: [*Kitāb-i Zabūr* [*-i Dā'ūd*]

The Book of the Psalms [*of David*]

کتاب زبور داود

CONTENTS: A Persian translation of the Book of Psalms by an unnamed translator.

It is the same anonymous translation that is preserved in MS 105 (Entry No. 33) of St John's College and also in two Bodleian Library manuscripts: MS Laud Or. 141 and MS S. Clarke 10. This anonymous translation was certainly made sometime before 1640—a date that appears with Archbishop Laud's ownership entry in Bodleian Library, Oriental Collections, MS Laud Or. 141. The ending of this particular copy (MS 133 at St John's College) is the same as Bodleian MS Laud. Or. 141 but differs slightly from St John's MS 105, though the translation is substantially the same. The Bodleian Library MS S. Clarke 10 is an incomplete transcription, possibly of MS Laud Or. 141, made by Samuel Clarke, who died in 1669.

Two 17th-century Persian translations are known to have been made. In 1027/1618 Shah ʿAbbās I ordered that a translation of the Psalms be prepared, and this was done from the Hebrew by John Thaddeus, Carmelite bishop of Isfahan, whose name is given as assisted by three Muslim mullahs and one Jewish rabbi. Thaddeus' translation is preserved in three Bodleian Library manuscripts: MS Greaves 4, MS Bodl. Or. 130, and MS Bodl. Or. 439, where the Portuguese friar John Thaddeus is referred to as Padre Juan (پادری جوان); see SEB I, cols. 1050–1 nos. 1827, 1828, and 1829.

The second translation was made from the Vulgate Bible by Jeronimo Xavier during the reigns of the Mughal rulers Akbar I (reg. 1556–1605) and Jahāngīr (reg. 1605–27). No manuscript copies of this translation, however, are recorded as being preserved today.

The anonymous translation in the two copies at St John's (MS 105 and MS 133) is different from that made by John Thaddeus. Whether or not it might be the translation made by Jeronimo Xavier has not been determined.

For other copies: see St John's College, Oxford, MS 105 (Entry No. 33); Bodleian Library, Oriental Collections, MS Laud Or. 141, which ends with Psalm 150 (SEB I, col. 1052 no. 1830), and MS S. Clarke 10, which ends with Psalm 138 and is in Samuel Clarke's handwriting (SEB I, col. 1052, no. 1831).

For Persian translations in general, see J. Thomas, 'Bible.iii: Chronology of Translations of the Bible' and Kenneth J. Thomas and Fereydun Vahman, 'Bible.vii: Persian Translations of the Bible', in *EncIr*, iv. 203–6 and 209–13.

PHYSICAL DESCRIPTION:

99 leaves (fos. 1b–99b)

Beginning (fo. $1b_{1-3}$):

کتاب زبور
فصل اول سعادت‌مند مردی که بتدبیر — ۱ ظالمان نرفت • وبر راه خطاکاران نه ایستاد • وبر تخت
<<کاران crossed out>> ((طاغیون in margin)) نه نشست

Ending (fo. $99b_{13-16}$, Psalm 150):

ستایش گویید اورا در چنگهای خوش‌اواز ستایش گویید — ٦
اورا درچنگهای خوشی همه روح ستایش گوید خداوندرا
حال لوئیه
تمت
تم

The copy is undated and unsigned. The general appearance of the script, paper, and ink suggests a date of the 16th to 17th century.

Persian. Dimensions: 23.0 × 12.6 (text area 16.8 × 6.8) cm; 16 lines per page. The text area has been frame ruled, with the indentations quite visible. It is written in an elegant, professional, medium-small Naskh script in dense black ink with headings in warm red and small red-dot text-stops. The line numbers are indicated by standard numerals written in the margins. There are catchwords at the bottom of the verso of every folio.

The thin, glossy, beige paper has a thickness of 0.09 and an opaqueness factor of 6. It has unevenly distributed fibres, and there are globular inclusions and occasional thin patches. There are indistinct sagging vertical laid lines and no visible chain lines. The paper is very similar to that in MS 105 (Entry No. 33).

Marginalia and owners' notes: There are a few marginal corrections by the scribe, but no other marginalia.

Volume contents: The volume consists of 101 leaves and one front and one back endpaper (i + 101 + ii). Folio 1a (foliated as ii), the same paper as the main treatise, is blank. Folios

100 and 101 (old iii and iv) are also blank but are of the same paper as the treatise itself and have been ruled as if for text to be added. Folio i is the same paper as the pastedowns, blank except for a pencilled notation *The Psalms in Persic*. Folio ii (old v) is a blank endpaper of the same type as the pastedown.

Binding: The volume is bound in a Persian binding of red leather over pasteboards; the spine has been repaired. The covers each have a scalloped mandorla central medallion with two shield-shaped pendants, block stamped with a floral and leaf design. The medallions and pendants are filled with gilt paper, and a linking design has been painted in gold paint, which was also used to form a gold frame of two thin fillets with simple corner leaf designs. The envelope flap has a similar frame and a block-stamped shield-shaped medallion, similar to but larger than the pendants on the cover; the gilt paper infilling is now missing from the envelope flap. The doublure of the envelope flap is marbled paper of green on white with a printed orange leaf design; the lining of the fore-edge is red leather. There are modern pastedowns and endpapers. The numeral *193* has been inked on the fore-edge of the manuscript.

Provenance: No information available.

References

Coxe, 40 entry CXXXIII.
Bernard, *Catalogi*, A.14 (*in abaco secundo*).
Pearson, *Oriental Collections Great Britain*, 49 (no description given).
Pearson, *Oriental Manuscripts Europe*, 308 (no description given).

2

HEBREW MANUSCRIPTS

Peter E. Pormann

Entry No. 35

MS 143

CONTENTS: This is a 13th-century bilingual Latin–Hebrew manuscript made in England, containing four books of the Old Testament: Joshua, Judges, Song of Songs, and Ecclesiastes. The Latin translation in the margin is the Vulgate, while the interlinear one translates each word literally, and is thus much closer to the Hebrew. Hebrew proper names are transliterated rather than given their known Latin form. The Hebrew was obviously written first, not only suggested by the Hebrew catchwords, but also by the entire layout of each page.

The manuscript belongs to a group of bilingual Latin–Hebrew manuscripts produced for the study of Hebrew. See G. Dahan, 'Deux psautiers hébraïques en latin', *Revue des études juives,* 158 (1999), 62–87, esp. 84–7; R. Loewe, 'The Mediaeval Christian Hebraists of England: The *Superscriptio Lincolniensis*', *Hebrew Union College Annual*, 28 (1957), 205–52; R. Loewe, 'Latin *Superscriptio* MSS. on Portions of the Hebrew Bible Other than the Psalter', *Journal of Jewish Studies*, 9 (1958), 63–71; S. Berger, *Quam notitiam linguae Hebraicae habuerunt Christiani medii aevi temporibus in Gallia* (Nancy: typis Berger-Le-Vrault, 1893); and Judith Olszowy-Schlanger, 'The Knowledge and Practice of Hebrew Grammar among Christian Scholars in Pre-expulsion England: the evidence of "bilingual" Hebrew–Latin manuscripts', in Nicholas de Lange (ed.), *Hebrew Scholarship and the Medieval World* (Cambridge: Cambridge University Press, 2001), 197–28.

For similar manuscripts in Oxford, see Corpus Christi College MSS 5 and 7–9.

The first folio of the volume, when it came into the possession of St John's College, was subsequently found to be a missing folio of a Hebrew manuscript in Lambeth Palace. In

1954 it was reunited with the Lambeth MS 435, and this volume (MS 143) was then refoliated. It is important to note that after the removal of the original first folio which belonged to the Lambeth manuscript, someone pencilled in a new foliation while published references continued to be made to the old *pagination.* All references here are to the new foliation. Formulae for conversion are p = 2f + 1, adding 1 for verso pages, and f = ½(p − 1), with a remainder of ½ indicating a verso.

The following is an example of the *superscriptio* from fo. $1v_{1-6\ (1-11\ \text{Latin})}$, giving the text of Joshua 1: 1–2 (see Plate 11):

	ויהי
et factum	mortem post
est ut post	אחרי מות
mortem mo	servi mose
ysi servi do	משה עבד
mini loqueretur do	ad dominus loquebatur et domini
minus ad iosue filium	יהוה ויאמר יהוה אל
nuni ministrum moy	moisi ministrum nun filium iehousuha
si et diceret	יהושע בן נון משרת משה
ei.	mortuus meus servus Mose dicens
Moyses servus meus	לאמר משה עבדי מת
mortuus est surge et	surge nunc et
…	ועתה קום …

PHYSICAL DESCRIPTION:

172 leaves (fos. 1r–74r, 75r–172r)

Beginning (fo. $1r_{1-11}$; only eleven lines are written on fo. 1r) – Joshua 1: 8b–11b:

את דרכיך ואז תשכיל
הלא צויתיך חזק ואמץ
אל תערץ ואל תחת כי
עמך יהוה אלהיך בכל
אשר תלך
ויצו יהושע את שטרי
העם לאמר עבדו בקרב
המחנה ויצוו [*sic*] את העם
לאמר הכינו לכם צדה כי
בעוד שלשת ימים אתם
עבדים את

Ending (fo. $172r_{1-11,\ 1-13\ \text{Latin}}$ – Eccl. 12: 13b–14); see Plate 12. All Latin abbreviations have been resolved except *ar*[*ticulus*], denoting either the article or the *nota accusativi*:

audiamus omnes ar
הכל נשמע ואת
ar time dominum ar
[*sic*] האלהים ירא את מצ
omnis hic quod observa eius mandata
מצותיו שמר כי זה כל
factum omne ar quod homo
האדם כי את כל מעשה
iudicium in adducet deus ar
האלהים יביא במשפט
bonum si abscondito omni super
על כל נעלם ואם טוב
omnes ar sermonis finem malum si et
ואם רע סוף דבר הכל
time deum ar ar audiamus
נשמע את האלהים ירא
hic quod observa eius mandata ar
את מצותיו שמר כי זה
homo omnis
כל האדם
חזק

finem loquendi
omnes pariter
audiamus
deum time et
mandata illius
observa hic est enim
omnis homo et
cuncta que fiunt
adducet deus in iu
dicium pro omni er
ratu sive bonum
sive malum
sit.

The manuscript is undated and unsigned. The appearance of the vellum, ink, and script suggests that it was written in the 13th century, probably in England.

Hebrew and Latin. Dimensions: 21.3 × 15.4 cm (many leaves irregular); 17 lines of Hebrew and 37 lines of Latin per page. The Hebrew is written in a central area 14.3 × 6.8 cm, and the Latin in a column near the outside edge, measuring 14.5 × 2.6 cm. The folios have been ruled in brown ink, with both horizontal and vertical guidelines extending to the edges of the leaves.

Folio 1r has Joshua 1: 8b–11b. The entire book of Joshua occupies fos. 1v–74r. Folios 75r–138v contain the Book of Judges, fos. 139r–149v$_4$ the Song of Songs, and fos. 149r$_5$–172r the Book of Ecclesiastes.

Both the Latin and the Hebrew scripts are careful and even calligraphic in execution. The Hebrew hand is that of a non-Jewish writer and has the hallmarks of an English script. It is carefully vocalized. The Latin, which is smaller than the Hebrew, is also typically insular. The spaces for initial letters (or miniatures) both in Hebrew and in Latin have not been filled; see, for example, fo. 1v (see Plate 11).

Dr Alison Salvesen, after recently examining the manuscript, has suggested that the hand has all the hallmarks of an Ashkenazi scribe of the 13th century and differs very little in style (though rather more in quality) from that of the Worms Mahzor (dated 1272, Germany; see Malachi Beit-Arié, *The Makings of the Medieval Hebrew Book*

(Jerusalem: Magnes Press, Hebrew University, 1993), 174, 178, 180. However, the scribe is more careless. The error on fo. 1r, where he has begun to write the third page of text on the blank sheet *preceding* the start page of Joshua, is much more typical of a Jewish scribe than a Christian. Although the quires were designed to be bound in a codex opening left to right, after writing the beginning of Joshua on fos. 1v and 2r, leaving 1r blank for the beginning of the book, the scribe has automatically moved to the blank folio leftwards (fo. 1r), as one would for a Hebrew book, instead of to the next blank one to the right (fo. 2v). The commonest way in which the first scribe fills the line to the left margin is to use a blank space followed by something resembling a large colon at the margin: one square penstroke above a slightly slanted penstroke. Less commonly the consonants Lamedh, Daleth, and Taw are elongated to fill the space when they occur at the end of the line. Overall, in this respect of filling the line to the left, the scribe shows a certain lack of style. One slight curiosity is the lack of *daghesh*, the point within Hebrew consonants that shows whether they are to be pronounced hard or fricatively. It hardly appears at all, and has not been added either by the scribe of the consonantal text, or by the second scribe who has evidently added the vowel points.

Dr Salvesen also takes the second main scribe to be Jewish, not merely because of his ability to vocalize the Hebrew (though not always very accurately) and to correct the Hebrew text of the first scribe, but also for the following reason. The first scribe has made the remarkable error of adding the Divine Name of God (YHWH) to the text of Judges in two verses on fo. 98v, making the Lord the subject of two verbs which otherwise have no explicit subject (Judg. 9: 29b: 'and *the LORD* said to Abimelech, "Increase your army greatly and go forth" '; Judg. 9: 31 'and *the LORD* sent messengers to Abimelech in Tormah'). The scribe even elongates the form of those two verbs immediately preceding the Name, perhaps because he is conscious that he is about to write the Divine Name, though this is a procedure not found elsewhere in this manuscript. The second scribe, who was unafraid to cross out a phrase that the first scribe had written in error on fo. 142v, does not strike out the two Divine Names on fo. 98v out of respect for their sanctity. Instead he encloses each in a frame to show that they have been written in error. This method of dealing with the problem reflects Jewish rather than Christian sensibilities regarding the sacred name of God. It is of course possible that both main Hebrew scribes were Jewish converts to Christianity in adulthood, having learned Hebrew and scribal practices in their youth, along with a reverence for the Divine Name that would not lightly be shed. However, there is no way of telling from the text whether the scribes were still religiously Jewish or not when they wrote the book.

Judith Olszowy-Schlanger, in a recent publication analysing in detail this and fifteen similar bilingual manuscripts, presents convincing arguments for the manuscript having been produced in England around 1250 in a Christian milieu, and that while the Latin was certainly written by Christian scribes, the Hebrew (of which she distinguishes three hands) was probably written by those trained in a Jewish context, though she notes that the question has been debated in the scholarly literature.

Dark-brown to black ink was used for the Hebrew and the Latin in the accompanying columns. The interlinear Latin is in a lighter brown ink. The manuscript has been foliated (and previously paginated) and bound as a Western manuscript. There are Hebrew catchwords at the start of each eight-leaf quire, written at lower right corner (e.g. fos. 8v, 16v, 24v).

The manuscript is made of vellum; there is stitching on some leaves (e.g. fo. 56) and occasional holes (fo. 57). Near the vertical edge, each leaf has been punctured with a series of holes as part of the ruling process. There is some damp staining, and the volume is soiled with grime and thumbing.

Marginalia and owners' notes: There are small and carefully written Latin marginal notes, most of which have been partially cut off when the edges of the manuscript were trimmed for rebinding. There are occasional Latin annotations written in a quite large script, in light-brown ink, at the bottom of some folios, and also some faded fistnotes (e.g. fo. 25a, 114b, 148a).

Volume contents: The volume consists of 172 leaves, with one blank endpaper (172 + i). Folios 74v and 172v are blank. At the bottom of fo. 1r there is the pencilled annotation: *Initium paginæ tertiæ | errore Scribæ hic positum.*

Binding: The volume is bound in a 17th-century Western library binding of brown leather over pasteboards, with five cords on the spine. The numeral *143* is stamped in gold on the spine. The covers have a blind-stamped central frame formed of three fillets and scallops with shells. There are flower-head pendants at each corner of the central frame, which is then enclosed by a larger frame formed of two simple fillets. The binding has been damaged and repaired. There are relatively modern paper pastedowns and one endpaper. The front pastedown has a pencilled note by H. M. Colvin regarding the return of the first folio to the Lambeth Palace manuscript as well as the following Latin note:

E Libris Coll[egii] Do[mini] Jo[annis] Bapt[istæ] Oxon[ii].

Pars | Bibliorum Hebræorum, | continens 4 sequentes Libros, | Josuam, | Judices, | Cantica, | Ecclesiasten: | Cum duplici Versione Latinâ, nempe, | Vulgatâ, & alterâ magis ad literam factâ; | quarum illa marginem occupat, hæc inter lineas scribitur.

Codex Ærâ caret; sed non videtur valdè | antiquus. Incipit à sinistrâ, & pergit ad | dextram; Ordine scil. contrario ei, qui in | Hebraicis cæterisq^{ue} Orientalibus scriptis | observari solet. – Voces initiales desunt.

Provenance: The volume was given to St John's College by Edward Bernard in 1667. At the top of fo. 1r there is written: *Liber Coll[egi] Do[mini] Joannis Bapt[istæ] Oxon[ii]. Ex dono Edvardi Bernardi Socii 1667.*

References

Coxe, 43 entry CXLIII.

Bernard, Catalogi, B.26 (*in abaco tertio*).
Pearson, *Oriental Manuscripts Europe*, 56 (no description given).
D. Neubauer, *Catalogue of Hebrew Manuscripts in the Bodleian Library and in the College Libraries of Oxford*, Catalogi Codd. Mss. Bibliothecae Bodleianae Pars XII (Oxford: Clarendon Press, 1886), col. 862 no. 2439.
Malachi Beit-Arié, *Catalogue of the Hebrew Manuscripts in the Bodleian Library: Supplement of Addenda and Corrigenda to Vol. 1 (A. Neubauer's Catalogue)*, ed. R. A. May (Oxford: Clarendon Press, 1994), col. 478 no. 2439.
Hanna, *St. John's Catalogue*, 206–7.
Judith Olszowy-Schlanger, *Les Manuscrits hébreux dans l'Angleterre médiévale: étude historique et paléographique* (Paris: Peeters, 2003), 224–8 entry no. 14.

Entry No. 36

MS 253 (item 51)

TITLE: *The Copy of a Hebrew Conveyance of Land in Gamlingay from William of Leicester, to Walter de Merton, the Founder of Merton College, Oxon. In ye time of K. Hen. 3^d. The Founder purchasing Land of a Jew, The Jew wou'd have ye Leases drawn in his Own Language. These Leases now translated into Latin by M. Gagnier.*

CONTENTS: These leaves constitute the transcription and translation of two Hebrew deeds of conveyance whose originals are in the possession of Merton College, Oxford (shelfmark: D.1.57(i)). This transcription and translation was prepared by Jean Gagnier (d. 1741), the Lord Almoner's Professor of Arabic at Oxford. The original documents transcribed here are dated the Wednesday before Pentecost in 1268 (= 23 May 1268). The transaction to which they relate is the conveyance of land owned by William de Leicestre and mortgaged to Josce, son of Bendit, to Walter de Merton and his house of scholars—i.e. Merton College.

In the first conveyance, one Jose filius Bendit [Benedict] makes over to Walter de Merton two debts of 43 pounds and 16 mark which William de Leicestre of Gamlingay owed to the late Abraham filius Vives, who was the former husband of Jose filius Bendit's wife Esther and which she had brought him in her dowry. In the second document, Jose filius Bendit relinquishes to Walter de Merton all his claims on the estate of William de Leicestre in Gamlingay in respect to the above debts.

In the transcriptions of the Latin incipits and explicits that follow, the material in parentheses and brackets is in the translation itself.

Beginning of first deed of conveyance:

Hebrew (fo, $62b_{1-5}$):

אני חתום מטה מודה הודאה גמורה שמכרתי והנחתי ממני ומיורשי ומכל הבאים מכחי לשיר גוטייר דמירטון כבר חותֵם אדוננו המלך וליורשיו ולבאים מכחו כל דין ותביעה וערעור שהיה לי ושיכול להיות על חוב מארבעים ושלשה לטרין שגילם דליציסטר מגמלינגיאה נתחייב לאברם בן ויוש ...

Latin translation (fo. $63a_{1-7}$):

Ego infra scriptus confiteor confessione perfectâ me vendidisse et concessisse a me & ab hæredibus meis et a posteris meis Sir Waltero (Heb. Gautier) de Merton, quondam Cancellario Domini nostri Regis, et hæredibus eius, et posteris eius totum ius & postulationem et prætentionem, quæ erat mihi & potuit esse super debitum quadraginta et trium librarum, quas William de Leicestre de Gamelegaye debebat Abramo filio Vives (or Vios) ...

Ending of first deed of conveyance:

Hebrew (fo. $62b_{2-5}$):

אקט יום ד בשבוע פנטקושט שנת חמשים ושתים למלכות הנקו' ומה שהודיתי חתמתי יוסי בן בנדיט בנדיט בן יוסי עד חיים דניקול עד

Latin translation (fo. $63b_{13-17}$):

Actum die quartâ in septimana Pentecostes Anno quinquagesimo secundo Regni supradicti. Atque hoc quod confessus sum sigillo meo munivi, Jose filius Bendit. Bendit filius Jose Testis. Chajim de Nikol [Lincoln] Testis.

Beginning of second conveyance:

Hebrew (fo. $64a_{1-3}$):

אני חתום מטה מודה הודאה גמורה שפטרתי ומחלתי לשיר גוטייר דמירטון כבר חותם אדוננו המלך וליורשיו ולבאים מכחו כל דין ותביעה וערעור שהיה לי ושיכול להיות לי על קרקעות

Latin translation (fo. $65a_{1-5}$):

Ego infra scriptus confiteor confessione perfectâ me dimississe et cessisse Sir Waltero (Hebr. Gautier) de Merton, quondam Cancellario Domini nostri Regis, et hæredibus eius et posteris eius totum ius & postulationem, quæ erat mihi vel potuit esse mihi super fundos ...

Ending of second conveyance:

Hebrew (fo. $64a_{20-21}$):

ומה שהודיתי חתמתי יוסי בן בנדיט בנדיט בן יוסי עד חיים דניקול עד

Latin translation (fo. $65b_{7-10}$):

Atque id quod confessus sum sigillo meo munivi Jose filius Bendit. Bendit filius Jose Testis. Chajim de Nikol [Lincoln] Testis.

PHYSICAL DESCRIPTION:

5 leaves (pencilled foliation, fos. 61a–65b)

Hebrew and Latin. Dimensions: 40.7 × 19.3 (text area *c.*27 × 17) cm. The Hebrew is written on sheets of paper ruled with pencil, 23 lines per page on fo. 62a (continued on 62b for 5 lines) and 21 lines on fo. 64a. The Latin is not written on ruled sheets; the number of lines varies and no margins are maintained.

The title is given on fo. 61a, in the handwriting of Gagnier. Folio 62a is blank. The two Hebrew documents occupy fos. 61b (and finishing on 62b) and 64a (64b is blank). Gagnier's Latin translation is on fos. 63a–b and 65a–b.

The matt-finished, ivory paper has fine horizontal laid lines, single chain lines, and is watermarked (initials AI, and a cubical tomb with a cross and dagger).

Volume contents: This Hebrew and Latin document is item 51 in a miscellaneous collection of autographs, ancient documents, and palaeographical curiosities formed by John Pointer (1668–1754) and bequeathed by him to the College. The volume is labelled *MUSÆUM POINTERIANUM, Vol. 4, Being a Collection of several Papers of Antiquity & Curiosity.*

Provenance: The volume was bequeathed to the College by John Pointer (1668–1754) of Merton College. Because St John's College already had the nucleus of a museum of curiosities, John Pointer was motivated to bequeath his own such collection to the College. His collection, which became known as the *Musaeum Pointerianum*, was then housed under the northern end of the Laudian Library in the College until the Museum of the History of Science was established in the Old Ashmolean, at which time most of his collection was transferred there. This bound volume, however, remained in the library of the College. See Costin, *History of St. John's College*, 188, and Gunther, *Early Science in Oxford*, iii. 336–41.

References

Pointer, Oxoniensis Academia, 92–4:

> There being such a Collection of Curiosities in this College already, has induc'd me to bequeath my own collection to be added to it, hoping it may be a Maintenance (or at least a Help towards one) for some young Scholar in shewing 'em; a Scholar to be appointed by the President, to whom he shall administer an Oath to keep all Things safe. A Short Specimen of which is as follows
> . . . [amongst others in the list] . . .
> *A Deed of Conveyance of Landes to the Founder of Merton College, in Hebrew.*

In the unpublished typescript, Coxe–supplement, 12, there is the following description:

> (f.51) transcript and translation of a Hebrew 'starr' dated 23 May 1268, whereby Jose fil' Benedict assigns to Walter of Merton two debts which William de Leicester of Gamlingay owed to the late Abram fil' Vives, formerly husband of Jose's wife Antera [*sic*]; (f. 53), transcript & translation of a Hebrew `starr' whereby Jose fil' Benedict relinquished to Walter of Merton all his claims on the estate of William de Leicester in Gamlingay by reason of the above debts.

Gagnier's Latin translation as well as the Hebrew original of the present transcription are published by Peter E. Pormann, 'Two New Starrs Relating to the History of Merton College, Oxford', *Journal of Jewish Studies*, 55 (2004), 101–17.

3

TURKISH MANUSCRIPTS

Tim Stanley

Entry No. 37

MS 253 (item 7)

CONTENTS: This document is an official letter in Turkish from a senior member of the Ottoman government, whose name appears in the stylized signature, or *penche*, inscribed near the upper right side of the text, with a seal stamped nearby.

As will be shown below, it was written in Constantinople in 1618, during the reigns of Sultan Osman II (1027–31/1618–22) and King James I (1603–25).

The letter (see Plate 13) is from the Kaymakam Pasha, the man who acted as head of government in the capital while the Grand Vizier was absent on campaign. It is addressed to: 'That paragon among the lords of Christendom, the chief reliance of the leaders of the Christians, our friend, the vizier of the King of England—May he end his days as a Muslim!'

Summary of contents:

His Imperial Majesty Sultan Osman Khan has charged us with the post of Kaymakam of the Grand Vizier, and we are now settling matters that need our attention.

It so happens that the ambassador from your Sovereign to the Threshold of His Imperial Majesty had given notice that he had been summoned home and would need to appoint someone to stand in for him, and he was granted leave to do so. Now, at the accession of His Imperial Majesty it is a long-established custom that the rulers of all friendly powers send a delegation to deliver a letter of congratulation and amity, but so far this nicety has not been observed. A letter with regard to this matter, couched in amicable terms, has been sent to our friend your Sovereign, and a letter of a friendly nature has also been written to you. Please ensure that, in future, protocol is observed, and in this way you will be able to maintain your privileged position in relations with the Threshold of His Imperial Majesty.

Previously, when the Grand Vizier, Halil Pasha, had turned his attention to the campaign in the East, a gentleman was sent to the Porte with a letter expressly in order to settle certain affairs of one of your merchants, but the needs of the army took precedence, and that matter was not dealt with. This matter will now be settled in a manner reconciled to our principles and to the agreements between us, and you may be assured that no detail will be neglected in matters affecting our mutual relations. God willing, you will henceforth see many fine manifestations of the friendship between us and your Sovereign.

Analysis:

The letter was, as one would expect, written at Constantinople, but it contains no date. It must have been drawn up after 1016 [= 1607–8], since this date appears on the ink seal of the Kaymakam Pasha that has been applied in the top right margin, beneath his signature (*penche*). Both signature and seal contain the name of Muḥammad, or Mehmed, and we may identify the signatory as Öküz Mehmed Pasha (d. 1029/1620), who first received the rank of pasha in 1016/1607–8. Öküz Mehmed was himself Grand Vizier between 17 October 1614 and 17 November 1616 [Ramaḍān 1023–Dhū al-Qaʿdah 1025 H] and again between 18 January and 23 December 1619 [Ṣafar–Dhū al-Ḥijjah 1028 H], and he held the post of second vizier in the interim, when the Grand Vizier was Kayserili Halil Pasha (d. 1038/1629). The latter was clearly the Halil Pasha referred to in the letter, in whose absence Öküz Mehmed was acting as Kaymakam.

Halil Pasha departed for the eastern front on 15 June 1617 [10 Jumādá II 1026 H], and he was away on campaign when Sultan Ahmed I died on 22 November [23 Dhū al-Qaʿdah] and was succeeded by his brother Mustafa I. Halil Pasha was still away when, because of his incapacity, Mustafa was replaced by Ahmed's son Osman II, on 26 February 1618 [1 Rabīʿ I 1027 H]. The Grand Vizier's successes on campaign led to a peace treaty with Iran concluded on 26 September 1618 [6 Shawāl 1027 H], but when he returned to the capital in the following January, he was dismissed and replaced by Öküz Mehmed Pasha.

This letter was therefore written between Osman II's accession on 26 February 1618 and Halil Pasha's dismissal on 18 January 1619. This dating is supported by the identity of the ambassador involved.

According to Alfred Wood, who based his account on English official sources, Paul Pindar was appointed to this post by the Levant Company on 26 November 1611 and reached Constantinople by 20 December. His letter of recall is dated 25 January 1618, and he named a merchant to act as his agent as part of the preparations for his departure, which was set for July of the same year.

This part of the story is in accord with the letter, but it seems that, although Pindar had been recalled, and his recall had been approved by the Ottoman government, he had not yet left Constantinople when the letter was written. According to Wood, the Ottoman government prevailed on Pindar to remain, and the Levant Company did not appoint Sir John Eyre as a successor until 1619, so that Pindar did not leave Constantinople until about April 1620, when Eyre arrived.

Plate 1. MS 103, fo. 180a: colophon dated 4 Ramaḍān 752 [25 Oct. 1351], al-A'raj al-Nīsābūrī, *Tawḍīḥ al-Tadhkirah*

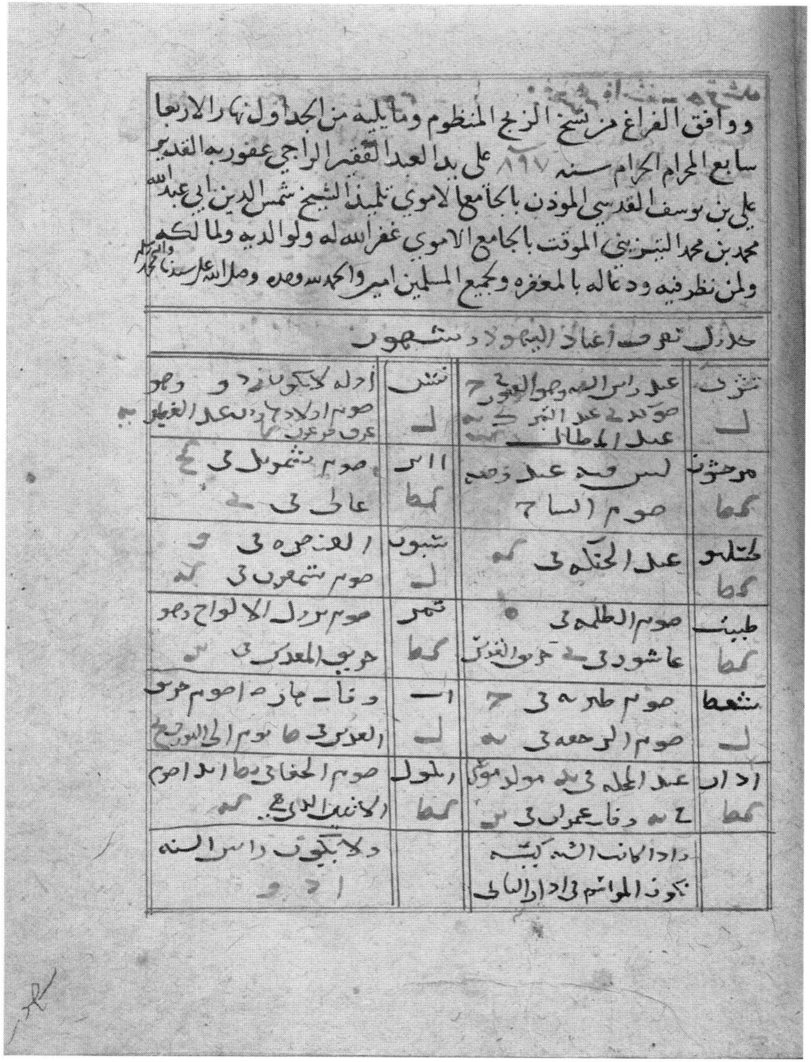

Plate 2. MS 156B, fo. 90a: colophon dated 7 Muḥarram 897 [10 Nov. 1491], attributed to Abū al-Fidā', *Kitab al-Sirr al-maktūm fī al-'amal bi-l-zīj al-manẓūm*

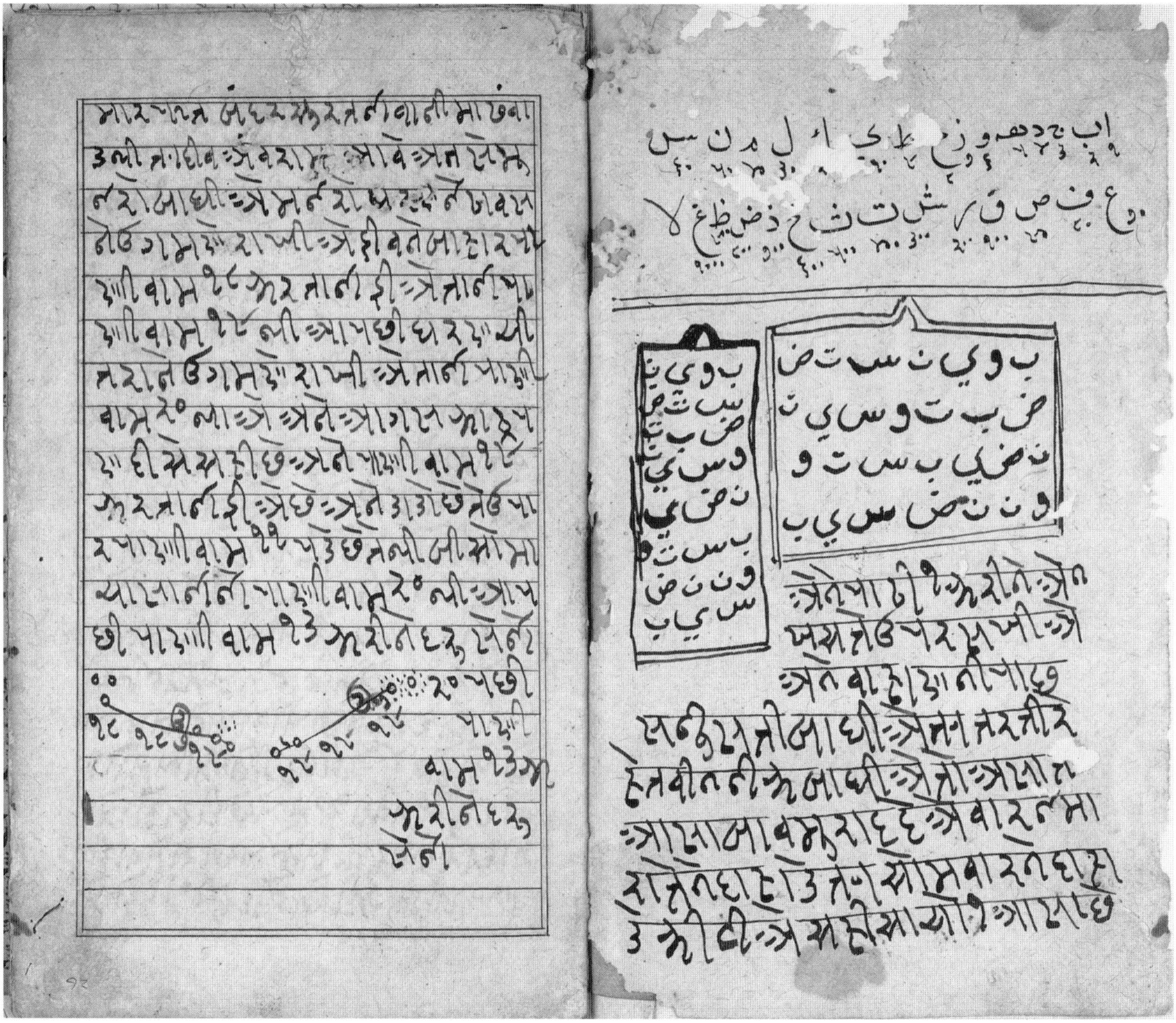

Plate 16. MS 254, item 45, fos. 25b–26a: opening of a Gujarati navigational text, with a design for a talismanic tablet to be affixed to a ship (Gujarat, 17th–18th cent.)

Bibliography:

A. H. de Groot, 'Khalil Pasha, Kaysariyyeli', *EI*[2], iv. 970–2.
A. H. de Groot, 'Mehmed Pasha, Öküz', *EI*[2], vi. 998–9.
Alfred C. Wood, *A History of the Levant Company* (Oxford: Oxford University Press, 1935; second impression London, 1964), 80 n. 1.

PHYSICAL DESCRIPTION:

Turkish. Dimensions: 43.5 × 42.5 cm; 20 lines. A single sheet. One side has now been folded in and then the paper folded in half. It is evident from fold marks that it was at one time folded to fit a very small and narrow rectangular case or pocket.

It is written with dense black ink, sprinkled with gilt. The text has not been ruled; the lines sweep upward at the ends.

The biscuit paper has vertical laid lines and no chain lines. The edges are damaged, and there are some holes at fold lines.

The verso of the document is blank, except for a note in a 17th- or 18th-century hand giving the following totally incorrect description:

A letter from the Sophi of Persia to K. Ch. 1
written upon Paper made of ye Bark of Trees

Volume contents: This Turkish document is item 7 in a miscellaneous collection of autographs, ancient documents, and palaeographical curiosities formed by John Pointer (1668–1754) and bequeathed by him to the College. The volume is labelled *MUSÆUM POINTERIANUM, Vol. 4, Being a Collection of several Papers of Antiquity & Curiosity.*

Provenance: The volume was bequeathed to the College by John Pointer (1668–1754) of Merton College. Because St John's College already had the nucleus of a museum of curiosities, John Pointer was motivated to bequeath his own such collection to the College. His collection, which became known as the *Musaeum Pointerianum*, was then housed under the northern end of the Laudian Library in the College until the Museum of the History of Science was established in the Old Ashmolean, at which time most of his collection was transferred there. This bound volume, however, remained in the library of the College. See Costin, *History of St. John's College*, 188, and Gunther, *Early Science in Oxford*, iii. 336–41.

References

Unpublished, except for the following inaccurate listing in Pointer, *Oxoniensis Academia*, 92–4:

> There being such a Collection of Curiosities in this College already, has induc'd me to bequeath my own collection to be added to it, hoping it may be a Maintenance (or at least a Help towards one) for some young Scholar in shewing 'em; a Scholar to be appointed by the President, to whom he shall administer an Oath to keep all Things safe. A Short Specimen of which is as follows

. . . [amongst others in the list] . . .
Another Letter from the Sophi of Persia to King Charles I.

This incorrect description of the document as a letter from a Persian ruler to King Charles I was repeated in Coxe-supplement-1, 12.

4

SYRIAC MANUSCRIPTS

Peter E. Pormann

Entry No. 38

MS 70

AUTHOR: [anonymous]

TITLE: *Kṯāḇā d'ellat koll 'ellān*

The Book of the Cause of All Causes

CONTENTS: This is an incomplete copy of the first four books (out of seven surviving) of a treatise known as *Causa causarum* by an anonymous author of possibly the 10th century.

The treatise has been edited by C. Kayser, *Das Buch der Erkenntniss der Weisheit oder der Ursache der Ursachen* (Leipzig: Hinrichs, 1889). The St John's manuscript was not used in this edition.

For other copies: See A. Baumstark, Geschichte der syrischen Literatur (Bonn: A. Marcus und E. Webers Verlag, 1922), 280–1; R. Payne Smith, *Catalogi codicum manuscriptorum Bibliothecae Bodleianae. Pars sexta: Codices Syriacos, Carshunicos, Mendaeos, complectens* (Oxford: e typographeo Clarendoniano, 1864), col. 585; and Vatican, Syriac MS 191, fos. 89a–128b (G. Furlani, *Rivista degli studi orientali*, 23 (1948), 37–45).

PHYSICAL DESCRIPTION:

108 leaves (fos. 1a–100a, 101a–108a)

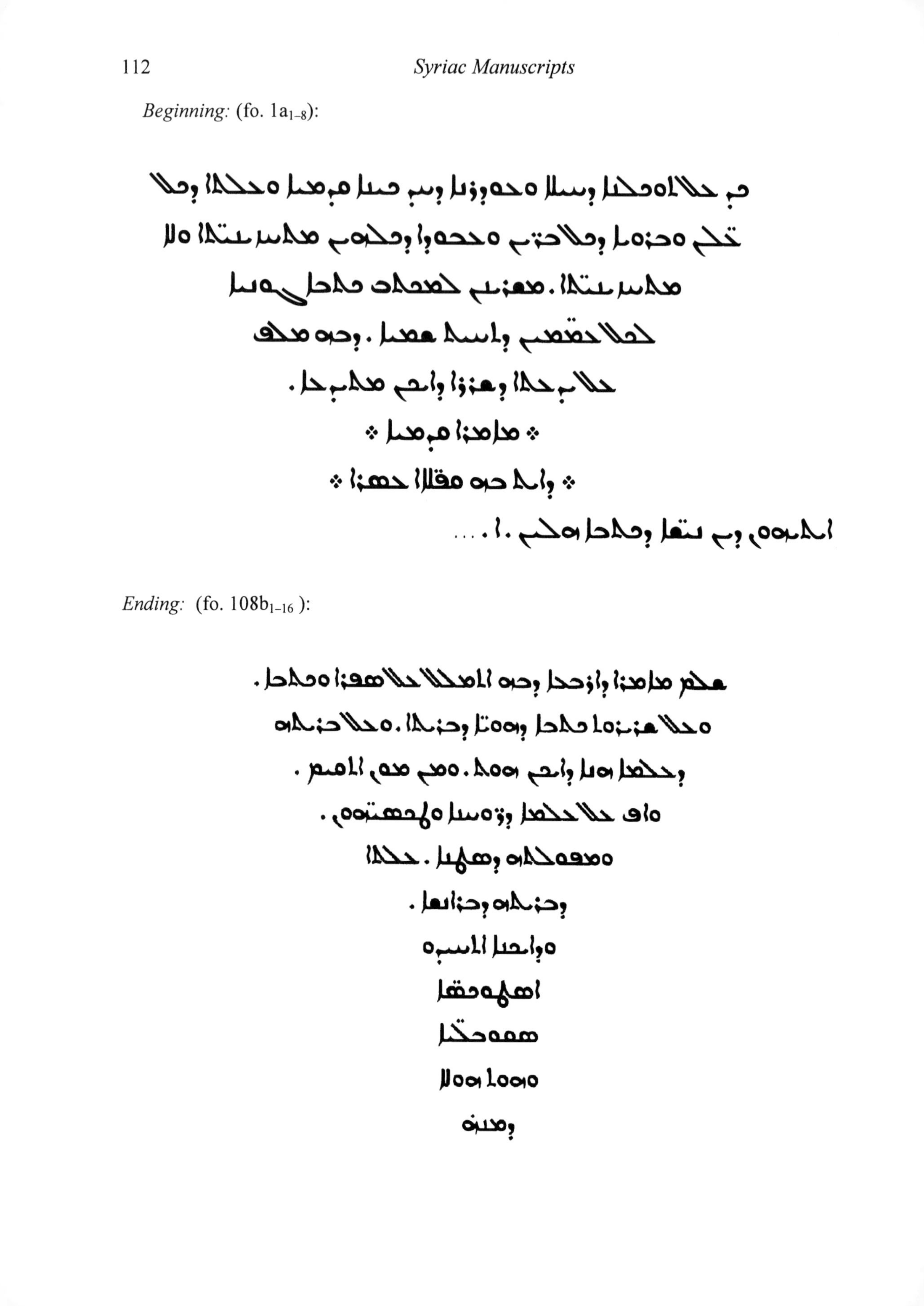

Beginning: (fo. $1a_{1-8}$):

[illegible]
[illegible]
[illegible]
[illegible]
[illegible]
[illegible]
[illegible]
[illegible]

Ending: (fo. $108b_{1-16}$):

[illegible]
[illegible]
[illegible]
[illegible]
[illegible]
[illegible]
[illegible]
[illegible]
[illegible]
[illegible]
[illegible]
[illegible]

ܐܬܚܡ ܟܠܗ ܀

ܕܡܬܚܐ

ܒܗܘܐ

ܒܪܬܐ

܀

The copy is undated and unsigned. The nature of the paper, ink, and script suggests a date of the 16th century. It was donated to St John's in 1639, thus providing a date *ante quem* it was produced.

Syriac. Dimensions: 28.6 × 21.4 (text area 22.5 × 14.4) cm; 29 lines per page, with the catchwords occupying the 29th, ruled, line. The text area has been frame ruled.

The copy is incomplete, with the text ending at a point equivalent to the bottom of p. 184 in the edition by C. Kayser.

The four Memre contained in the copy, with their corresponding Kephalaia, occupy the following folios; the equivalent pages of the edition by Kayser [= K] have been indicated:

1a–41	List of contents, Memre I–IX		(= K, 2–6)
4a–7b	Preface		(= K, 6–13)
8a Memra I			
	8a–9b	Kephalaion 1	(= K, 13–17)
	10a–12b	Kephalaion 2	(= K, 17–22)
	12b–13b	Kephalaion 3	(= K, 22–3)
	13b–20a	Kephalaion 4	(= K, 23–36)
	20b–25a	Kephalaion 5	(= K, 36–46)
	25b–29b	Kephalaion 6	(= K, 46–53)
	29b–33b	Kephalaion 7	(= K, 53–61)
	33b–35a	Kephalaion 8	(= K, 61–4)
	35a–39b	Kephalaion 9	(= K, 64–72)
	39b–44b	Kephalaion 10	(= K, 72–82)
44b Memra II			
	44b–46a	Kephalaion 1	(= K, 82–5)
	46a–48a	Kephalaion 2	(= K, 85–9)
	48a–50a	Kephalaion 3	(= K, 89–92)
	50a–51b	Kephalaion 4	(= K, 92–5)
	51b–53b	Kephalaion 5	(= K, 95–9)
	53b–54b	Kephalaion 6	(= K, 99–100)

	54b–56b	Kephalaion 7	(= K, 100–4)
	56b–62b	Kephalaion 8	(= K, 104–14)
62b	Memra III		
	62b–67a	Kephalaion 1	(= K, 114–21)
	67a–70a	Kephalaion 2	(= K, 121–7)
	70a–75b	Kephalaion 3	(= K, 127–35)
	75b–80a	Kephalaion 4	(= K, 135–42)
	80a–82a	Kephalaion 5	(= K, 142–5)
	82a–82b	Kephalaion 6	(= K, 145–6)
	82b–84a	Kephalaion 7	(= K, 146–8)
	84b–85b	Kephalaion 8	(= K, 148–50)
	85b–86a	Kephalaion 9	(= K, 150–2)
86b	Memra IV		
	86b–87b	Kephalaion 1	(= K, 152–4)
	87b–88b	Kephalaion 2	(= K, 154–5)
	88b–92a	Kephalaion 3	(= K, 155–60)
	92a–103b	Kephalaion 4	(= K, 160–77)
	103b–108b	Kephalaion 5	(= K, 178–84)

(100b was left blank because the ink on 100a had bled through).

The text is written in a medium-large *serṭō* script, possibly by a European scholarly hand, in a dark-brown ink; there is a Western way of indicating a transposition on fo. 52b, instead of the normal Syriac one of three points arranged in a triangle above each word, and likewise there is a distinctive use of a symbol for an insertion on fo. 68b. There are text-stops drawn in dark-brown ink, formed of four small dots surrounding a small central dot, sometimes with small strokes between the four large dots, giving it a flower-like appearance. There are catchwords on every page (both sides of folio) written by the copyist.

There is a diagram on fo. 105a of the four elements (clockwise: fire, air, water, earth) with two cardinal qualities attached to each (i.e. fire: dryness and heat; air: heat and moisture; water: cold and moisture; and earth: dryness and cold) around the word: ܗܘܠܐ (= ὕλη). This is comparable to the diagram *n* on p. 180 of Kayser's edition.

ܚܡܝܡܘܬܐ . ܢܘܪܐ . ܝܒܫܐ ܀ ܪܛܝܒܘܬܐ . ܐܐܪ . ܚܡܝܡܘܬܐ ܀ ܪܛܝܒܘܬܐ . ܡܝܐ . ܩܪܝܪܐ ܀

ܩܪܝܪܐ . ܐܪܥܐ . ܝܒܫܐ ܀

The ivory, matt-finished paper has a thickness of 0.17–0.20 mm and an opaqueness factor of 4. It has fine, slightly wavy, vertical laid lines and single but closely spaced (2.2 cm) chain lines (slightly wobbly). There are watermarks (cluster of grapes? finger?), mostly in the gutter of the manuscript. There is some creasing of paper. There are a few small smudges and grease spots, but otherwise little soiling or deterioration of the manuscript.

Marginalia and owners' notes: There are two marginal notes. On fo. 5a₋₄: ܘܐܬܬܟܪܘ , and on fo. $8b_{18}$: ܫܘܣܝܐܠ , *non parcé*, with the Latin characters in the same ink as the main text.

Volume contents: The volume consists of 108 leaves plus two preliminary leaves and two endpapers (blank and of different watermarked paper from main text) in addition to front and back flyleaves of marbled paper (i–iii + 1–108 + iv–vi). Folios 100b and 108b are blank. The front flyleaf has the annotation: [*1753. Abac. ij. 15. olim*] *nunc 70*; there is a similar note on the back flyleaf: *Abac:ij, N°.15* (*1753*).

Binding: The volume is bound in a European binding (six cords) of pasteboards covered with brown leather. The covers have frames formed of two gold fillets; the spine is decorated with gold-stamped decorative devices incorporating four small fleur-de-lis around a circular design with spokes. The front edges of the boards are perforated by two holes to which are attached green silk ties with which the volume may be tied shut. The doublures and flyleaves are of European marbled paper. The numeral *70* has been inked on the fore-edge of the manuscript.

Provenance: The volume was given to the College in 1639 by Matthias Turner. At the top of fo. 1a there is the annotation: Liber Coll[egi]i D[i]: Ioannis Bapt: Oxon[ii], et dono M[ri] Matthiæ Turner, Sac: Theol: Bacchalaurei, et Coll[egi]i Commensalis. 1639.

References

Coxe, 20 entry LXX.
Bernard, Catalogi, A.15 (*in abaco secundo*).
Pearson, *Oriental Collections Great Britain*, 31 (no description given).
Pearson, *Oriental Manuscripts Europe*, 91 (no description given).

5

ETHIOPIC MANUSCRIPTS

Edward Ullendorff

Entry No. 39

MS 228 (item 1)

TITLE: [not given]

AUTHOR: [not given]

CONTENTS: The text, written in classical Ethiopic (Geʿez), opens with a Hymn to God, beginning 'I bow to your divinity who have created darkness before making light'. This is followed by sixteen praises for creating the various parts of the world as indicated in the first chapter of Genesis.

For a comparable Hymn to God, see Getachew Haile, *Catalogue of Ethiopian Manuscripts* (Collegeville, Minn.: St John's College, 1993), x, no. 4316.

PHYSICAL DESCRIPTION:

4 leaves (fos. 4r–7r)

Beginning (fo. $4r_1$):

እሰግድ ፡ ለመለኮትከ ፡ ዘፈጠርከ ፡ ጽልመተ ፡ እምቅድመ ፡ ትግበር ፡ ብርሃነ ።

Each of the subsequent sixteen praises begins with the same phrase:

እሰግድ ፡ ለመለኮትከ ፡

The copy is undated and unsigned. The nature of the script and general condition indicate conclusively that it was produced in the 19th century.

Classical Ethiopic (Geʿez). Dimensions: *c.*22 × 20.5 (text area, 2 columns each 14.5 × 7.2) cm; usually 18–19 lines per page.

The text is written in black ink, in a rather unattractive hand. It was transcribed by the same person who transcribed fos. 63r–70v of the volume (see Entry No. 38). The text and column areas are ruled by hardpoint.

The texts are written on vellum, with leaves of varying sizes.

Volume contents: The volume consists of 72 leaves. Folios 1–3 and 71–2 are blank leaves of vellum (essentially endleaves), while fos. 7v and 62v are also blank. Folios 4r–7r (item 1) contain the item here catalogued, and fos. 8r–70v (item 2, Entry No. 40) contain the 'Miracles of Jesus Christ'. The texts occupy eight unnumbered quires, consisting of 4, 8 10, 8, 8, 10, 11, and 8 leaves respectively.

Binding: The volume is bound in wooden boards. The front cover is formed of three pieces of wood stitched together with leather or cloth cords running through twelve bored holes. The back cover is formed in a similar manner of two pieces of wood. There is no spine. The eight quires and preliminary and back endleaves are stitched together with cords passing through eight bored holes in each cover.

Folios 15, 31, and 59 have a thread place-marker inserted at the top of the folio. Between fos. 14 and 15 there is a loose piece of printed cotton apparently serving as a bookmark.

The bound manuscript is kept in a dark-brown leather pouch, measuring *c.*22.5 × 23.5 × 5 cm (see Plate 14). The back, front, and sides are formed of one piece of leather, except for a narrow gusset set into one side seam. A triangular flap (composed of two pieces of leather stitched together) is sewn to the top back edge of the pouch, and this flap comes over the top and can be passed under a stiff leather horizontal band attached by thongs to the two sides. Also attached to the side panels are two narrow strips of leather forming a shoulder or belt strap, which at one time could be attached to the small thongs on the lower back of the pouch. On the front side of the pouch, the area under the flap is a lighter shade of brown, not having darkened with age and exposure to light as the other exterior surfaces have done.

Provenance: No information is available on when or by what route the volume came to be at St John's College.

The names of some owners with traditional Ethiopian personal nomenclature are indicated, several of which were subsequently erased to make room for new owners, but quite often these lacunae have not been filled in. None is dated.

On the first endleaf there is a pencilled annotation giving an earlier shelfmark, *MSS. 214*.

References

Unpublished. The manuscript is listed in the Coxe-supplement-1 (unpublished typescript), 5, though this item is not mentioned.

Pearson, *Oriental Manuscripts Europe*, 116 (a simple statement that St John's College has a single Ethiopic manuscript; no shelfmark or description is given).

A brief, but accurate, handwritten description was first offered by the Revd. Dr. Charles Fox Burney of St John's College (Lecturer in Hebrew), then domiciled at 17 Bradmore Rd, Oxford. This undated typed material was found inside the pouch and is now kept separately in a plastic sleeve.

Entry No. 40

MS 228 (item 2)

TITLE: *Miracles of our Lord and God and Saviour Jesus Christ*

AUTHOR: [not given]

CONTENTS: This is a collection of Ethiopic miracles. There is no author as such, but the collection is a long-established traditional composition which usually consists of 42 miracles. In this particular copy, there are only 32 miracles (see below for details of omissions).

For other copies: see Edward Ullendorff, *Catalogue of Ethiopian Manuscripts in the Bodleian Library* (Oxford: Clarendon Press, 1951), vol. ii. The treatise is well represented in other collections in Britain, including the British Library, Cambridge University Library, and the John Rylands University Library, Manchester.

The text of the present copy conforms closely with that printed by William Wright, *Catalogue of the Ethiopic Manuscripts in the British Museum Acquired since the Year 1847* (London: Trustees of the British Museum, 1877), 43–4, MS Or. 620, Entry LXVII.

PHYSICAL DESCRIPTION:

63 leaves (fos. 8r–70v)

Beginning (fo. 8r, following the trinitarian formula, Plate 15):

ተአምር ፡ ዘገብረ ፡ እግዚእነ ፡ ወአምላክነ ፡ ወመድኃኒነ ፡ ኢየሱስ ፡ ክርስቶስ ፡ ...

The copy is undated and unsigned. The nature of the script and general condition indicate conclusively that it was produced in the 19th century.

Classical Ethiopic (Geʿez). Dimensions: *c.*22 × 20.5 (text area, 2 columns each 16 × 7.5) cm; 19–23 lines per page.

The text is written in black ink, in a rather mediocre hand. **ኢየሱስ ፡** and **ማርያም ፡**, as well as chapter beginnings, are rubricated. Folios 8r to 62r were written by one copyist, while fos. 63r to 70v were transcribed by a different copyist (the same person who copied item 1 of this volume, fos. 4r–7r; see Entry No. 39). The text area and columns have been ruled by hardpoint for 19 lines of text per column, but the ruling has not always been followed, with some folios (e.g. 10v) having as many as 23 lines of writing.

Contents and titles:

Fo. 8r:	1st miracle
Fo. 17r:	2nd miracle: Remembering the birth of our Lord Jesus Christ
Fo. 19r:	3rd miracle: Our Lord in his childhood
Fo. 19v:	4th miracle: When our Lord was born of the twice blessed Virgin Mary
Fo. 24v:	5th miracle: About our Lord's coming into the Temple
Fo. 25v:	6th miracle: When the Magi came to Bethlehem
	[miracles 7 and 8 are missing]
Fo. 26r:	9th miracle: There was a man who had a lot of cattle
Fo. 27r:	10th miracle: Our Lord on Lake Tiberias (Sea of Galilee)
Fo. 28r:	11th miracle: Our Lord in the Galilee region
Fo. 29r	12th miracle: When our Lord came from Tiberias and wished to go up to Jerusalem
Fo. 30r:	13th miracle: When our Lord went towards Nazareth together with Joseph
Fo. 31v:	14th miracle: When our Lord ascended to Jerusalem and came to the Temple with many people from among the Jews
Fo. 35r:	15th miracle: When our Lord was in Jerusalem, at one time, there gathered around him the learned among the Jews
Fo. 35v:	16th miracle: When our Lord passed Samaria to visit the graves of the fathers Abraham, Isaac, and Jacob
Fo. 37v:	17th miracle: When our Lord passed the region of Magdala which is in the country of the Philistines (Matthew 15: 39)
Fo. 39r:	18th miracle: When our Lord came to Jerusalem, City of God, he saw a man who was blind from birth (John 9: 1)
Fo. 40r:	19th miracle: When our Lord came to the village of Nain (Luke 7: 11–12) with his disciples
Fo. 40v:	20th miracle: When our Lord ascended to Jerusalem on the feast of Tabernacles
Fo. 43r:	[21st; unnumbered] miracle: When our Lord went to the City of David which is Jerusalem there were with him Simon, Andrew, and James, and John
Fo. 44v:	22nd miracle: On one day our Lord went from Jerusalem to Bethlehem as he wished to visit the graves of the children whom Herod had killed (cf. Matthew 2: 16)
Fo. 46r:	23rd miracle: When our Lord was at Caesarea with his disciples . . . [the text has Caesarea of the Philistines—instead of Philippi?]
Fo. 47r:	24th miracle: When our Lord went to Galilee with his disciples [incorrectly spelt] and with a multitude of the people of the Jews

Fo. 48v: 25th miracle: One day when our Lord went to the region of እሌጎጸር ፡ [?]

Fo. 50v: 26th miracle: The people of Galilee and Judah lived for four years and a half sowing and when the time of harvesting arrived the locusts consumed it all with nothing left over

Fo. 52v: 27th miracle: There were many lions in the region of Askalon, so much so that the people of that place could not come from the gates of their houses after sunset

Fo. 53v: 28th miracle: And when our Lord went to Jericho he gathered his disciples and said to them, you are the children, the heirs of God

Fo. 56v: 29th miracle: And when our Lord went again to the Mount of Olives and with him were John and James, the children of Zebedee

[The second column of folio 57r and the first column of 57v are blank, but the continuity of the text seems not to be disturbed.]

Fo. 59v: 30th miracle: After all this our Lord said to his disciples: Know that the Kingdom of Heaven is near

[Fo. 62r is blank, apart from seven lines at the top, and fo. 62v is blank altogether. Fos. 63r–64v deal with John the Evangelist. Fo. 65v returns to the Miracles of our Lord.]

Fo. 65v: 31st miracle: And it was in the village of Cana in Galilee that the wedding of Nathanael took place (cf. John 1: 45 and 2: 1)

Fo. 67v: 32nd miracle: Afterwards our Lord went to Bethany on the way to the Jordan … his disciples said to him 'Lazarus, our friend has died; let us go to him to awake him' (cf. John 11: 1, 11)

The texts are written on vellum, with leaves of varying sizes. The three front and two back endleaves are also of vellum. Folio 19 has stitched repairs, and there are holes in fos. 28, 50, 53, 56, and 57. The outside edges of fos. 8–62 have punched holes used in ruling. The leaves are water damaged and soiled through thumbing. The vellum has some worm-eaten holes (e.g. fos. 50, 57).

Volume contents: The volume consists of 72 leaves. For the other item in the volume, as well as the binding and provenance, see Entry No. 39.

References

Unpublished. It is listed in the Coxẹ-supplement-1 (unpublished typescript), 5, where it is suggested that it is an 18th-century manuscript.

Pearson, *Oriental Manuscripts Europe*, 116 (a simple statement that St John's College has a single Ethiopic manuscript; no shelfmark or description is given).

A brief, but accurate, handwritten description was first offered by the Revd Dr. Charles Fox Burney of St John's College (Lecturer in Hebrew), then domiciled at 17 Bradmore Rd, Oxford. This undated typed material was found inside the pouch and is now kept separately in a plastic sleeve.

6

GUJARATI MANUSCRIPTS

Samira Sheikh

Entry No. 41

MS 254 (item 45)

TITLE: [not given]

AUTHOR: [not given]

CONTENTS: A Gujarati navigational text, consisting of a map of the coast of Gujarat, sailing instructions, a list of ports and their latitudes, and talismanic designs to be attached to a ship in order to ensure safe passage.

It is unlikely that the manuscript was made before the first half of the 17th century, for some of the place names on the map and in the lists of ports, such as Muzaffarabad, were built or came into prominence only after the end of the 16th century. On the other hand, it must have been produced before the middle of the 18th century, since it was placed in the scrapbook compiled by John Pointer, who died in 1754.

PHYSICAL DESCRIPTION:

10 leaves (5 bi-folios), with pencilled foliation 25r–35v.

Gujarati. Dimensions: folios 25–8 and 32–5, 19.8 × 11.8 (text area 16.7 × 9.5) cm; 19 lines per page. Folios 30–1 (map), 20.0 × 11.7 (text area 17.4 × 19) cm, the map being drawn on a folded sheet of original size 20 × 23.5 cm.

The folios have been bound in upside down in a volume containing a large number of other, unrelated, items. The folios are ruled with inked lines and the text is written within black-inked frames (two fillets). At the centre of four bi-folios a Gujarati map (with some Arabic script) has been placed, occupying fos. 29–31. The script and numerals are Devanāgārī. The texts are written in dense black ink. While Devanāgārī script reads left to right, and the sequence of folios is usually left to right, in this instance the sequence of folios is right to left.

The paper has no laid or chain lines and no watermarks; there are many thin patches. The paper is worm-eaten.

Structure and analysis:

Fo. 25a: Blank except for label: *A Chinese MS.*

Fo. 25b (illustrated in Plate 16): At the top, the letters of the Arabic alphabet are written with Devanāgārī numerals beneath, giving the numerical values of the Arabic letters in the *abjad* sequence of letter-numerals. Beneath that, and separated by a double line, are two magical tablet designs with patterns of Arabic letters. Both employ the same seven letters, ب و ي ن س ت ض , written in rotations commonly found in a type of magic square known as a 'Latin square' (see Maddison and Savage-Smith, *Science, Tools, & Magic*, 106–7). In the *abjad* sequence of letter-numerals, given at the top of the page, these seven letters have the values: 2 + 6 + 10 + 50 + 60 + 400 + 800, yielding a sum of 1328. This sequence of letters has no recognizable meaning.

The text below reads (in Gujarati in the Devanāgārī script): 'After making it into one board, [we] write that constellation upon it and tie it swinging to the back of the vessel, tied close enough that it floats, then God on High (الله تال) [will] grant desires. Do this on Friday night and day [and] on the day of Monday. Right and true is the one God (Allah).'

Fo. 26a (Plate 16): A description of nautical manoeuvres to reach the port of Surat, beginning: 'To go to Surat port, Māndhvād to Dīv . . . when . . . comes, we take bearings (*mujro*/*majro*). Bearings . . . [illegible]. We sail towards the rising Khaval [an asterism]. Outside Dīv we proceed, doing 18 fathoms of water. After the fresh water has become 19 fathoms, we sail towards the asterism Cītrā [Spica in Virgo] . . .'

These instructions are accompanied by a diagram depicting relative depths. The term used for 'fathom' is *vām*, a rough equivalent; for this and other terminology regarding the asterisms, see B. Arunachalam, 'The Haven-Finding Art in Indian Navigational Traditions and Cartography', in S. Chandra (ed.), *The Indian Ocean*: *Explorations in History, Commerce, and Politics* (New Delhi: Sage Publications, 1987), 191–221, published earlier as 'The Haven Finding Art in Indian Navigational Traditions and its Applications in Indian Navigational Cartography', *Annals of the National Association of Geographers, India*, 5 (1985), 1–23.

Fos. 26b–27a: A description of manoeuvres to reach Jeddah [Jidā].

Fo. 27b: An itinerary. The place names are accompanied by Pole Star altitudes as latitudes for each locality. The following are the place names, presented in two columns as they are in the text and with modern names (where identifiable and different) given in parentheses:

Surat
Hāsot (Hānsot)
Bharuch
Gandhār
Khabhāt (Khambhāt/ Cambay)
Goghā
Div Navalakhu (Diu)
Māgarol (Māngrol)
Jagat (Jagat-Dwārka)
Munādā (Manorā, near Karachi)
Sarjāsak (Sirja)
Harmuj (Hormuz)
Katīph
Bāhārān (Bahrain)
Nīl
Jāchhe cākubān
Rās
Jajiro Bālāchhe

Libādbā (Liwa/Lima?)
Maskat (Masqat)
Dada Kalat (Kelat)
Machhira (Masirā, off coast of Oman)
Ārā chīkarā (Ra's Sawqirah?)
Hervān
Khorīā morīā (Kuria Muria Islands/ Jazira Khuryā Muryā)
Dophār (Dhufar)
Partak (Fartak)
Karsan
Herij
Seher Mukalā (al-Shihr, al-Mukalla)
Kanākanī
Enanhavar (Ahwar)
Dār chīno
Āndan (Aden)
Bāmb madap (Bāb al-Mandab)
Mukhā

Fo. 28a: Itinerary continues:

Kubā (Khawba, north of Kamaran)
Lohīā (al-Luhayya, north of Kamaran)
Kamrān
Khornānāk
Hālībīn ākub (Hali?)
Bandarjīdā (Jedda)
Mankamubarak (Mecca)
Madīnāmubarāk (Medina)
Jabal Kubes
Rās Devārī
Martān
Savākīn ...? Suves (Suakin)
Akik (Ra's Aqiq [Sudan])
Dehelak (Dahlak)
Jelā (Zula [in Eritrea])
Barbarā (Berbera)

Bartakī (Bayt al-Faqih?)
Hāphun (Raas Xaafuun, Somalia)
Mor Kabir (Raas Macbar?, Somalia)
Rās Lādh
Jedāl
Kodīnchā
Phostarib
Mugadasā (Mogadishu)
Markhu (Marka)
Barāvā (Baraawe)
Rās'u
Daman u Tad ugamanu
Jām ghāndā
Māhem par (Mahim)
Tak Māhemnī (Mahim's ...?)
Vasī (Vasai)

Meth (Maydh)	Cheval (Cheul)
Phīlak (Felik / Raas Felug [Somalia])	Dādārājapharī
Garadaphun (Guardafui)	Dābhol par (on Dabhol)

Fo. 28b: Itinerary continues:

Sīgotar Rās Momīn	Socotra (Ra's Momin, east Socotra)
Sīgotar Rās …	
Sīgotar Rās Sohelī	Gub Jajīrā
Khādī bījī (second gulf)	Tak par
Takagāj [?]	Gub par (on Gub)
Khādī par (on the gulf)	Khādī nā chhedā (shore of the gulf)
Dandan vāsīā	Gubnā māthā bījā (second head of the Gub)
Hinor par (on Hinor [Honovar])	Gub sakhī
Kānadā Māgrol (Mangalore)	Gub par darjā
Kalīkot (Calicut/Kozhikode)	Thok par
Kochī (Cochin/Kochi)	Sunārgām (Sonārgāon)
Koljā/Kolamjā (Quilon/Kollam)	Khādī par (on the gulf)
Kuārī (Kanyakumari)	Sātīgām (Sātgāon/Chittagong)
Kalikot (Calicut)	Tak Satigam ni (Tak of Satigam)
Jāor	Khādī par (on the gulf)
Pāliādh	Khādī (gulf)
Tak par	Tok
Godāvarī	Thok Sunāgām

Fo. 29a: Blank

Fo. 30a: Blank

Fo. 30b–31a (illustrated in Plate XXI): A Gujarati coastal map showing the Gulf of Khambhat, drawn on a grid.

'Khambhāt' is written at the top of the map, next to the two lighthouses. Reading left to right along the coast, the localities named are (with modern equivalents in parentheses): Madhvād, Dīv (Diu), Simbar (Simbor), Madapharābāj (Muzaffarabad/Jafrabad), Chānch, … [illegible], Sīāl Bet, Sartanpor [?], Sotio (Soshia), Kuta (Kuda), Gudī [?], Ghogho (Ghogha), Rog [?].

Reading top to bottom along the right-hand coastline: Gandhār, Bharuch, Hānsot, Bhagvā, Vāriāv, Rānder, Surat, Gamnī nī Khādī (Gulf of ?), Navsārī, Ghandīvī (Gandevi), Valsād, Pālnoro (Parnera), Umarsādī, Kolak, Daman, Barād [?], Dehenu (Dahanu), Muslī-o [?].

Sandbanks, notorious in the Gulf of Khambhat, are indicated by stippling. The grid contains numerals (in integers and fractions, written in Devanāgārī) which indicate depth soundings in the Gulf. The last two rows have the word *kādav*, meaning mud or mire, and the word *dādo* (quicksands or shoals), both written with numerals alongside, to indicate depth.

The map was drawn on a large sheet of paper (20 × 23.5 cm) which was folded in half. As a result, fo. 31 is a doubled leaf, with the fold forming the right-hand edge of fo. 31. Folio 29 is the extension of the folded underside of 31. Folio 29 and fo. 30a are blank, as are the inside areas of the doubled fo. 31.

It is a carefully delineated double-page map drawn on a grid of 11 × 13 cells of equal size (each 1.5 cm^2). It is drawn and labelled in black ink, with green opaque watercolour used for highlighting the coast and red opaque watercolour used to highlight the lighthouses and topographical features such as the inner coastlines. In the lower right corner there is an annotation in Arabic script: هذا يا متليقع , whose meaning is unclear.

Fo. 31b: Blank

Fos. 32a–34b: All have a ruled and framed text area, but no text.

Fo. 35: Blank

No nautical maps from South Asia are known to have been produced before 1662, and few have survived. The map, itinerary, and sailing instructions in the St John's manuscript appear to have been part of a *rehmāni* or pilot's guide (also called *roznāma*) compiled by residents in the port towns of Gujarat. These manuals contained shoreline silhouettes, directional instructions (often in the form of riddles), and sometimes various calculations. A *roznāma/rehmāni* written no later than 1664 in the Kutchi language using Gujarati script, and containing five maps showing portions of the south-west Indian coast, is now in the National Museum in New Delhi. Those maps, however, do not employ a grid, but rather use stellar rhumb lines with constellation symbols at the end of the lines to indicate sailing directions, with Pole Star altitudes given for many of the ports. The decorative devices in those maps also differ from the ones in the St John's map, though they do employ a similar method of indicating elevations of landmasses (closely placed dots or small dashes). The maps now in New Delhi also have only one area in which the profile of the inner coastline is shown in red, while on the present map such a representation of the coastline dominates.

This map now in St John's is closer in design to another nautical map of Gujarati origin that was acquired in 1835 by Sir Alexander Burnes from a local pilot (now in the Royal Geographical Society, London, inv. no. Asia S.4). In the latter map, which is undated but probably of the 18th or early 19th century, the coloration (red shading of inner coastline and dotted method of indicating elevations) is similar to the map now at St John's. The present map here catalogued, however, lacks the English annotations (no doubt added later) and rhumb lines connecting locations, as well as the black ink drawing of ships with red sails and the various flags with red panels. For illustrations of the map now at the Royal Geographical Society, see Joseph E. Schwartzberg, 'South Asian Cartography', in J. B. Harley and David Woodward (eds.), *The History of Cartography*, ii/1: *Cartography in the Traditional Islamic and South Asian Societies* (Chicago: University of Chicago Press, 1992), plate 40 and 18.9.

The cartographic technique employed in this Gujarati map is strikingly different from those on other Indian nautical maps. The use of a grid on the present map appears to be unusual amongst the Indian maps so far recorded. No other Indian map is known to have a geographical grid (except those of Ṣādiq Iṣfāhānī, which are of Persian derivation and are in any case not nautical coastal maps). Furthermore, the St John's map, unlike the other coastal maps described above, is oriented with north at the top.

For maps of Gujarat, see in Sezgin, *GAS* X, 575–80. For Indian coastal maps in general, see Schwartzberg, 'South Asian Cartography', cited above, 472–508, and, for European accounts of Indian mapping, 324–7. See also Susan Gole, *Indian Maps and Plans: From Earliest Times to the Advent of European Surveys* (New Delhi: Manohar, 1989).

Volume contents: This Gujarati manuscript is part of item 45 in a miscellaneous collection of autographs, ancient documents, and palaeographical curiosities formed by John Pointer (1668–1754) and bequeathed by him to the College. The volume is labelled 'Addition of Curiosities to Vol. III'.

Item 45 in MS 254 has several additional leaves, all of them vellum, having non-consecutive pencilled foliation. The other leaves include part of a late 14th-century Book of Hours recovered from the binding of a book, a charter of Thomas Earl of Warwick (d. 1242) granting 13 acres of land on Blackmore Heath (Warwickshire) to Simon Fitz Simon, and letters of Peter Mews, Bishop of Bath and Wells, conferring the office of sub-dean of Wells on William Levinz, MD, 25 March 1679.

Provenance: Bequeathed to the College by John Pointer (1668–1754) of Merton College. Because St John's College already had the nucleus of a museum of curiosities, John Pointer was motivated to bequeath his own such collection to the College. His collection, which became known as the *Musaeum Pointerianum*, was then housed under the northern end of the Laudian Library in the College until the Museum of the History of Science was established in the Old Ashmolean, at which time most of his collection was transferred there. This bound volume, however, remained in the library of the College. See Costin, *History of St. John's College*, 188, and Gunther, *Early Science in Oxford*, iii. 336–41.

References

Unpublished, except for the following inaccurate listing in Pointer, *Oxoniensis Academia*, 92–4:

> There being such a Collection of Curiosities in this College already, has induc'd me to bequeath my own collection to be added to it, hoping it may be a Maintenance (or at least a Help towards one) for some young Scholar in shewing 'em; a Scholar to be appointed by the President, to

whom he shall administer an Oath to keep all Things safe. A Short Specimem of which is as follows

. . . [amongst others in the list] . . .

A China MS. and Map

In the unpublished typescript, Coxe–supplement-1, 15, there is the following description: 'a MS. itinerary in Gujerati, with a map of the Gulf of Cambray, c. 1700'.

A fuller discussion of the item will appear in a study by Samira Sheikh, 'Maps, Magic and Maritime Skills: Cartography and Navigation in the Indian Ocean Region, *c.*1750', in Z. Hirji and D. Parkin (eds.), *Traditions of Learning and Networks of Knowledge in the Indian Ocean* (London: Routledge).

II

INCIDENTAL ARABIC POETRY

Geert Jan Van Gelder

Filling up empty leaves or occasionally an empty margin, incidental verse is marginal in more than one sense. The material is extremely diverse. Some scholars have studied particular types of incidental poems found in manuscripts: Gotthold Weil presented poems on the lending of books ('Arabische Verse über das Ausleihen von Büchern', Islamica, 2 (1926), 556–61); Max Weisweiler discussed epigrams on books and writing in his article on 'scribes' verses' ('Arabische Schreiberverse', in R. Paret (ed.), *Orientalistische Studien Enno Littmann . . . überreicht . . .* (Leiden: Brill, 1935), 101–20); and Franz Rosenthal published ' "Blurbs" (Taqrīẓ) from Fourteenth-Century Egypt' (*Oriens*, 27–8 (1981), 177–96). All these poems may be called relevant and appropriate to their context. However, the larger part of the incidental poetry one finds in the manuscripts here described (and they are by no means untypical) is wholly unrelated or only tenuously related to the content of the manuscripts or the practice of writing and copying, lending and borrowing. As a result the following contribution, unlike the studies mentioned before, lacks any unifying theme but at least offers a more accurate and representative picture of what may be expected. I have copied, transliterated, and translated (as far as possible) all the incidental Arabic verse I have found, twenty-three pieces altogether. The Arabic reproduces more or less faithfully what is found in the source, mistakes and all (the vocalization, if present, has been reproduced only partially). The transliteration presents a 'regularized' version, which conforms to the rules of Arabic orthography, grammar, and prosody; it is meant to give an accurate representation of the sounds and the prosody, rather than the orthography of a 'correct' version. This implies, for instance, that the hamza is always rendered as ', even at the beginning of a word, and that short vowels are lengthened whenever the metre requires it (as in rhyme-words).

The manuscripts in the collection also contain non-incidental poetry, particularly in al-Ḥarīrī's Maqāmāt and al-Sakkākī's handbook on syntax, rhetoric, poetics, and prosody. A non-literary, didactic poem, with a versification of astronomical matters, is contained in MS 156B. It is attributed to the well-known writer and prince Abū al-Fidā' (672–732/1273–1331), who wrote poetry and works on history, geography, and various other subjects. He is known to have versified a juristic work, but the present poem is not otherwise known.

MS 91 (catalogue Entry No. 6)

A panegyric distich, using celestial diction appropriate to the present text which contains astronomical tables, is found on fo. 2a. The two lines of *basīṭ* metre, by an unknown poet, read and translate as follows:

I.

لا زلت تسعد بالايام مغتبطا   ما دام للسايرات السبعة احطامُ
ماه ومهر وكيوان وكاتبه   والمشتري وانا هيد وبهرامُ

Lā zilta tas'adu bi-l-'ayyāmi mughtabiṭan
mā dāma li-s-sā'irāti s-sab'i 'aḥkāmū:

Māhun wa-mihrun wa-kaywānun wa-kātibuhū
wa-l-mushtarī wa- anāhīdun wa-bahrāmā.

May you always be happy, rejoicing in your days,
as long as the seven planets exercise their rule:
Moon, Sun, Saturn, Mercury,
Jupiter, Venus, and Mars.

The names of the planets are an interesting mixture, for five of them are Persian, although necessarily equipped with Arabic case endings. Only Jupiter and Mercury have Arabic names, the latter not the customary *'uṭārid* but *al-kātib* (here with pronominal suffix as if Mercury were Jupiter's scribe), a form that belongs to the west of the Arabic world rather than the eastern parts (P. Kunitzsch, entry 'al-Nudjūm', in *EI*[2], viii. 101). The macaronic flavour is no doubt the result of the strictures of metre and rhyme.

MS 103 (catalogue Entry No. 2)

Three anonymous epigrams are written on fo. 2b: they have little in common, apart from using celestial diction or imagery, in keeping with the contents of the manuscript.

1. A dūbayt 'two-liner', which in Persian would be called 'quatrain', paradoxically with an Arabic word *rubā'iyya*, rather than the Arabo-Persian term *dūbayt*. The metre, not part of traditional Arabic prosody, is typical for the quatrain/*dūbayt*.

II.

قد اشرقت الدنيا من كاس محيانا   والنجم لنا ساق والبدر ثريانا

من كان له شوق فالمجلس مثواه   من كان له ذوق اياه وايانا

Qad 'ashraqati d-dunyā min ka'si muḥayyānā
wa-n-najmu lanā sāqin wa-l-badru thurayyānā
Man kāna lahū shawqun fa-l-majlisu mathwāhū
man kāna lahū dhawqun 'iyyāhu wa-'iyyānā

The world shines from the cup of Our countenance,
the Pleiades are Our cupbearer, the full moon is Our chandelier.
He who has a yearning will have a resting place in the party;
he who has (a mystical) taste: Let him heed Us!

There is some playing on words: *al-najm*, 'the star', is very often used for the Pleiades, as it is here, while the 'proper' name of the Pleiades, *al-Thurayyā*, is used in its derived sense of 'chandelier'. Bacchic themes are often combined with celestial imagery mentioning the moon or the Pleiades (many examples in Paul Kunitzsch and Manfred Ullmann, *Die Plejaden in den Vergleichen der arabischen Dichtung*, Beiträge zur Lexikographie des klassischen Arabisch 9 (Munich: Verlag der Bayerische Akademie der Wissenschaften: In

Kommission bei Beck, 1992), *passim*; the present epigram is not found there). The last hemistich is rather obscure, as befits a mystical poem. I am not certain that the expression *iyyāka wa-* with the accusative ('Beware of ...!') can be changed to the third person singular, nor do I see why someone with *dhawq* should be warned. A more fitting but possibly far-fetched solution would be to see a reference to two nearly identical Qur'anic phrases: *in kuntum iyyāhu ta'budūn* 'if it be Him that you serve' (2: 172, 16: 114, 41: 37) and *mā kuntum iyyānā ta'budūn* 'not Us were you serving (10: 38). Since the emphatic Him and Us both refer to God, the poem may suggest that the difference between persons is immaterial and that God is one with His creation.

2. A distich in *wāfir* metre:

III.

رات قمر السما فاذكرتني   ليالي وصلنا بالرقمتين

كلانا ناظر قمرا ولكن   رايت بعينها ورات بعيني

Ra'at qamara s-samā'i fa-'adhkaratnī
layāliya waṣlinā bi-r-Raqmataynī
Kilanā nāẓirun qamaran wa-lākin
ra'aytu bi-'aynihā wa-ra'at bi-'aynī

She saw the moon in the sky. She made me think
of our nights together in al-Raqmatān.
Each of us was looking at a moon, but
I saw with her eyes and she saw with mine.

Al-Raqmatān is a place near Medina mentioned in pre-Islamic poetry (e.g. Zuhayr's *Mu'allaqah*) as well in later poetry (e.g. Ibn al-Fāriḍ). The interpretation of the last line is not altogether clear: does the poet say that the girl is the 'real' moon? There may, as in the preceding poem, be a hint at the interchangeability or even identity of lover and beloved. The lines are quoted anonymously, with a commentary, in 'Abd al-Ghanī al-Nābulsī, *Nafaḥāt al-azhār 'alá nasamāt al-asḥār* (Būlāq, 1299/1822), 170.

3. A distich in *basīṭ* metre:

IV.

يا من تحلّق حتى صار مرتفعا   من السمأ الى اعلى مراقيها

لا تامنن انحطاطا وارع حرمتنا   وانظر الى الارض واذكر كوكننا فيها

Yā man taḥallaqa ḥattā ṣāra murtafi'an
mina s-samā'i 'ilā 'a'lā marāqīhā
Lā ta'mananna nḥiṭāṭan wa-r'a ḥurmatanā
wa-nẓur 'ilā l-'arḍi wa-dhkur kawnanā fīhā

You who have soared until you have risen

up in the sky unto its highest elevation:
Do not feel secure against a fall; respect our rights,
and look towards the earth, remember that we live on it.

MS 145 (catalogue Entry Nos. 19, 20, 21)

An appropriate epigram in praise of Euclid, of three lines in *kāmil* metre, is found on fo. 1a. It is introduced by *li-l-shaykh al-ra'īs quddisa sirruhu*, which suggests that Ibn Sīnā is their author. However, they are in fact by a rather less famous scholar, Abū ʿAlī al-Muhandis al-Miṣrī (Abū ʿAlī, the Engineer, the Egyptian, or, as an old Latin hand in the manuscript has correctly identified him, [*Carmen*] *Abu Ali Geometri Æyptii*). The lines are found in al-Qifṭī's biographical dictionary of scholars, *Ikhbār al-'ulamā' bi-akhbār al-ḥukamā'* (ed. Muḥammad Amīn al-Khanjī, Cairo: Maṭbaʿat al-Saʿādah, 1326/1908, 269), which has a variant in the last line (*'akrim bi-dhāka* for *li-llāhi darru*) and an extra line (here given between brackets). Perhaps the copyist thought that this line, with its earthy materialism, jars with the rest. It is to be noted that as in English the personal name 'Euclid' has become the science itself. It is spelled *Ūqlīdisu* in the manuscript, which is unmetrical and has been corrected in the following transliteration:

V.

اُوقليدس العلم الذي يحوى به   ما في السماء معا وفي اللآفاق

هو سُلم وكانما اشكاله   درج الى العلياَ للطرّاق

ترقى به النفس الشريفة مرتقى   للهِ درّ المرتقى والراقي

'Uqlīdisu l-'ilmu lladhī yuḥwā bihī
   mā fī s-samā'i ma'an wa-fī l-'āfāqī
[*Tazkū fawā'iduhū 'alā 'anfāqihī*
   yā ḥabbadhā zākin 'alā l-'anfāqī]
Huwa sullamun wa-ka-'annamā 'ashkāluhū
   darajun 'ilā l-'alyā'i li-ṭ-ṭurrāqī
Tarqā bihī l-nafsu sh-sharīfatu murtaqan
   li-llāhi darru l-murtaqā wa-r-rāqī

Euclid is the science by which is encompassed
what is in heaven and within the horizons.
[Its benefits exceed what one has spent on it:
How splendid, a thing that exceeds expenses!]
It is a ladder, and its (geometrical) figures are like
steps to higher things for those that tread upon them:
The sublime soul rises with its rising;
How splendid, the rising and he who rises!

MS 175 (catalogue Entry Nos. 1, 7, 9, 11, 12, 13)

Folio 44a, between treatises on astronomy and calendars, has been filled with material that is miscellaneous indeed. At the top of the page one finds a recipe in prose for *mawz murabbā*, bananas in syrup, which is recommended for its aphrodisiacal qualities. After that, one line of *ṭawīl* is found, which at first sight seems to be wholly unrelated to either bananas or stars. Neither the meaning nor, indeed, the reading is wholly clear:

VI.

همو زينوا زهْري طريا يرى حياً حمدت زماني والندي هو ها هونا

ا ب ج د ه و ز ح ط ى يا يب

Humū zayyanū zahrī ṭariyyan yurā ḥayyan
ḥamidtu zamāni wa-n-nadā huwa hā hūnā

They have adorned my flowers, fresh, seen alive (?);
I praised my time, while dew was here (?).

Instead of *yurā ḥayyan* one might think of, for instance, *yurī ḥayā* 'showing fertile rain', which would be better metrically, even though the manuscript indicates the ending *-an.* I suspect that *hūnā* is a mistake for *hunā.* In fact, the meaning and these readings are unimportant, for it turns out that the verse is a mnemotechnic acrostic, and relevant to the preceding treatise. What matters is that there are twelve words in the line, and that the numerical value of the letters beginning each word give a sequence:

h	*z*	*z*	*ṭ*	*y*	*ḥ*	*ḥ*	*z*	*w*	*h*	*h*	*h*
5	7	7	9	10	8	8	7	6	5	5	5

Each word is given its serial number, from 1 to 12, written in *abjad* underneath the words; they stand for the months. A carelessly written instruction in bad Arabic prose follows, beginning 'Deduct the letter of the month from 20 [written in red as the letter *kāf*], remains (?) the day of the transition (*taḥwīl*). These letters are the months, the first of them being Ādhār (March), in succession ...'. Apparently the verse is used to calculate the day in the (Christian) month on which a new zodiacal sign begins.

Folio 74b, too, is filled with mixed matters: five poems and a line in prose. Four of the poems are 'number epigrams', all of them on the number three. This 'number wisdom' is very common in Arabic, in prose or poetry. Al-Thaʿālibī (d. 429/1038) devoted a short anthology to them: *Bard al-akbād fī al-a'dād* (in *Khams rasā'il*, Constantinople: Maṭbaʿat al-Jawā'ib, 1301/1883, 101–41); the following poems are not found there.

1. A *rajaz* couplet, which looks as if it is meant to rhyme; but the rhyme is defective (the fault would be termed *ikfā'*):

VII.

ثلاثة ليست لهم أمانة　　العلق والقحبة والحمامه

Thalāthatun laysat lahum 'amānah
'al-'ilqu wa-l-qaḥbatu wa-l-ḥamāmah

Three things that are untrustworthy:
a catamite, a whore, and a pigeon.

The word *'ilq*, 'precious one', is a euphemism. In modern Egypt it is still a coarse word for passive homosexual; see Martin Hinds and El-Said Badawi, *A Dictionary of Egyptian Arabic: Arabic–English* (Beirut: Librairie du Liban, 1986), 593. It is possible that 'pigeon', too, is a euphemism here (it may mean 'penis', as readers of Nefzawi's *The Perfumed Garden* will remember, a sense that seems to fit here). After all, real pigeons are not particularly noted for being untrustworthy. There is in fact a saying *āman min ḥamām Makka* 'more reliable than the pigeons of Mecca' (Aḥmad ibn Muḥammad al-Maydānī, *Majma' al-amthāl*, Beirut: Dār al-Kutub al-'Ilmīyah, 1988, i. 420).

2. A line in *sarī'* metre with internal rhyme:

VIII.

ثلاثة ليسا لهم عاريه　　المشط والسواك والجاريه

Thalāthatun laysā lahum 'āriyah
'al-mushṭu wa-s-siwāku wa-l-jāriyah

Three things that must not be lent:
a comb, a toothbrush, a slave-girl.

The strange dual *laysā* should read *laysa* (the metre accommodates both). *Siwāk* or *miswāk* is often translated as 'toothpick', which is possible. Normally it is a twig, one end of which is chewed until it resembles, in its appearance and use, a toothbrush rather than a toothpick.

3. A line that looks like an internally rhyming *basīṭ* trimeter:

IX.

ثلاثة للرجالى مهلكات　　طوزا قيْـــنــرْ اقرات

Thalāthatun li-r-rijāli muhlikāt
ṭwz 'qynr 'qrāt

Three things that lead men into perdition:
... ... ??

Unfortunately, the second hemistich is wholly incomprehensible.

4. Two lines in *wāfir* metre:

X.

ثلاثة مهلكه الانام   وداعية الصحيح الاسقام

دوام مدامة ودوام   وطي وادخالو الطعام على الطعام

Thalāthatun muhlikatu l-'anāmī
wa-dā'iyatu ṣ-ṣaḥīḥi 'ilā saqāmī
Dawāmu mudāmatin wa-dawāmu waṭ'in
wa-'idkhālu ṭ-ṭa'āmi 'alā ṭ-ṭa'āmī

Three things that lead mankind to perdition
and cause the healthy to be sick:
Always drinking wine and always copulating,
and 'inserting food upon food'.

The last thing seems to refer to taking another mouthful before swallowing a previous one, deemed greedy and bad manners. The first hemistich of line 1 does not scan; one would expect e.g. *Thalāthun muhlikātun li-l-'anāmī*. The second half of the line seems to have *al-asqām*, which does not scan and is syntactically odd. I have assumed that *alif-lām-alif* is an ignorant spelling of *ilā* (compare the similar spelling of *'alā* on fo. 44a by what might be the same clumsy hand). *Idkhālu* is misspelled *idkhālū*.

5. The last poem, seven lines of doggerel verse in *sarī'* metre; versified Shiʿite Ḥadīth on a very practical matter. The orthography is extremely defective and has been regularized in the following transliteration:

XI.

أبدأ بُيمناكَ وفي الخِنْصَرِي   في قَصِك الاذْفاري وسْتــبْصِر

وثني بالوُصْطا وَثلث بما   قد قيل في الإبَهمِ والبِنْصَرِ

وخْتِمْ بسَبَباتِها هاكِذا   في اليد والرجْل ولا تزْدَرِ

ثُم ابْدا بالإبهام من بعد ذا   والاصبع الوُصطا وبالخِنْصَرَ

وبعدَها سَبابةٌ وَجْعَلْ   بِنْصَرَها خَتِمة الايسَرِ

فذالِك اَمنٌ لك ان رُمْتَه   من رَمْدِ العين فلا تزْدَرِ

قد صح هذ عن علي الرضا   انقلل العِلم عن المُنْذر

'Ibda' bi-yumnāka wa-bi l-khinṣarī
fī qaṣṣika l-'aẓfāri tastabṣirī
wa-thanni bi-l-wusṭā wa-thallith bi-mā
qad qīla fī l-'ibhāmi wa-l-binṣarī
wa-khtim bi-sabbābatihā hākadhā
fī l-yadi wa-r-rijli wa-lā tazwarī (*tazdarī ?*)

thumma bda [for *bda'*] *bi-l-'ibhāmi min ba'di dhā*
wa-l-'iṣba'i l-wusṭā wa-bi-l-khinṣarī
wa-ba'dahā sabbābatun wa-j'al [unmetrical]
binṣarahā khātimata l-'aysarī
fa-dhāka 'amnun laka 'in rumtahū
min ramadi l-'ayni fa-lā tazdarī
qad ṣaḥḥa hādhā 'an 'Aliyyi r-Riḍā
... l-'ilma 'ani l-mundhirī.

Begin with your right hand, and with the little finger
when you cut your nails, then you will be reasonable.
Secondly, your middle finger, thirdly, what
has been said about the thumb and the ring finger.
And finish with the index finger; thus
with the hand and the foot, and do not deviate (or: scorn [this]?).
Next, begin with the thumb after that,
and the middle finger and with the little finger
And after it the index finger, and make
the ring finger the conclusion of the left.
That gives you protection, if you should wish it,
against eye disease, so do not scorn it.
This is an authentic report coming from ʿAlī al-Riḍā (the eighth Imam),
(transmitting?) knowledge from the Warner (the Prophet).

I do not know whether the rhyme word in line 3 should be read *tazwarī* or *tazdarī* (as in line 6). In the last line *hādhā* is written without *alif.* The unclear word in this line seems to be a form of the root *NQL* (one would expect e.g. *'an-nāqili l-'ilma*).

The last line on the page, apparently again on paring one's nails, is difficult to read. Perhaps *Qallimū aẓāfīrakum* [spelled *adhafīrakum*!] *bi-l-sunnati wa-l-ādābi yā . . . min yasār . . .* 'Pare your nails in accordance with the Sunna and good manners . . . from the left . . .' It does not seem to be metrical.

MS 370 (catalogue Entry No. 25)

At the end of this copy of al-Ḥarīrī's famous *Maqāmāt* one finds a series of short poems, all anonymous except for one attributed to Bahā' al-Dīn Zuhayr. Folio 143a contains two epigrams with wordplay on al-Ḥarīrī's name and on the title of his *Maqāmāt*, followed by two 'blurb' epigrams praising the *Maqāmāt*:

1. A distich in *sarī'* metre:

XII.

أهوى حريريا مقاماته   تعلو مقاماتِ بديع الزمانْ

مشتغِلا في العقد ما ضَرّهُ   لو حلّ عندي ساعة في مكانْ

'Ahwā ḥarīriyyan maqāmātuhū
ta'lū maqāmāti Badī'i z-Zamān
Mushtaghilan fī l-'aqdi mā ḍarrahū
law ḥalla 'indī sā'atan fī makān

I love a silk-maker, whose 'standings' are
superior to the *Maqāma*s of Badīʿ al-Zamān (al-Hamadhānī),
Who is busy knotting the braids; it would not harm him
if he unwound with me for a while in one place.

There is a play on words, too, in the use of *'aqd* (knotting, braiding; a technical term in weaving and making silk cords) and its antonym *ḥall* (loosening, dwelling); the translation attempts to echo this.

2. A distich in *wāfir* metre:

XIII.

تعلق خاطري بهوى حريري   تكرر نحو منـــزله مسيري

وقفت ببابه خمسين يوما   وقلت كذا مقامات الحريري

Ta'allaqa khāṭirī bi-hawā ḥarīrī
takarrara naḥwa manzilihī masīrī
Waqaftu bi-bābihi khamsīna yawman
wa-qultu kadhā Maqāmātu l-Ḥarīrī

My mind has become attached to the love of a silk-maker
to whose dwelling I have been going repeatedly.
I stood at his door for fifty days
and said, Thus are the standing places/*Maqāmāt* of al-Ḥarīrī.

The reference is, of course, to the 50 *Maqāma*s. This poem is also written, in a different hand, on fo. 143b. Amatory epigrams on craftsmen and other professionals were a very popular sub-genre especially from the Mamluk period onward.

3. A distich in *sarī'* metre:

XIV.

أقسم بالله واياته   ومشْعر الحجّ وميقاته

ان الحريريّ حريّ بأن   تكتب بالبتر مقاماته

'Uqsimu bi-llāhi wa-'āyātihī
wa-mash'ari l-ḥajji wa-mīqātihī

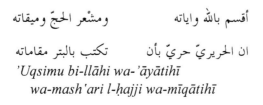

'Anna l-Ḥarīriyya ḥariyyun bi-'an
taktuba bi-t-tibri Maqāmātihī

I swear by God and his Signs
and by the rite of Pilgrimage and its appointed times
That al-Ḥarīrī is worthy that
you write down his *Maqāmāt* in gold.

The rhyme does not allow the last verb to be read as a passive, which would sound somewhat more normal.

4. A distich in *wāfir* metre:

XV.

مقام الفضل ليس له نظير   يصير العبد فيه كالأمير

ومن ذا في الأنام له مقامٌ   اذا ذكرتْ مقامات الحريرِ

Maqāmu l-faḍli laysa lahū naẓīrun
yaṣīru l-'abdu fīhī ka-l-'amīrī
Wa-man dhā fī l-'anāmi lahū maqāmun
'idhā dhukirat Maqāmātu l-Ḥarīrī

The standing of excellence is matchless:
with it a slave becomes like a prince.
And who among mankind has any standing
when al-Ḥarīrī's *Standing Places* are mentioned?

Folio 143b offers, apart from the repeated epigram (no. 2 above), three anonymous poems unrelated to al-Ḥarīrī or his *Maqāmāt*:

1. A *dūbayt* with internal punning rhymes and an unusually long metre (17 syllables per hemistich instead of the usual 12 to 14):

XVI.

في بحر هواك صار راسي راسي يا كل المرام

من ينجدني ولست ناسي ناسي والجسم كلام

أصبحت بدمعي لكاسي كاسي من غير مدام

ابكي وأصيح كم اقاسي قاسي يبخل يلام

Fī baḥri hawāka ṣāra rāsī / rāsī / yā kulla marām
man yunjidunī wa-lastu nāsī / nāsī / wa-l-jismu kilām

'Aṣbaḥtu bi-dam'ī li-kāsī / kāsī / min ghayri mudām
'Abkī wa-'aṣīḥu kam 'uqāsī / qāsī / yabkhulu (or *bi-bukhlin*?) *yulām*

In the sea of love for you my head
 is anchoring, O you, all my desire!
Who will help me? I will not forget
 my people, though my body be full of wounds.
Now I have with tears covered
 my cup, without wine.
I weep and cry: How much longer must I endure
 a cruel one who is stingy and blameworthy?

The last two hemistichs are metrically deviant.

2. Five lines in *basīṭ* trimeter:

XVII.

قد فتح الله المواهب — وجاد بالنصر والمآرب
واصبح الكون في سرور — وفي أمانٍ من المتاعب
ونحن بالله لا بزيد — ولا بعمرو ولا بصاحب
ولا كبير ولا صغير — ولا بجاه ولا بجانب
الكل ظلٌّ يزول لكن — قامت بأحكامه المواهب

Qad fataḥa llāhu bi-l-mawāhib
 wa-jāda bi-n-naṣri wa-l-ma'ārib
Wa-'aṣbaḥa l-kawnu fī surūrin
 wa-fī 'amānin mina l-matā'ib
Wa-naḥnu bi-llāhi lā bi-Zaydin
 wa-lā bi-'Amrin wa-lā bi-ṣāḥib
Wa-lā kabīrin wa-lā ṣaghīrin
 wa-lā bi-jāhin wa-lā bi-jānib
'Al-kullu ẓillun yazūlu lākin
 qāmat bi-aḥkāmihī l-mawāhib

God has granted gifts
 and has generously given support and fulfilled desires
Now the world is rejoicing
 and secure from troubles.
We exist through God, not through Tom
 or Dick or Harry, or any friend,
Nobody old or young,
 nor through high rank or importance.

Everything is a shadow that will pass, but
gifts exist by His decrees.

3. Six lines in *basīṭ* metre:

XVIII.

اشكو الى الله قوما لا خلاق لهم   ان رمت اظهار علم بينهم جهلوا
وان عريت يقولوا جاء مكتذبا   وان تسرولت قالوا قد زهى الرجل
وان جيت منبسطا سميت مسخرة   او جيت منقبضا قالوا به ملل
وان تجالسهم قالوا به طمع   وان تجانبهم قالوا به خلل
يتفاخرون باجداد لهم سلفت   نعم الجدود ولكن بيسما نسلوا
من لي بخلق وخلق يرتضون به   لا بارك الله فيهم كلهم سفلوا

'Ashkū ilā llāhi qawman lā khalāqa lahum
'in rumtu 'iẓhāra 'ilmin baynahum jahilū
Wa-'in 'arītu yaqūlū jā'a muktadhiban
wa-'in tasarwaltu qālū qad zahā r-rajulū
'In ji'tu munbasiṭan summītu maskharatan
wa-'in ji'tu munqabiḍan qālū bihī malalū
Wa-'in tujālis'humū qālū bihī ṭama'un
wa-'in tujānibhumū qālū bihī khalalū
Yatafākharūna [sic] *bi-'ajdādin lahum salafat*
ni'ma l-judūdu wa-lākin bi'samā nasalū
Man lī bi-khalqin wa-khulqin yartaḍūna bihī
lā bāraka llāhu fīhim kulluhum safulū

I complain to God about people who are a bad lot:
if I want to display knowledge among them they are stupid.
If I am naked they say, He has come as a swindler;
and if I put on trousers they say, The man has got conceited.
If I come in a cheerful mood I am called a clown,
and if I come while downcast they say, He is bored.
If you sit down with them they say, He wants something;
and if you avoid them they say, There's something wrong with him.
They boast of their ancestors from the past:
splendid forefathers, but bad progeny!
Who can give me a body and a character that will please them?
May God not bless them, they are all despicable.

The obvious emendation of the unmetrical *yatafākharūna* is *yufākhirūna*.

Folio 144 contains five poems, two attributed and three anonymous.

Fo. 144a:

1. A distich in *kāmil* metre attributed to Bahā' al-Dīn Zuhayr (581–656/1186–1258), a very popular Egyptian poet, whose *Dīwān* was edited and translated in rhymed verse by E. H. Palmer (*The Poetical Works of Behà-ed-Dìn Zoheir of Egypt*, Cambridge: Cambridge University Press, 1876–7). His translation is quoted here (see p. 41, Arabic text p. 35). In the *Dīwān* the poem continues with seven further lines.

XIX.

لبها الدين زهير

عتب الحبيب فلم أجد سبباً لذاك العتب حادث

بالامس لي الى يومي لم اره وها ذا اليوم ثالث

'Ataba l-ḥabību fa-lam 'ajid
sababan li-dhāka l-'atbi ḥādith
Bi-l-'amsi lī 'ilā yawmī lam (?)
'arahū wa-hādhā l-yawmu thālith

The loved one chides, I know not why
I've fallen into such disgrace
But two clear days have now gone by
Since last I looked upon his face.

The second line of our text is corrupt; Palmer's text has *Wa-l-yawma lī yawmāni lam | 'arahū*.

2. One line in *kāmil* metre:

XX.

دع عنك تعنيفي وذق طعم الهوى واذا عشقت فبعد ذلك عنفي

Da' 'anka ta'nīfī wa-dhuq ṭa'ma l-hawā
wa-'idhā 'ashiqta fa-ba'da dhālika 'annifī

Stop chiding me, and taste yourself the flavour of love;
and when you have become a passionate lover, chide me then.

The final imperative is incorrectly written with final *yā'*, making it feminine.

Fo. 144b:

3. Ten lines in *mujtathth* metre, attributed to al-Būrīnī. On Badr al-Dīn al-Ḥasan ibn Muḥammad al-Būrīnī (963–1024/1556–1615), historian and poet, see *EI*[2] s.v. (C. Brockelmann) and Brockelmann, *GAL*, ii. 290, S ii. 401.

XXI.

للبوريني

يا راشق القلب مني   اصبت فاكفف سهامك
ويا كثير التجنّي   قطعت حتى سلامك
وخنت ذمة عبد   ما خان قط ذمامك
فاردد عليّ منامي   فلا سُلبت منامك
فمن راى سوء حالي   بكى عليّ ولامك
بمن احلّك قلبي   ارفع قليلا لثامك
وابسمْ لعلي احيى   اذا رايت ابتسامك
يا خمرة ما أُحيلا   للعاشقين التثامك
بكيت دالا وميما   لمّا تامّلت لامك

Yā rāshiqa l-qalbi minnī / 'aṣabta fa-kfuf sihāmak
Wa-yā kathīra t-tajannī / qaṭa'ta ḥattā salāmak
Wa-khunta dhimmata 'abdin / mā khāna qaṭṭu dhimāmak
Fa-rdud 'alayya manāmī / fa-lā sulibta manāmak
Fa-man ra'ā sū'a ḥālī / bakā 'alayya wa-lāmak
Fa-law 'aradta ḥayātī / lamā hazazta qawāmak
Bi-man 'aḥallaka qalbī / 'irfa' qalīlan lithāmak
Wa-bsim la-'alliya 'aḥyā / 'idhā ra'aytu btisāmak
Yā khamratun mā 'uḥaylā / li-l-'āshiqīn ltithāmak
Bakaytu dālan wa-mīman / lammā ta'ammaltu lāmak

You who shoot at my heart: you have hit it, now stop your arrows.
You, with all your mean behaviour, have even stopped greeting me.
You have betrayed the trust of a servant who never betrayed your trust.
So give me back my sleep—may you not be robbed of your sleep!
He who sees my bad state will cry for me and blame you.
If you wanted me to live, you should not have swayed your body.
By Him Who made you dwell in my heart: lift your veil a little,
And smile, so that perhaps I may live when I have seen your smile.
O wine, how sweet is it for lovers to kiss you!
I have wept *b*, *l*, *o*, *o*, and *d* when I looked at your *l*!

The last *l*, or rather its elegantly curved Arabic equivalent, conventionally stands for the beloved's locks at the side of the head. Conventional, too, is the use of masculine forms and pronouns for the beloved. A boy may well have been intended, although the veil suggests a girl or woman. Of course, the poem may be read as a mystical poem (al-Būrīnī wrote a commentary on Ibn al-Fāriḍ's *Dīwān*, which has been printed), but there is no compelling reason to do so.

4. (Part of) a *mukhammasa* in *khafīf* metre:

XXII.

يا اخا الحزم قد تحير امري   في امور على الخليقة تجري

بين عفو ونعمة ضاع فكري   لست ادري ولا المنجم يدري

ما يريد القضاء بالانسان

صرت احتار بين فتق ورتق   ولساني ابى يفوه بنطق

وفؤادي حوى سريرة صدق   غير اني اقول قولا بحق

وارى الغيب فيه رأي عيان

كل نفس تجزى بما اسلفته   من قبيح وصالح فعلته

صح في النقل عن ثقاة روته   كل من كان محسنا قابلته

بجميل سوابق الاحسان

Yā 'akhā l-ḥazmi qad taḥayyara 'amrī
Fī 'umūrin 'alā l-khalīqati tajrī
Bayna 'afwin wa-ni'matin ḍā'a fikrī
Lastu 'adrī wa-lā l-munajjimu yadrī
   mā yurīdu l-qaḍā'u bi-l-'insānī
Ṣirtu 'aḥtāru bayna fatqin wa-ratqī
Wa-lisānī 'abā yafūhu bi-nuṭqī
Wa-fu'ādī ḥawā sarīrata ṣidqī
Ghayra 'annī 'aqūlu qawlan bi-ḥaqqī
   wa-'arā l-ghayba fīhi ra'ya 'iyānī
Kullu nafsin tujzā bi-mā 'aslafat'hū
Min qabīḥin wa-ṣāliḥin fa'alat'hū
Ṣaḥḥa fī n-naqli 'an thiqātin rawat'hū
Kullu man kāna muḥsinan qābalat'hu
   bi-jamīlin sawābiqu l-'iḥsānī

My prudent friend, I am confused
About matters that happen to all creatures;
my thoughts are lost between forgiveness and blessing. (?)
   I do not know, nor does the astrologer know,

what the Divine Decree wants with Mankind.
I am bewildered, between rending and mending,
While my tongue refuses to utter a word,
And my heart harbours the secret of truthfulness,
But I will speak words in truth
and see the Unseen from eye to eye.
Every soul is recompensed for what it has done before,
Of evil things and good things it has done.
This has correctly been transmitted by reliable authorities:
Everyone who has done good deeds,
his former good deeds will requite him handsomely.

On the form, see e.g. the entries 'Takhmīs' (P. F. Kennedy) and 'Musammaṭ' (G. Schoeler) in *EI*[2]. Most likely, an original poem rhyming in *-ānī* (italicized in the translation) was amplified later with three hemistichs for each verse. A *mukhammasa* is usually a longish poem, and it is therefore likely that only part is quoted here.

5. Two lines in *ṭawīl* metre, written in the margin:

XXIII.

تمتعتما يا مقليّ بنظرة　　　　واورثتما قلبي الموارد

اعيناي كنا هن فؤادي فانه　　　　من الظلم سعى اثنان في قتل واحد

Tamatta'tumā muqlatayya bi-naẓratin
wa-'awrathtumā qalbī (...) l-mawāridī
'A-'aynāya kunnā 'an fu'ādī fa-'innahū
mina ẓ-ẓulmi sa'yu thnāni fī qatli wāḥidī

You have, my eyes, enjoyed a glance
and you have bequeathed to my heart (...) of places.
O eyes of mine, conceal it from my heart, for
it is unjust that two should strive to kill one.

The second hemistich, though not showing a visible lacuna, is incomplete. Instead of *thnāni* in the last hemistich one should expect *thnayni*.

APPENDIX I

CONCORDANCE OF MANUSCRIPTS

Manuscript		Folios	Title | Author | Entry No.
MS 33		402 fos.	*Kitāb Durrat al-tāj li-ghurrat al-Dubāj* | Quṭb al-Dīn Maḥmūd ibn Mas'ūd al-Shīrāzī | **Entry No. 24**
MS 70		108 fos.	*K̲ṯāḇā d'ellat koll 'ellān* [*Causa causarum*] | anon. | **Entry No. 38**
MS 72		382 fos.	The *Qur'ān* | **Entry No. 30**
MS 83		192 fos.	*Kitāb al-Ḥiyal fī ḥurūb wa-fatḥ al-madā'in wa-ḥifẓ al-durūb* | pseudo-Alexander the Great [Muḥammad ibn Manglī] | **Entry No. 22**
MS 91		92 fos.	[*Zīj-i jadīd-i sulṭānī*] | Ulugh Beg | **Entry No. 6**
MS 103		174 fos.	*Tawḍīḥ al-Tadhkirah* | al-A'raj al-Nīsābūrī | **Entry No. 2**
MS 105		103 fos.	*Kitāb-i Zabūr* [*-i Dā'ūd*] | The Book of Psalms | **Entry No. 33**
MS 107		204 fos.	The *Qur'ān* | **Entry No. 32**
MS 122		253 fos.	*Miftāḥ al-'ulūm* | al-Sakkākī | **Entry No. 23**
MS 133		99 fos.	*Kitāb-i Zabūr* [*-i Dā'ūd*] | The Book of Psalms | **Entry No. 34**
MS 143		172 fos.	A bilingual Latin–Hebrew copy of four books of the Old Testament (Joshua, Judges, Song of Songs, and Ecclesiastes) | **Entry No. 35**
MS 145	[1]	1b–203a	*Taḥrīr Kitāb Uṣūl al-handasah li-Uqlīdis* | Naṣīr al-Dīn al-Ṭūsī | **Entry No. 20**
	[2]	204a–208a$_4$	[*dhayl*] | Naṣīr al-Dīn al-Ṭūsī | **Entry No. 21**
	[3]	208a$_5$–213b, 214b–215a	*Sharḥ muṣādarāt li-kitāb Uqlīdis* | Ibn al-Haytham | **Entry No. 19 [MAIN ENTRY]**
MS 151	[1]	1b–131b	[*Zīj-i jadīd-i sulṭānī*] | Ulugh Beg | **Entry No. 5 [MAIN ENTRY]**
	[2]	132a–148a	[untitled miscellany on nativities | anon. | **Entry No. 14**
	[3]	149a–180b	[untitled collection of astronomical tables] | anon. | **Entry No. 15**
MS 155	[1]	1a–9b	[untitled collection of astronomical tables] | anon. | **Entry No. 4 [MAIN ENTRY]**
	[2]	11a–12a	[untitled set of calendric conversion tables] | anon. | **Entry No. 10**
MS156B	[1]	1a–17b, 19a–23b, 29a–83b, 87a–90a$_5$	*Kitab al-Sirr al-maktūm fī al-'amal bi-l-zīj al-manẓūm* | [attributed to] Abū al-Fidā' | **Entry No. 3 [MAIN ENTRY]**

Manuscript		Folios	Title | Author | Entry No.
MS156B	[2]	18b, 28b, 84–6, $90a_6$–91b, 92b–93a, 94a–103a	[untitled collection of astronomical tables and notes] | anon. | **Entry No. 16**
	[3]	24b–26b	[untitled collection of astronomical material] | anon. | **Entry No. 17**
	[4]	27a–b	*Bāb fī ma'rifat kusūf al-shams* | anon. | **Entry No. 18**
MS 175	[1]	1b–10a	*Risālat al-jāmi'ah lil-'urūḍ kullihā* | anon. | **Entry No. 9**
	[2]	11a–12a	[astronomical and calendrical tables] | anon. | **Entry No. 11**
	[3]	12b–39b	[*al-Shakkāzīyah*] | Abū Isḥāq Ibrāhīm ibn Yaḥyá al-Zarqāllu | **Entry No. 1** [MAIN ENTRY]
	[4]	40a–43b	[miscellaneous astronomical and mathematical notes] | anon. | **Entry No. 12**
	[5]	44b–56a	*Nuzhat al-nāẓir fī waḍ' khuṭūṭ faḍl al-dā'ir* | Shams al-Dīn Muḥammad ibn Abī al-Fatḥ al-Ṣūfī al-Miṣrī | **Entry No. 7**
	[6]	56b–74a	[untitled collection of astronomical tables] | anon. | **Entry No. 13**
MS 186		60 fos.	*Rasā'il fī 'ilm al-mīqāt* | Badr al-Dīn Muḥammad Sibṭ al-Māridīnī | **Entry No. 8**
MS 201		332 fos.	The *Qur'ān* | **Entry No. 28**
MS 215		392 fos.	The *Qur'ān* | **Entry No. 31**
MS 228	[1]	4r–7r	Ethiopic 'Hymn to God' | **Entry No. 39**
	[2]	8r–70v	A collection of Ethiopic miracles | **Entry No. 40**
MS 253	[7]	1 fo.	A Turkish *firman* | **Entry No. 37**
	[51]	61a–65b	A Hebrew conveyance of land | **Entry No. 36**
MS 254	[45]	25r–35v	[untitled Gujarati navigational text] | **Entry No. 41**
MS 304		417 fos.	The *Qur'ān* | **Entry No. 29**
MS 367		170 fos.	[*al-Muqaddimah al-Ghaznawīyah fī furū' al-Ḥanafīyah*] | al-Ghaznawī |**Entry No. 27**
MS 369		512 fos.	*Kitāb al-Jāmi' al-ṣaḥīḥ* | Muḥammad ibn Ismā'īl al-Bukhārī | **Entry No. 26**
MS 370		143 fos.	[*Maqāmāt al-Ḥarīrī*] | al-Ḥarīrī | **Entry No. 25**

APPENDIX II

CONCORDANCE BY AUTHOR

Abū al-Fidā', Ismā'īl ibn 'Alī ibn Maḥmūd ibn Muḥammad ibn Taqī al-Dīn 'Umar ibn Ayyūb, al-Malik al-Mu'ayyad 'Imād al-Dīn (d. 732/1331)
Kitab al-Sirr al-maktūm fī al-'amal bi-l-zīj al-manẓūm MS 156B (item 1); Entry No. 3.

Alexander the Great (pseudo-)
Kitāb al-Ḥiyal fī ḥurūb wa-fatḥ al-madā'in wa-ḥifẓ al-durūb MS 83; Entry No. 22.

A'raj Nīsābūrī (al-), Niẓām al-Dīn al-Ḥasan ibn Muḥammad ibn al-Ḥusayn (*fl.* 711/1311)
Tawḍīḥ al-Tadhkirah / Shayḥ al-Tadhkirah MS 103, Entry No. 2.

Bukhārī *see* Muḥammad ibn Ismā'īl al-Bukhārī

Ghaznawī (al-), Jamāl al-Dīn Aḥmad ibn Muḥammad ibn Maḥmūd ibn Sayyid (d. 593/1197)
al-Muqaddimah al-Ghaznawīyah fī furū' al-Ḥanafīyah MS 367; Entry No. 27.

Ḥarīrī (al-) (d. 516/1122)
Maqāmāt al-Ḥarīrī MS 370; Entry No. 25.

Ibn Abī al-Fatḥ al-Ṣūfī al-Miṣrī, Shams al-Dīn Muḥammad (*fl.* 878/1473)
Nuzhat al-nāẓir fī waḍ' khuṭūṭ faḍl al-dā'ir MS 175 (item 5); Entry No. 7.

Ibn al-Haytham (d. 431/1041 or 430/1039)
Sharḥ muṣādarāt li-kitāb Uqlīdis MS 145 (item 3); Entry No. 19.

Ibn Manglī *see* Muḥammad ibn Manglī

Māridīnī (al-) *see* Sibṭ al-Māridīnī

Miṣrī *see* Ibn Abī al-Fatḥ al-Ṣūfī al-Miṣrī

Muḥammad ibn Ismā'īl al-Bukhārī (d. 256/870)
Kitāb al-Jāmi' al-ṣaḥīḥ / Kitāb al-Ṣaḥīḥ / Kitāb Ṣaḥīḥ al-Bukhārī MS 369; Entry No. 26.

Muḥammad ibn Manglī (*fl.* 778/1376–7)
Kitāb al-Ḥiyal fī al-ḥurūb wa-fatḥ al-madā'in wa-ḥifẓ al-durūb MS 83; Entry No. 22.

Naṣīr al-Dīn al-Ṭūsī (d. 672/1274)
Taḥrīr Kitāb Uṣūl al-handasah li-Uqlīdis Entry No. 20, MS 145 (item 1).
[no title; a *dhayl*] MS 145 (item 2); Entry No. 21.

Niẓām al-Dīn al-Ḥasan ibn Muḥammad ibn al-Ḥusayn, known as al-A'raj al-Nīsābūrī *see* A'raj Nīsābūrī

Quṭb al-Dīn Maḥmūd ibn Mas'ūd al-Shīrāzī (d. 710/1311)
Kitāb Durrat al-tāj li-ghurrat al-Dubāj / Unmūdhaj al-'ulūm MS 33; Entry No. 24.

Sakkākī (al-), Yūsuf ibn Abī Bakr ibn Muḥammad (d. 626/1229)
Miftāḥ al-'ulūm MS 122; Entry No. 23.

Sibṭ al-Māridīnī, Badr al-Dīn Muḥammad (d. 912/1506)
Rasā'il fī 'ilm al-mīqāt MS 186; Entry No. 8.
Iẓhār al-sirr al-mawḍū' fī al-'amal bi-l-rub' al-maqṭū'
Risālah mubārakah nāfi'ah fī ṭarīq al-'amal bi-l-khayṭ

Hidāyat al-sā'il fī al-'amal bi-l-rub' al-kāmil
al-Risālah al-Fatḥīyah fī al-a'māl al-jaybīyah
Laqṭ al-jawāhir fī ma'rifat al-dawā'ir

Ulugh Beg ibn Shāhrukh ibn Tīmūr Gurgān (d. 853/1449)
Zīj-i jadīd-i sulṭānī [Persian] MS 151 (item 1); Entry No. 5.
Zīj-i jadīd-i sulṭānī [Arabic] MS 91; Entry No. 6.

Zarqāllu (al-), Abū Isḥāq Ibrāhīm ibn Yaḥyá al-Zarqāllu al-Ṭulayṭulī (d. 493/1100)
al-Shakkāzīyah MS 175 (item 3); Entry No. 1.

Zarqēllo *see* Zarqāllu

Anonymous

Entry No. 4, MS 155 (item 1)
Entry No. 9, MS 175 (item 1)
Entry No. 10, MS 155 (item 2)
Entry No. 11, MS 175 (item 2)
Entry No. 12, MS 175 (item 4)
Entry No. 13, MS 175 (item 6)
Entry No. 14, MS 151 (item 2)
Entry No. 15, MS 151 (item 3)
Entry No. 16, MS 156B (item 2)
Entry No. 17, MS 156B (item 3)
Entry No. 18, MS 156B (item 4)
Entry No. 38, MS 70
Entry No. 39, MS 228 (item 1)
Entry No. 40, MS 228 (item 2)
Entry No. 41, MS 254 (item 45)

APPENDIX III

CONCORDANCE OF DATED MANUSCRIPTS

Date	Copyist	Location	Manuscript	Entry Nos.
732, 23 Rajab 20 Apr. 1332	Badr al-Sarāyī	Khwārazm	MS 122	23
752, 4 Ramaḍān 25 Oct. 1351	ʿAbd Allāh al-Qayṣarī		MS 103	2
897, 7 Muḥarram 10 Nov. 1491	ʿAlī ibn Yūsuf al-Qudsī	Damascus	MS 156B, item 1	3
901, 23 Shawwāl 5 July 1496	Aḥmad ibn Shams al-Dīn ibn Fakhr al-Dīn al-Jahramī *mawlidan* al-Juwaymī *aṣlan*	Iranian province of Fārs	MS 369	26
915, 23 Rabīʿ II 8 Aug. 1509	Abū al-Qāsim ibn Muḥammad ibn ʿAlī al-Khaddām al-Andalusī		MS 173, items 1, 3, 4	1 9
938, Jumādá II Jan. 1532	[not given]		MS 151, items 1, 3	5
939, 20 Ṣafar 21 Sept. 1532	[not given]		MS 91	6
1036 1626–7	[not given]		MS 72	30
1071, Dhū al-Ḥijjah 4 Aug. 1661	[not given]		MS 105	33
[1618]		Constantinople	MS 254, item 7	37
1186, 7 Dhū al-Ḥijjah 1 Mar. 1773	[not given]		MS 367	27

INDEX OF TITLES

INDEX OF PREVIOUS OWNERS AND DONORS

GENERAL INDEX